EUROPEAN THEATRE 1960–1990

EUROPEAN THEATRE
1960–1990

Cross-cultural perspectives

Edited by Ralph Yarrow

London and New York

First published 1992
by Routledge
11 New Fetter Lane, London EC4P 4EE

Simultaneously published in the USA and Canada
by Routledge
a division of Routledge, Chapman and Hall Inc.
29 West 35th Street, New York, NY 10001

Typeset in 10 on 12 point Garamond by
Witwell Ltd, Southport
Printed in Great Britain by
TJ Press (Padstow) Ltd, Padstow, Cornwall

British Library Cataloguing in Publication Data

European theatre 1960–1990: cross-cultural perspectives.
1. Europe. Theatre, history
I. Yarrow, Ralph
792.094

Library of Congress Cataloging in Publication Data

European theatre 1960–1990: cross-cultural perspectives/edited
by Ralph Yarrow.
p.   cm.
Includes bibliographical references and index.
1. Theater–Europe–History–20th century.   2. Theater and
society–Europe.   3. European drama–20th century–History
and criticism.   I. Yarrow, Ralph.
PN2570.E84   1991 1992
792'.094'09045–dc20   91–3661

ISBN 0–415–00047–5

CONTENTS

v

CONTENTS

NOTES ON CONTRIBUTORS

Christopher Cairns is Reader in Italian Drama at the University College of Wales, Aberystwyth, United Kingdom. He edits the series 'Italian Origins of European Theatre' and 'Studies in the Commedia dell'Arte', and organized the 1988 London conference on 'The Commedia dell'Arte from the Renaissance to Dario Fo'. He has worked as interpreter/assistant with Carlo Boso at *commedia dell'arte* workshops in London, Cardiff and Venice, and with Adriano Iurissevich in Aberystwyth and Coleraine as director of Goldoni's *La Locandiera* and Aretino's *Talanta*. He has worked on and with Franca Rame and Dario Fo and is preparing the authorized biography of Dario Fo in English.

Susanne Chambalu studied Drama at the University of Vienna, Austria, and is researching a thesis on Michelene Wandor and women in British theatre. She is also studying dance, acrobatics and mime.

Gwynne Edwards is Professor of Spanish at the University College of Wales, Aberystwyth, United Kingdom, and a specialist in Spanish theatre and cinema. Critical studies include *Lorca: The Theatre beneath the Sand* (London, 1980) and *Dramatists in Perspective: Spanish Theatre in the Twentieth Century* (Cardiff, 1985). Two volumes of his translations of Lorca have been published: *Lorca: Three Plays* (London, 1987) and *Lorca: Plays Two* (London, 1990). Professional productions include Lorca's *Blood Wedding*, Contact, Manchester, 1987; *Doña Rosita*, Bristol Old Vic, 1989; *When Five Years Pass*, Edinburgh (Fringe First), 1989; and Carlos Muñiz's *The Ink Well*, Battersea Arts Centre, London, 1990.

Anthony Frost is Chair of Drama at the University of East Anglia, Norwich, United Kingdom. He has published, with Ralph Yarrow,

Improvisation in Drama (London, 1990), and is working on a new approach to theatre history.

Theo Girshausen is Assistant Professor at the Theatre Institute, Free University of Berlin, Germany. His publications include: *Die Hamletmaschine. Heiner Müllers Endspiel* (Cologne, 1977); *Realismus und Utopie. Die frühen Stücke Heiner Müllers* (Cologne, 1982); *B. K. Tragelehn – Theater arbeiten: Shakespeare/Molière* (Berlin, 1988). He has written theatre reviews and essays on theatre in both former FRG and GDR for *Theater heute* and *Theaterzeitschrift*.

George Hyde is Lecturer in English and Comparative Literature at the University of East Anglia, Norwich, United Kingdom. He was Reader in Contemporary English Literature at Marie Curie University, Lublin, Poland, from 1976 to 1979, and his publications include a book on Nabokov (London, 1978), two books on D. H. Lawrence (1981 and 1990), translations of Russian and Polish texts, and numerous essays on aspects of modernism and literary theory. He is currently writing a book on Russian Formalism.

David Jeffery is Head of the School of Languages at Chichester College of Technology, United Kingdom, has directed and written articles about Alfred Jarry's *Ubu*, directed Gabriel Cousin's *Descente sur Récife* and Jean Anouilh's *L'Invitation au Château*, and has made two videos on contemporary French life.

Martin Sorrell is Lecturer in the Department of French, University of Exeter, United Kingdom. He has published a number of articles on contemporary French theatre and has translated plays for use on the professional stage. He has also written a full-length study of the poet Francis Ponge. A bilingual anthology of modern French poems, using his verse translations, is forthcoming. He is a co-founder of the Bac to Bac French-speaking theatre-in-education company, based originally in Exeter and now in London.

Margareta Wirmark is Professor of Comparative Literature at Lund University, Sweden. She has written several books on theatre and drama: *Nuteater. Dokument från och analys av 70-talets gruppteater* (about the independent theatre groups of the 1970s; Stockholm, 1976); *Den kluvna scenen. Kvinnor i Strindbergs dramatik* (about women's role in Strindbergian drama; Stockholm, 1989); and *Kampen med döden. En studie över Strindbergs 'Dödsdansen'* (about the theme of death in Strindberg's *The Dance of Death*, with a summary in English; Stockholm, 1989).

Ralph Yarrow is Lecturer in Drama and European Literature at the University of East Anglia, Norwich, United Kingdom. He has published articles on the functioning of consciousness in relation to reception theory, modernist writing and fantasy. He has devised and edited a *Nouveau Roman Handbook* (Norwich, 1984) for teachers and students, has published with Anthony Frost *Improvisation in Drama* (London, 1990), and is writing a book on traditional Indian theatre and co-writing another on literature and spirituality. He has acted in English, French and German, and directed Strindberg, Jarry and Expressionist drama.

ACKNOWLEDGEMENTS

Thanks are due to the following, in addition to those mentioned at specific points in the text: the School of Modern Languages and European History, University of East Anglia, for financial assistance with research; Michael Robinson; Louise Evans, for typing and comments; and Helena Reckitt at Routledge, for her editorial patience and expertise.

1

INTRODUCTION

Ralph Yarrow

This book looks as though it sets out to tell the story of theatre in Europe during thirty years. But that already poses questions. There may be more than one story; there is more than one way of telling. Each of the chapters shows different angles and implies the possibility of a different method. That diversity is deliberate, although it is also in a way fortuitous. A second question: why this period? Again the answer is slightly different depending on the location, although in a general sense it can be said that the period starts after an era of post-war reconstruction or recovery; and there have been important shifts in the way almost all aspects of theatre, from finance to actor-training, have been viewed. It is a period in which censorship is abandoned in several countries, in which the outburst of political and personal awareness of the 1960s occurs, and in which Europe experiences a variety of political swings. It also ends, fortuitously but appropriately, with a 'year of revolutions' in Eastern Europe which will make the situation significantly different in the future (particularly, no doubt, in Germany and Poland). Economic and political alliances in Europe (EEC, NATO) are already having to adjust to these events, and where these political 'theatres' are required to change, it will not be long before the artistic equivalents reflect the process.

More than one story. Although the major historical events are common, different countries experience them in different ways. Post-war reconstruction tends to want to institutionalize culture as part of the statement of social values; a phase of consolidation then leads to the unrest of the late 1960s. But just as 1968 is not the same everywhere, so there are also various ways in which theatre responds or is involved. Do we tell the story of censorship and its demise? Or give an account of new buildings, public investment in theatres as visible temples of national culture? Do we concern ourselves with new

1

writing, new attitudes to the business of directing, new kinds of training for actors, new understandings of 'performance'? The answer must be that we need to do all these. They have different weighting according to the country concerned, and to the interest and expertise of the writer. This kind of plurality is inevitable, but it is also appropriate. It is not possible, in what is to a large extent a fairly brief summary, to cover everything everywhere. So the juxtaposition is important: what is not given so much importance in one chapter (the historical chronology, for instance; or an account of new writing) is dealt with in others. Many influences are common: the repertoire of established theatres, let alone that of the 'alternative' scene, has always been open to a certain extent to the range of European activity. Actors, directors, styles, all circulate. But where in some cases (particularly German or Swiss theatre) it is difficult to speak of a 'national' theatre, it is necessarily even more so to use the term 'European' too readily. Here too the juxtaposition of frameworks in separate chapters and sections is intended to prevent over-simplification.

Alongside the various accounts of forms and developments runs a thread, sometimes explicit, sometimes implied, of questions about those directions. People who work in theatre have always, at least implicitly, asked these questions, about the place of theatre in society, about its function as mirror or as challenge, about its origins in communal play or in ceremony, about how it works and why. 'Performance theory', which has focused many of these issues, in one sense merely foregrounds what the theatrical activity of many ages and cultures has been concerned to produce. During the period 1960–90, are there identifiable general trends in performance style, shifts in repertoire, and so on? Has the relationship between theatre and society markedly changed, and if so what relevance does this have to the political and cultural context? Have new ways of thinking about theatre (such as performance theory, semiology, feminist theory) significantly affected the ways in which it makes cultural statements and the nature of those statements? Is the operation of theatre still largely an elitist, a marginal, a radical or a conservative enterprise?

The functions of the book are, first, to provide some kind of historical and descriptive account of developments, and second to permit an overview across national boundaries, to try to identify common developments and to analyse their meanings. What has occurred? In what contexts has it taken place? How can it be understood? The method is to take samples rather than to attempt to be totally comprehensive: that is the job of encyclopaedias of world theatre.

There is an imbalance in the length of sections and chapters. This arises partly from the vagaries of putting together a collection of essays by different authors in several countries; but the distinctions in length and approach can be useful. The longest chapters, on West Germany and Poland, for instance, offer detail that is not generally well known outside these countries (George Hyde's precise and instructive accounts of Kantor in performance, for instance), or that exemplifies trends also occurring elsewhere but not so fully documented: Theo Girshausen's careful review of the interweaving of political and aesthetic factors in the growth of new working practices in Frankfurt in the 1970s allows us to eavesdrop on debates which were going on in many theatre companies and institutions at the time. The shorter contributions have their own appropriate shape: the economy and clarity of Gwynne Edwards's account of the period in Spain allows the central fact of Franco's death to stand out; Margareta Wirmark's useful notes on Sweden enable us to perceive interesting parallels relating to the awareness of the need to open theatre to new audiences and discover new styles; they also tell of a national Arts policy perhaps more solidly supported financially than is the case anywhere else (though city and state subsidies in Germany and Switzerland are substantial). The chapter on Austria is particularly short and does not attempt to cover all aspects of the state of Austrian theatre, but the chapter format has been retained for the sake of consistency.

One way of attempting to illustrate developments across the board is to draw up a list of names of people and places who have been of major significance (see Table 1). There is an immediate difficulty in classifying them into categories, because by the nature of their intention and operation many of them transcend such boundaries. And no list is comprehensive; this one does not attempt to be. It offers examples, and it is followed by an alternative account which is more chronological and discursive. The categories themselves are unsatisfactory: 'established' hides much that is innovative; 'alternative' includes fringe, mobile and ethnic.

One look at the 'established' column immediately makes it clear that many of the most innovative performers and directors (Strehler, Stein, Brook, Mnouchkine, for example) do not fit neatly into this category any more than names like Grotowski or Lecoq can be restricted to one kind or area of activity. The example of Fo is left to

Table 1 Major names in European theatre

Established	Alternative	Training	Writing
Barbican	Avignon	Eugenio Barba/Odin Teatret	(Antonin Artaud/Bertolt Brecht/modernism)
Roger Blin ↓	Augusto Boal →	Peter Brook ↓	Fernando Arrabal
Dario Fo	Bread and Puppet	(Jacques Copeau/Michel Saint-Denis tradition) ↓	Samuel Beckett
Intendantenteater	Peter Brook/Bouffes du Nord →	Jerzy Grotowski	Caryl Churchill
National Theatre	Centre Ocean Stream	Jacques Lecoq	Sarah Daniels
Trevor Nunn	Cheek by Jowl ↓		Tankred Dorst
Piccolo Teatro	Complicité		Friedrich Dürrenmatt
Roger Planchon/Villeurbanne	Edinburgh Festival (alternative/Fringe)		Dario Fo
RSC/Peter Hall	Dario Fo		Max Frisch
Peter Stein/Peter Zadek	Gardzienice ↓		Witold Gombrowicz
Giorgio Strehler	Hull Truck		Vaclav Havel
Teatri stabili	Keith Johnstone ↑		Eugène Ionesco
	Joan Littlewood ↑		Elfriede Jelinek
	Living Theater		Tadeusz Kantor
	Mediaeval Players ↓		Milan Kundera
	Ariane Mnouchkine ↑ ↓		Mike Leigh
	Mummenschanz		John Osborne
	Jérôme Savary		Harold Pinter
	Zbigniew Stok/Erika Hänssler		Gerlind Reinshagen
	Teatr Osnia Dnia		Richard Schechner
	Theatre Machine		Peter Weiss
	Trestle		Arnold Wesker
	Trickster		
	Jean Vilar/TNP ↓		

Notes: In film one could also mention Ingmar Bergman, Harold Pinter and Pier Paolo Pasolini
Arrows indicate movement towards another category

4

stand for this transference across boundaries which is to some extent a characteristic of all theatre activity, and which seems particularly prevalent in the period under consideration.

Several things already emerge from this inadequate attempt, which to some extent reflect the bias of my own awareness and to some extent indicate useful connections. Not all the names are European in the strictest sense – Boal is South American, Bread and Puppet are a North American company. Both however have roots in Europe (the latter via Lecoq's Paris school) and have been important influences. There is a preponderance of names in the 'Alternative' column, which in part reflects my sense – supported at least in part, yet not entirely, by the essays in the book – that 'more' was happening in this area. Yet other histories or accounts would deal largely or even exclusively with the more established forms of theatre, and would be able to draw valuable conclusions. It is doubtless true that there was 'more' in terms of variety of performance styles and organizational structures, and perhaps in the sense that much of the energy for change derived from here. Other points to note are that many of the directors who worked in relatively 'established' institutions had a hand in innovative development also – Brook and Vilar to name but two (the latter in a way confirmed by the subsequent appointment of Jérôme Savary to the Théâtre National Populaire, TNP); and that not a few writers worked with companies to develop new approaches to performance in line with, for instance, a feminist or socialist intention: Caryl Churchill with Joint Stock, Mike Leigh with actors as part-creators of the eventual script.

Some useful remarks about the European situation in the 1950s and 1960s can be found in Ferdinando Taviani's introductory essay to *The Floating Islands*, Barba's reflections on theatre. 'The 50s', says Taviani, 'were the years of the Berliner Ensemble, of the Piccolo Teatro of Milan, of Jean Vilar's Théâtre National Populaire. Theater was thought of as a representation and analysis of great historical and class conflicts, a public cultural "service" for all citizens.'[1] However, these relative certitudes gave way in the 1960s before the rediscovery of Artaud and the eruption onto the scene of the Living Theater, and, less dramatically but perhaps more profoundly, the work of Grotowski – from which emerged Barba's experiments and tours with Odin Teatret, and, in combination with an Artaudian view of physicalization, much of Peter Brook's early work. Grotowski's *Towards a Poor Theatre* was not published until 1968, though his work had already become influential;[2] and 1968 itself was of course a form of living theatre in many countries. Even in Britain, which as usual woke up rather late to events in Europe, censorship was abolished in that year. Barrault was forced to resign from the Théâtre de l'Odéon, seen as part of the establishment, which ironically meant that Odin Teatret's planned visit could not take place. In 1968 too, Dario Fo began to develop his *Mistero Buffo*, a one-man *tour de force* linking popular tradition with political topicality. In the 1960s Jacques Lecoq opened his school in Paris (and worked with Fo earlier to develop important aspects of his physical skills). Brook's *The Empty Space* was published in 1968 as well, and distinguishes 'Holy' and 'rough' theatre from the deadly variety.[3] These developments quickly communicated themselves throughout much of Europe, although their full effect was not felt until the latter part of the 1970s and the 1980s in terms of changes in performance style. But already Brook worked on *US* with the RSC in 1966, Ariane Mnouchkine produced *1789* with the Théâtre du Soleil at the Cartoucherie in Paris, again in 1968. Theatre was taking place in different locations, establishing different relationships with its audience, demanding more from its performers, politicizing its message in ways distinct from, but equally aggressive as, those of Brecht. A kind of thoroughgoing renovation was in progress, and the list of writers and directors whose work was being performed during the 1960s indicates the range and depth of what was taking place. The 1960s, not untypically, brought a whole battery of new theoretical and practical propositions which (as, for instance, the chapter on German theatre points out) profoundly affected the nature of much in the organization and operation of theatre, although the 1950s had seen some important developments and consolidations also.

It was during the 1950s that, alongside the consolidation of financial support and theatre buildings, live theatre had to meet the growing challenge of television, together with an albeit temporary resurgence of film. In some cases this led to fruitful interchange (the case of Ingmar Bergman, for example), and at the very least it made it easier for performers to earn a living; but there were negative effects also. Possibly the need to face the challenge had a part to play in stimulating a greater readiness to experiment. Administrators, performers and writers were more prepared to experiment with new models. From the vantage-point of 1990 it looks as if the impetus has faded, but this may in part be because the things that happened during the period 1965–85 (roughly) were so important. A period of retrenchment or assimilation is inevitable, although in some cases other factors appear even more significant. Permanent theatres and rep in Britain, for instance, face serious economic problems; there is a 'crisis' in West German theatre; little new writing is making a general impact; even in Poland, where theatre activity has displayed intense and ingenious forms of questioning, theatre has been upstaged by the events of the 1989 'revolutions' of Eastern Europe – there may be less incentive when there is less obviously to protest about. That last point, however, is speculation; we are more concerned with the changes that have taken place in the period under discussion.

An overview of the 'story' might suggest that it goes something like this since the late 1950s: in *actor-training* it's more about physical readiness, attention, play, mutual responsibility (Grotowski, Lecoq, Johnstone, Brook, Barba); less about personal charisma, operatic vocalization, projection; in *directing* more about working *with* actors and writers, being a workshop leader or catalyst, less about total domination of text or production (the names mentioned above, plus Littlewood, Stein, Mnouchkine); in *organization* more about co-operatives, companies choosing repertoires and methods/styles (Stein again; Fo's companies; Gardzienice); in *financial structure* – in some places – towards greater independence and flexibility, cultural and political, but perhaps correspondingly greater insecurity; in others, towards increasing subsidy (Sweden) or unequal distribution of public money (Britain, Switzerland). Whether this holds good in all contexts can be explored through the succeeding chapters. We might then ask whether there is such a thing as a 'post-modern' condition for theatre, although that rather academic issue is less important than a feel for the degree to which the plurality and richness of the experience called 'theatre' can still open people up to major human concerns.

It would be useful here to pick out a few of the major features that each chapter deals with. The tension between the established and the innovative, not surprisingly, is found everywhere, although the boundaries of what these terms define themselves shift, and the two are by no means entirely mutually exclusive.

In France there are moves towards decentralization and populariz-ation, with considerable 'official' support; the establishment of theatre in alternative spaces and modes (Brook at the Bouffes du Nord, Mnouchkine at the Cartoucherie, Vilar at the TNP, Savary, Plan-chon at Villeurbanne; the growing influence of Lecoq). Plenty of new directions here, although the setting-up and funding of regional theatre does not always escape from the tendency to fall back on familiar repertoires and styles.

In Germany theatre is heavily subsidized by the *Land* and/or the city, with little room for alternative structures; a part of the reconstruction of West German society, a necessary public cultural statement; but within the framework of a theatre largely operated by its managers, cracks and pressures emerge. Directors like Stein and Zadek seek new management styles as well as performance and repertoire innovations.

In Spain the central event is the death of Franco and the end of the sole surviving fascist regime in Europe; the end of theatre censorship is particularly significant here, and the emergence of theatre as social comment and of mobile theatre is directly linked to the closing phase of the regime.

Censorship ends in Italy also. This is important particularly in coinciding with the growing recognition in the work of Fo of the importance of re-establishing links with popular (*giullari*) traditions: theatre becomes physical confrontation with current issues in the wake of disruption instigated by the repressive attitude of the authorities to the visit of the Living Theater. The Established theatre, even though its principal proponents had, like Strehler, excellent credentials, is outpaced by more energetic and confrontational forms. There is also a significant expansion of opportunities for actor-training, with the establishment of schools in Milan, Bologna, Genoa, Florence and Rome.

Censorship ends in Britain and improvisation can be admitted to the stage: the effect is felt not just on performance but also on actor-training and on attitudes to the understanding of theatre as collective event. New building attempts to secure nationally prestigious theatrical institutions, and does offer new space for varied performance styles (the National Theatre with its plurality of stage/auditorium configurations, for example); perhaps more significant is the growth of small-scale touring theatre with (limited) Arts Council funding, and the parallel decline of more static repertory theatre.

In Poland the most crucial event may be the last: the as-yet-unknown effects of the 1989 political shift. But Polish theatre has already become known as a source of energy for Europe, even though its work – both the ascetic performance requirements of Grotowski and others, and the intense and difficult work of writers like Kantor – is known only to a restricted audience both inside and outside the country. A curiously potent charge seems to emerge from a theatre which is largely unofficial, even suppressed and persecuted, yet also in some way admitted as such.

In Scandinavia Bergman returns to the theatre and to some extent reclaims its importance in spite, or because, of his own use of film. Barba's work in Denmark is a marker for 'third theatre' everywhere – even as far away as India, where Badal Sircar uses the same term for his theatre in Calcutta – and for the interest in cultural exchange, in theatre as barter; like many other trainers of the period, he is less impressed by the need for traditional declamatory skill than by a requirement that the performer undergoes a kind of individual and group psychotherapy. Performance here, as for others, begins to emerge as a particular kind of model for personal and social interaction – the psychological and to some extent political inheritance of the 1950s articulating itself in terms of organizational and performance strategies. There are also important moves towards establishing theatre in the regions and opening it to those who would otherwise have little access or inclination to attend.

In all of this are we to adopt an Artaudian (psychological) or a Brechtian (political) view of the ways in which theatre reproduces or expresses personal and social being? Is performative action of the public kind theatre presents essentially an outburst of 'plague', a volcanic eruption of the pressures that the play of theatre allows to emerge, whereas the polite surface of the everyday does not? Are these eruptions to be understood as personal or collective? Does encouraging them defuse or escalate them? Is theatre part of the health of society or an expression of its sickness? These questions are, of course, not merely relevant to theatre of the period under discussion; but they emerge once again from a look at the events that took place during it, and they confirm that such issues are perennial for a consideration of the function of theatre. Since the period has also seen a huge upsurge in theorizing about theatre, they have been pushed once again to the forefront; but this upsurge is paralleled, by, or perhaps emerges from, a growing plurality of theatre forms. There are important issues to consider and there are important attempts to try to create theatre in new ways; the two are inextricable.

The chapters that follow raise these issues both explicitly and implicitly. Hopefully they will provide an insight into developments in an ambiguous and exciting period. If theatre 'speaks' to us directly, it does so as a total experience which may in some ways bypass the circumlocutions of verbal language; but that totality includes the many languages by which we construct and communicate our personal and social experience; it is a politics of performance and an articulation of being.

NOTES

1 Ferdinando Taviani, Introduction to Eugenio Barba, *The Floating Islands*, Holstebro, 1979: 10.
2 Jerzy Grotowski, *Towards a Poor Theatre*, Copenhagen, 1968; trans. various, London, 1969.
3 Peter Brook, *The Empty Space*, London, 1968, and Harmondsworth, 1972.

2

FRANCE

Towards *création collective*

David Jeffery

INTRODUCTION

Within eighteen months of de Gaulle's return to power in October 1958 and the promulgation of the Constitution of the Fifth Republic, a Ministère des Affaires Culturelles had been created under André Malraux, Planchon's Théâtre de la Cité de Villeurbanne had been designated the first Troupe Permanente within a new decentralization policy, and another Centre Dramatique had been created – in the Northern region at last – under André Reybaz. The years 1959–60 have been named 'ces années charnières où la promotion redémarre en province',[1] and the following decade under Malraux's direction – he was replaced in 1969 by Edmond Michelet – saw one of the most spectacular advances in government-subsidized cultural policies in the history of France.

In the years 1960–3 three new Centres Dramatiques and seven Troupes Permanentes had been established in the provinces. To these must be added a Maison de la Culture – in Caen – and a Théâtre National – Le Théâtre de l'Est Parisien. However, it would be convenient but erroneous to ascribe this surge of activity entirely to enlightened government intervention: several of these new enterprises had been in existence over a period of years and had been providing a Jean Vilar-type 'service public' to local inhabitants through a variety of cultural activities. It was as much to the credit of their directors, in their tenacity and dedication, as to the government in their wisdom, that their futures were put on a financially sound basis.

By the end of Malraux's period of office in 1969, there were fractionally more Troupes Permanentes than Centres Dramatiques in France – the respective totals being nine and eight. The Troupes

11

Permanentes were organizations complementary to the Centres Dramatiques but enjoying a lower level of government subsidy. In status they represented a middle echelon between the nationally recognized Centres and the regionally distinguished, but still amateur, drama companies. Some of the Troupes Permanentes became fully-fledged Centres later – this was the case with the Comédie de Caen and the Théâtre du Cothurne; others developed their activities to include performances at the later Maisons de la Culture, a third echelon of dramatic centres which were established from 1963 onwards.

The extent of the various subsidies allotted to the two major theatre organizations, the Centres Dramatiques and the Troupes Perma-nentes, analysed in detail in Raymonde Temkine's book,[2] illustrates the distinction between them. In 1965 the Centres were receiving, on average, four times as much money from the state as the Troupes. However, the Troupes received proportionally far more in local subsidy – from the 'collectivités locales' – than their senior counter-parts. Not infrequently their income from local sources surpassed that from the government – this was the case with the Comédie de Nantes, the Théâtre de Champagne and the Théâtre Populaire de Flandres – while the subsidies received from the two sources by the Comédie des Alpes were roughly equal. These financial points illustrate the importance of the local community to the Troupes Permanentes – an importance which is reciprocated by the presentations of the compa-nies themselves in terms of their repertoire and localized orientation.

Such *rapports*, however, lead directly to problems both for the theatre directors and for the community they serve and these problems in their turn have a bearing on the repertoires of the companies. In general, the accusation of cultural paternalism may be levelled at any government intervention in the arts; in France, during the period of decentralization, this criticism tended to be counteracted by the very real and practical results of the rapid expansion of dramatic activity within the tripartite system of Centres Dramatiques, Troupes Permanentes and Maisons de la Culture. In addition, as Bradby and McCormick have pointed out, 'the Maisons de la Culture were justified as part of a plan to promote the growth and prestige of French culture, the term "culture" being understood in a conser-vative sense.'[3] This promotion of French culture also spread abroad with the foreign tours of the companies of individual Centres Dramatiques.

The decentralization movement in the French theatre of the 1960s, therefore, consisted not only of a lateral, or geographical, expansion into the provinces, but also a vertical delineation of character, through the triple-level system of Centres Dramatiques, Troupes Permanentes and Maisons de la Culture. Nor were the provinces the only areas to benefit from this expansion: between 1960 and 1966, six theatres, all more or less experimental in character, opened in the suburbs of Paris.

The original Centres, all established by 1952, were joined by the Centre Dramatique du Nord in 1960, the Comédie de Bourges in 1963, the Théâtre de la Cité de Villeurbanne in 1963 and the Théâtre de l'Est Parisien in 1966. Sarrazin remarked of the new era under Malraux's ministry, 'En 1958, avec la décentralisation, le Théâtre National Populaire et les festivals, on recommence à respirer dans le théâtre.'[4]

Of all the original Centres Dramatiques, it was the Comédie de Saint-Etienne whose repertoire changed the most radically in the 1960s. Jean Dasté's last production of a Shakespeare play had been in 1958 and in subsequent seasons he regularly produced Molière, but his repertoire is significant for its introduction of the works of the newer French dramatists: Jamiaque in 1959, Vinaver in 1960, Cousin in 1962 and 1963, Gatti in 1966, Atlan in 1967, Audiberti in 1968 and Arrabal in 1969.

> Jean Dasté s'adresse tout spécialement à un public ouvrier, préoccupé par les problèmes que pose l'actualité. A ce public, il présente volontiers des œuvres représentatives du théâtre politique contemporain: *Les Coréens, Le Drame du Fukuryu-Maru, Un homme seul*. Brecht est fréquemment joué. Grâce aux efforts de Jean Dasté, un certain nombre d'ouvriers a compris que le théâtre pourrait être à la fois une distraction pour la masse et un instrument de libération.[5]

Other authors whose works featured in the repertoire more than once were Brecht, O'Casey, Gogol and Frisch. From these statistics, it is evident that Dasté was aiming to present drama with a social or political commitment; Dasté's own account of these years substantiates this view:

> Nous sentions la nécessité (en 1958) de jouer des œuvres d'auteurs vivants. Nous avions été jusque-là trop absorbés par la conquête d'un public (les tournées nous éloignaient de Saint-Etienne plusieurs mois dans la saison) pour avoir la possibilité

d'attirer en permanence de jeunes écrivains. Conscients de ce manque, nous décidons de faire tous nos efforts pour présenter, chaque saison, au moins une création au public.[6]

Two points of interest arise from this statement: first, that Dasté found himself too concerned about seeking an audience – suggesting that he would have preferred to create his own repertoire from choice and not out of necessity; second, that he now fully intended to act on a permanent basis as an outlet for new authors. Dasté's zeal as an innovator and experimental director had in no way diminished since his arrival in Saint-Etienne: in addition to their dramatic activities at Saint-Etienne, the Comédie had played during the summer of 1958 in a large circus tent, reminding Dasté of his period spent with the Copiaus in Burgundy; a young troupe presented a play for children in 1960 called *Les Musiques magiques*; Dasté himself continued his pastime of creating masks that represented politicians frequently seen on television, and also stressed the importance of masks in drama (especially in the recent production of Brecht's *Caucasian Chalk Circle*) and thus continued a tradition of the *commedia dell'arte* which was to be extended a few years later by Ariane Mnouchkine's company, Le Théâtre du Soleil.

Although differing in status from the Centres Dramatiques, the Troupes Permanentes operated similar programmes to, and possessed the same philosophy as, their senior counterparts to whose rank they all aspired. Their more itinerant nature, however, allowed them access to different audiences – such as local schools and small communities – and their resulting adaptability led to simpler sets and more modest presentations.

The statutes of the Centres Dramatiques and the Troupes Permanentes stipulated that they should produce four new plays each per season. After November 1965 this provision was changed to three new plays, of which one was to be classical, another a première. The minimum number of performances was to be 110 per season for each type of theatre: the overall pattern of their repertoires was therefore similar, the only major difference being in the smaller subsidies allowed to the Troupes Permanentes to fulfil those conditions.

In purely numerical terms, the Maisons de la Culture matched the Centres and the Troupes in importance: nine establishments were created in the 1960s. However, in terms of their function as purveyors of culture for all – as an adjunct to the notion of 'éducation permanente' perhaps, serving the whole community with a dazzling variety of cultural activities – they may be judged to have had a greater influence on the nation than their administratively senior counterparts.

Although the first Maisons at Le Havre, Caen and Bourges suffered from the constraints of being housed respectively in a museum, a municipal theatre and an outdated building, later Maisons at Amiens, Thonon, Rennes, Saint-Etienne, Firminy and Grenoble were designed individually to suit the needs of their communities. Despite some early political difficulties – including the unnecessarily premature change of administrators in Paris – the multi-media 'polyvalence' of the Maisons remained the fundamental principle on which they were all based. Facilities for drama formed the hub of their activities.

The granting of the status of a Maison to an area where an *animateur* had already acquired a following in an otherwise culturally barren region indicated that drama in general, and popular theatre in particular, was dictating the pace of development. *De facto* dramatic achievement preceded *de jure* recognition, and not vice versa, thus demonstrating the strength of the popular theatre movement as a whole. However, new or experimental drama could not provide the exclusive diet of the Maisons – nor would the public expect or want it to – but, conversely, the Maisons did offer an outlet for much of the new writing produced in the 1960s. Malraux's conception of the Maisons as purveyors of France's cultural heritage was another facet of their *raison d'être*; his other aim – to further the creation of works of art to enrich that heritage – more than adequately supplied the motive for them to practise new forms and fresh material. Not many of the Maisons were endowed with the finance or the talent to produce entirely home-based programmes, and their statutes, requiring a fifty–fifty financial share in their enterprise by state and municipality, inevitably ensured some outside influence. Many were receiving centres for itinerant groups such as the Franc-Théâtre or the Tréteaux de France; most attracted foreign companies or smaller groups of musicians, dancers, poets or players; all consciously and actively decentralized culture to the extent that local talent featured on programmes of activities side by side with nationally recognized artists.

An analysis of the repertoires of the Maisons de la Culture reveals that they are far less conservative and far more experimental than the Troupes Permanentes or the Centres Dramatiques: Molière, for example, appears only three times in the ATAC (Association Technique pour l'Action Culturelle) list of programmes for the nine

Maisons from 1967 until 1973; Shakespeare's plays were performed only at Thonon; only one Musset play and no Marivaux plays at all were put on by the Maisons in this period. In view of the fact that Molière, Shakespeare, Musset and Marivaux were four of the five most frequently performed authors in the new subsidized theatres – the other being Brecht – the Maisons can be said to have brought a new spirit of experimentation to the decentralization movement.

It was now possible to separate the functions of the well-endowed regional Centres and the more localized Maisons de la Culture, with the result that repertoires became more flexible, more suited to specific needs and more experimental in character. This brought benefits both for potential audiences and for the new dramatists emerging during this period; more important still, it allowed theatre to remain permanently up to date by providing social commentaries on certain issues, thus reacting against the hallowed notion of the theatre as a cultural museum-piece or as an archaic medium of communication and entertainment. In ten short years the theatre had descended from its elevated position as a bourgeois institution and had demystified its rituals to become the mouthpiece of the man-in-the-street with his everyday problems and his desire to communicate his experiences. The new Maisons were social meeting-places and initiators of a great variety of cultural experiences.

Experimentation was the order of the day; even the Théâtre National Populaire (TNP) was not immune from attempting new authors and new themes: in January 1967 Georges Wilson opened the Salle Gémier in the Palais de Chaillot with a production of Kateb Yacine's *Les Ancêtres redoublent de férocité*, a flamboyant and ritualistic treatment of the Algerian war. The Salle Gémier was to be an experimental theatre aimed at revitalizing the TNP repertory.

New York's Living Theater appeared for the first time in France in 1961 at the Théâtre des Nations festival in Paris. It introduced the French public to environmental theatre. A return tour in 1966 revealed a shift to radical, didactic theatre with a production of *The Brig, Mysteries* and *Smaller Pieces*.

Le Living Theater propose d'en finir non seulement avec les théâtres conventionnels et leurs structures à l'italienne, mais avec la forme traditionnelle du spectacle. Il faut faire violence au spectateur, provoquer une catharsis, communier avec la salle. Le public sera sollicité des manières les plus directes. Gesticulations, appels, provocations, exhibitionnisme essaieront d'établir sa participation profonde au jeu. Ici encore on tente de dépasser Artaud sur son propre terrain. La France a accueilli le Living avec intérêt et curiosité, bien qu'une partie de l'opinion ait jugé outrés et puérils ses moyens de 'mise en condition' des spectateurs. Le Living Theater a intéressé bon nombre d'animateurs qui croient à la communication gestuelle, à la participation du public au jeu dramatique.[7]

In 1968 the appearance of the Bread and Puppet Theater at the Sixth World Theatre Festival in Nancy caused a sensation, with its productions of *Fire* – a Vietnam protest piece – and two street-theatre shows, *Chairs* and *A Man Says Goodbye to His Mother*. Radical American theatre thus paved the way for new French groups also seeking to give back to the theatre its social function. Agitprop theatre showed that it was necessary to break not only with traditional ways of acting, but also with production methods. Françoise Kourilsky, in her book on the Bread and Puppet Theater,[8] explained the philosophy behind the art–life relationship: the technique of radical theatre lies in the commitment and understanding of the political nature of reality. It is not a question of making a 'cultural revolution' (a counter-culture to that of the Establishment, or local activities in which the spectators and actors are awakened to the reality surrounding them), but of making theatre *one* of the weapons of social revolution.

There was no doubt that, by 1968, a powerful momentum in the theatre was under way which drew dramatists and *animateurs* alike towards ever more experimentation and diversification of their activities: the enormously expanded programme of the Avignon Festival reflected these changes in French theatre. Indeed, France in the year 1968 might itself be regarded as the climactic point of a dramatic intrigue which had lasted for twenty years; tragically, the decentralization movement carried the seeds of its own destruction, namely, its propensity to become constantly more political – generally with left-wing tendencies – and this factor brought an inevitable clash with the authorities, both local and national. What 1968 probably demonstrated was that the people's theatre movement since Vilar had deluded itself into thinking that public-service theatre could somehow contribute actively towards unifying society itself. Such cultural evangelism has given way to individualistic experimentation – such as that of Gatti – and a healthy reassessment of theatrical form and style – such as practised by the Théâtre du Soleil. Much of the new style may be self-conscious or even derivative, borrowing from

Artaud, Brecht or the Absurdists, but it does demonstrate a vitality and diversity that is ensuring the theatre's survival as a living art-form in France today.

THE AVIGNON FESTIVAL

Jean Vilar's directorship of the Avignon Festival, lasting from its inception in 1947 until his death in 1971, represented, in a seminal way, the history of French theatre in the post-war period.

First, it established the concept of 'festival theatre' in France, a provincial base for nationally known actors attracting both tourists and others in the summer months to a brief season of quality theatre. As a venue, Avignon was ideal: Vilar's utopian desire to transcend class barriers and unite all the members of a community in a common appreciation of theatre was realized with facility in the warm and relaxed atmosphere of Provence, where theatre-goers enthusiastically attended the post-production discussions until the early hours.

Second, Vilar the *animateur* had so successfully stimulated a demand for theatre among the young – particularly in the Palais de Chaillot in Paris after 1951 – that his TNP became the focus of fashionable student activity both in Paris and Avignon, and the latter soon emerged as a Mecca for such groups from other countries. Indeed, the TNP charisma turned theatre-going into a ritual and the *habitués* of Avignon recall the 1950s not so much with nostalgia as with a quasi-religious veneration, worshipping Vilar as their god, and Gérard Philipe, the handsome *jeune premier* of Vilar's early productions, as their messiah.

Probably even more important for French theatre history was Vilar's contribution towards the popular theatre movement which emerged strongly in the 1960s and, while appealing to wider audiences, also contained the germs of a didactic approach such as Vilar had attempted with his repertoire of plays demonstrating a civic conscience among their heroes and inciting their audiences to consider their own moral and political responsibilities.

The Avignon Festival and the TNP shared a common destiny: both in the Palais de Chaillot and the Cour d'Honneur of Avignon's Palais des Papes, the audience numbered close on 3,000, but it was in Avignon that the real success of Vilar's venture could be measured: the audience of 5,000 who came to the first Festival in 1947 had increased to 30,000 by 1954, and 50,000 by 1963. In 1960 there were no less than fifty festivals throughout France, while Avignon itself had spawned numerous peripheral theatre activities such as lectures, debates and meetings between the actors and their public.

Vilar's philosophy thus pervaded the whole of the incipient decentralization movement since such activities became an integral part of the programmes of the Centres Dramatiques and Troupes Permanentes in existence by 1965. Equally, his political pre-occupations, never overtly expressed through his choice of plays but alluded to in such productions as Aristophanes' *Peace* and Giraudoux's *La Guerre de Troie n'aura pas lieu* at the time of the negotiations aimed at ending the Algerian war, laid the foundations for more explicitly political theatre under his successor at the TNP, Georges Wilson, who took over the company after Vilar's resignation from the position in 1963. Indeed, Vilar had sensed the changing times and Wilson acknowledged this:

> Notre théâtre, sur le plan idéologique, reste ce qu'il était: non un instrument de combat ou de parti, mais un moyen d'aider nos concitoyens à réfléchir sur les problèmes actuels. Que je conçoive ce moyen autrement que Vilar ne signifie pas pour moi une rupture, mais une continuation.[9]

Vilar could now devote his efforts towards the expansion of the Avignon Festival as he had long envisaged it: a vast festival of culture in which the cinema, music and dance could have a place beside that of theatre, and where topical problems raised by these events could take place between artists and spectators.

Some contacts had already been established: the first Rencontres Internationales de Jeunes were in 1955, and various other lectures, discussions, films and poetry-readings had been organized first by the association Les Amis du Théâtre Populaire, then by the TNP house-journal *Bref* until 1963. Vilar instigated the first Rencontres d'Avignon in 1964 which debated themes such as 'Pourquoi la culture? Pour qui?', 'Situation actuelle et avenir du public', 'La Culture est-elle rentable?', 'L'Etat doit-il avoir une politique culturelle?' Vilar, having decided not to direct any more plays, chose instead to select texts and to entrust their production to others. Paradoxically, his manifestly altruistic and libertarian approach to the Festival and its development was to cause him grave problems a few years later.

The real revolution in the history of the Festival came in 1966 – its twentieth anniversary – when Vilar decided to extend the period of the productions from a fortnight to one month and to open Avignon to new troupes. He invited Roger Planchon's Théâtre de la Cité de

Villeurbanne and Maurice Béjart's Ballet du XXe siècle to perform on equal footing with the TNP. Both troupes were triumphant, the former with their *Richard III* and the latter with a variety of set pieces and improvisations. For Claude Samuel of *Paris-Presse*, Avignon had now become 'le festival français le plus passionnant et le plus enrichissant de l'été' (*Paris Presse*, 12 August 1967). The total number of spectators at the Festival had risen from 53,000 in 1965 to 83,000 in 1966. It reached 100,000 the following year.

However, the mould had been broken: Planchon, refusing to play in the Cour d'Honneur of the Palais des Papes, the traditional venue of the TNP (but ceded to Béjart in 1966), had moved outside into the Place du Palais, symbolically instituting the movement of the whole Festival into and across Avignon itself. The second Avignon had begun, the Festival-cum-Fair, which slowly but inevitably absorbed the town, its host. New venues were needed to house the new activities: the Cloître des Carmes and the Cloître des Célestins were taken over in 1967 and 1968 respectively. A programme of films was inaugurated in 1967 with the world première of Jean-Luc Godard's *La Chinoise*, more contemporary pieces for the theatre were presented by Antoine Bourseiller's Centre Dramatique National du Sud-Est, while Planchon brought his revolutionary *Bleus, Blancs, Rouges ou Les Libertins*. Avignon's main square, the Place de l'Horloge, resembled a huge caravanserai and Jean Lacouture of *Le Monde* remarked that 'Avignon n'est plus une ville qui a un festival, c'est un festival qui a une ville' (*Le Monde*, 18 August 1967).

This new Festival – part Rio carnival, part Seville Feria – brought in street theatre, encouraged even more students to come to Avignon (a survey taken in 1967 showed 50 per cent of audiences to be under 25 years of age and from 57 different countries) and attracted new works to be performed. Against this positive background of cultural creativity, there were some reasons to feel disquieted: the TNP were absent from the Festival for the first time and Vilar himself detected signs of a change in the relationship between plays, players and audiences in 1967 ('J'ai constaté des changements, un nouveau type de relation entre le spectacle et le spectateur . . ., des poussées de fièvre assez inquiétantes, quelque chose de frénétique et d'indiscret').[10]

Such forebodings did not prevent Vilar – characteristically – from inviting an avant-garde troupe to the 1968 Festival which, as irony would have it, provided the focus for the protests of the Paris *enragés* who descended on Avignon that summer. Julian Beck and Judith Malina's Living Theater were offered the new venue of the Cloître des

Carmes for their production of *Paradise Now*, a spectacle inspired by Artaud and employing gesture akin to yoga or Zen Buddhism. However, despite the potential for hope and joy in this form of expression, and despite the novelty and stunning impression the company made on its audiences, it was the outward and more public image of the Living Theater performers that shocked the Avignonnais. The hippy looks and communal life-style of the group began to disquiet people and when, in addition, a protest play by Gérard Gélas's company Le Théâtre du Chêne Noir was banned by the Prefect of the Gard department, the Festival took on a distinctly political flavour, polarizing the forces already at work in French culture since May. The situation was exacerbated by the result of the local election campaign, in which the Republican candidate ousted the socialist mayor of Avignon, Henri Duffaut. Not only had the spirit of the Festival been compromised by this time, but Vilar found himself attacked by the protesters for running a 'cultural supermarket' for bourgeois reactionaries, and, by the right, for subsidizing questionably artistic productions from municipal funds. Riot police had even been called in to quell the demonstrations, thus adding to the chaos. The greatest irony for Vilar was that he had been denied freedom of speech by a handful of aggressive *contestataires* of dubious intellectual honesty in the very place (the Verger d'Urbain V) that he had created to provide such freedom.

Vilar's own position had been compromised when the Living Theater sided with the protesters, but their subsequent voluntary withdrawal from the Festival, together with Vilar's demands that no one should prevent the rest of the year's programme from continuing and the municipality's offer of a free buffet-dance for festival-goers, resulted in a calm and relaxed conclusion to the events of 1968. Six months later Vilar had his first heart attack.

Far from being a year of recuperation and moral stock-taking, 1969 was one of yet more innovation: a new art-form, the *théâtre musical* was introduced to the Festival, children's shows were put on, five young directors made their début, and four non-subsidized companies were also invited. The company which made the most impact was undoubtedly the Théâtre du Soleil which, with its 28-year-old director, Ariane Mnouchkine, toured around the suburbs of Avignon, giving twenty-five performances of their *Les Clowns* in a mobile fairground booth. Not only had popular theatre thus entered the Avignon Festival, but an alternative festival – 'le festival-off' – now began to compete with the official. Situated on the Ile de la Barthelasse in the

Rhône, its main poles of attraction were Gérard Gélas's company Le Théâtre du Chêne Noir and André Benedetto's Nouvelle Compagnie d'Avignon whose *Emballage*, a piece of collective Marxist writing on the theme of work, was presented in 1970. In the same year five new companies were invited to the official Festival, and, to Vilar's great personal satisfaction, a Picasso exhibition – showing his entire output for 1969 and 1970, amounting to 167 paintings and 50 drawings – was put on in the Grande Chapelle.

Vilar's death in May 1971 at the age of 59 ended an era, but not the doctrine with which he had single-handedly and single-mindedly endowed the Festival: it was, by the end of the 1960s, a cultural Mecca constantly being rejuvenated with new productions and new individual talents; a showcase, albeit an unnerving one for the uninitiated, of the best and the most interesting developments in a multitude of art-forms; above all, it was a show that had to go on and Vilar's chosen successor (as 'permanent administrator' rather than as creative artist) was Paul Puaux who dedicated himself to bringing to Avignon strong, uncomplicated drama for wide audiences. The 1971 programme had already been prepared by Vilar: it included the début of Théâtre Ouvert, the Théâtre de la Ville performing works by Giraudoux and Dario Fo, and a film retrospective of the work of Akira Kurosawa. True to character, Vilar had embraced the 'festival-off'; although he thus prevented the institutionalization of the Avignon Festival, his successors were left the task of centralizing and regulating the enormous number of alternative events that appeared each year.

Containing this output became Puaux's major task – almost every professional company now visited Avignon and there were up to 140 performances every day in both the official and 'off' festivals – and he attempted to inject some political or artistic coherence into each year's programme in order to rationalize the whole structure: in 1975 the accent was on young directors; in 1976, on minorities; in 1977 there was a concentration on the theatre of gesture, mime and clowning; in 1978 a greater international presence was stimulated.

In the later 1970s several companies brought Shakespeare to Avignon audiences; they were the Théâtre de l'Est Parisien, the Atelier théâtral de Louvain-la-Neuve, and the East Berlin Volksbühne. Puaux asked of the troupes he invited that they play a variety of their work, not simply one of their successful pieces. In 1978 Antoine Vitez produced four Molière plays at the Festival, while in 1979 Peter Brook had considerable success with his *Conference of the Birds*, and Ariane Mnouchkine's Théâtre du Soleil returned after a ten-year absence to stage their *Méphisto*.

In the field of dance, several overseas troupes were invited, including members of the Bolshoi in 1971 and dancers from the Ballet Malegot in Leningrad in 1976, the same year that the American Merce Cunningham brought his troupe and offered ticket-holders free seats at the rehearsals for their show *Events*. One of the outstanding productions of the period of the 1970s was the five-hour drama, music and dance production of the Bob Wilson company entitled *Einstein on the Beach* depicting eighty years of the scientist's life.

Throughout the 1970s there was close collaboration between the Festival and Théâtre Ouvert who acted as a bridge between Avignon and Paris where they also performed their experimental works by unknown authors. However, Puaux, contrary to expectations, did not invite them for 1979; unexpectedly too, he announced his withdrawal from the chief administrative post he had held for nine years; neither of these decisions has been fully explained. However, Puaux did retire in the knowledge that his project for a Maison Jean Vilar was complete: this is a centre for theatre studies in Avignon, housing documents of the Vilar period (1947–71) and giving professional people and researchers access to important source-materials.

The Avignon Festival now provides over a hundred presentations a day and has spread into every cellar, back-shop and courtyard in the town; it has crossed the Rhône into Villeneuve-lès-Avignon and suffers from a certain *gigantisme*, despite efforts by its administrators to limit its activities. The Festival has become the Cannes of the theatre world – without the prizes – attracting young and old, professional and amateur, and, as Vilar would have approved, people from all classes of society. Vilar would also have applauded the capacity of the Festival to continue to contain extremes in apparently peaceful co-existence; as in his day, people do not come to Avignon to see theatre but to talk about it, to live it, to let it overwhelm them – and these clear virtues of the Festival are Vilar's greatest legacy to us.

GABRIEL COUSIN'S *VIVRE EN 1968*: STREET THEATRE IN FRANCE

The work of Gabriel Cousin, a contemporary French dramatist whose plays are almost entirely unknown in Britain, is significant for two important reasons: first, his personal development as a dramatist encompasses both the pre-war ethos of Artaud and Copeau and the post-war experience of the Theatre of the Absurd while embracing a left-wing political stance towards the historical events of these two periods; second, his writing – part derivative, part intensely personal – typifies much of the drama dealing with socio-political themes and demanding a *prise de conscience* from spectators which characterized the repertoires of the decentralized theatres in France during the 1960s.

In his early plays Cousin dealt with such social and political issues as malnutrition and famine, racism, the H-Bomb and the alienation of individuals caused by over-automated work processes. His *Vivre en 1968*, described as 'une tentative de théâtre mobile par cheminement dans la rue', was France's first experiment in street theatre. It took place on Saturday 27 July 1968 in the town of Châtillon-sur-Chalaronne in the department of Ain, and consisted of eleven *séquences* performed in the manner of the Stations of the Cross at twelve different sites throughout the town. The production began at 9 p.m. and lasted for nearly two-and-a-half hours; it attracted some 600 spectators – one-fifth of the population of Châtillon and its surrounding villages.

Cousin wrote the text in a very short space of time: the scheme of the action had been finalized on 23 May and he completed the writing in ten days, then rehearsed with the thirty-five actors, dancers and singers for a further month until the performance. The action of the play was accompanied by a small orchestra consisting of a drum, a flute, a trumpet and an accordion, and it was heralded by torch-bearers who provided the initial link between the actors and the public by giving explanations of the contents of each Sequence and leading discussions on the issues raised.

The Prologue and first Sequence took place by the Porte de Villars at the entrance to the town. The Prologue reminded the inhabitants of Châtillon of the violence in the world outside their own peaceful existence, and of the expectations of men in other countries compared with theirs. Saint Vincent de Paul, a native of Châtillon in the seventeenth century, was introduced into the action here, calling upon the people of the town to awaken from their complacency and to become aware of the various forms of evil in the world. Actors dressed in monks' cowls and carrying banners proclaiming the areas where peace and liberty were currently lacking – Biafra, the Congo and Egypt – reminded the onlookers of the international scale of hardship. The effect of this scene was enhanced by having the actors drop to the ground as the death tolls from wars and torture were announced for each country and, as the players advanced and fell, so the spectators were obliged to walk over their bodies.

The second Sequence served as an introduction to the themes of Cousin's short play *La Descente sur Récife* which constituted the whole of the third Sequence and which was performed on a raised platform by the central market of Châtillon. The play concerns the plight of the poor peasants of Recife in Brazil's drought-ridden Nordeste region where, condemned to a state of endemic famine, they survive on a diet of crabs until their eventual and inevitable death from malnutrition. The theme of worldwide famine was again evoked in the following Sequence, a scene primarily of gesture and sound by the actors who moved among the crowd accompanied by drumrolls.

The following Sequences illustrated the evils of exploitation in various guises: the silkworkers of Lyon sang in protest at the Church and Government for whom they provided fine robes while they themselves barely had shirts to cover their backs; South America was again the setting for an illustration of US imperialism through economic exploitation and domination; the seventh Sequence portrayed India and its landowning maharajas who use religious fear to subjugate their employees.

The eighth Sequence recounted the genocide of the original Brazilian Indians in Amazonia: one group of actors represented capitalist society, enjoying an evening in a night-club listening to jazz; the other group were Indians living in primitive simplicity and dancing and singing to the flute. A sadistic scene followed, in which the capitalists intimidated the Indians, offered them drink to weaken them, then shot them dead. This scene was in the style of the Bread and Puppet Theater's representation of Vietnam put on at the Festival de Nancy earlier the same year. Simulated bomb explosions formed the transition to the next Sequence which demonstrated the potential and actual horrors of atomic warfare; examples were taken from contemporary events – the crash of an American bomber in Spain resulting in radioactive contamination of the region, the explosion of another bomber in Greenland, the disappearance of a nuclear submarine under the Atlantic.

The tenth Sequence took place outside the church and summarized the imminent tragedies of the world in statistical form: the over-population of underdeveloped countries, racial inequalities, social and political injustices in many countries, including France. In Brechtian manner, slide projections presented the texts spoken by an unseen actor. The sequence ended with a balletic form of a play showing the power-struggles of three different ethnic groups, the whole scene dominated by one actor brandishing a whip. The performance ended with a simulation of total global destruction; all the actors paused for meditation until, from inside the church, a voice proclaimed

> Qui veut gagner sa vie la perdra,
> Qui veut perdre sa vie la gagnera.

A negro spiritual began as the whole cast processed into the church, where the final Sequence took place.

The last scene is one of exaltation: it is a plea for strength to accomplish the tasks necessary to combat the evils in the world. It is an optimistic and encouraging ending, expressing hope for the causes espoused in the play itself. The programme of *Vivre en 1968* echoed this sentiment:

> En exaltant le bonheur de l'homme, en dénonçant ce qui provoque son malheur, pourrons-nous ce soir du 27 juillet, trouver un grand élan d'amitié universelle, signe de paix, de dialogue et de compréhension?

Despite the complexities of production which street theatre necessarily entails – *Vivre en 1968* suffered from technical problems associated with the larger-than-expected crowd who witnessed it – it is clear from the subsequent press reports that the play's impact was considerable:

> Le public fut tantôt émerveillé, épaté, transporté, tantôt frappé, outré.[11]

> L'impact sur la population, certains recevant comme une révélation, d'autres ne supportant pas et même organisant une pétition contre. Tous ont été provoqués au point d'être concernés et non plus consommateurs. Ce spectacle était le leur.[12]

The play's impact was equally strong on outsiders: 'C'est parmi vous que j'ai vécu l'événement théâtral de l'année' stated Henry Delmas, returning to Paris after attending the Avignon Festival, and Claude Garbit, in his long and critically favourable report of *Vivre en 1968* in *Le Dauphiné Libéré*, described the play as 'un bouleversant spectacle' and 'un déchirant réquisitoire contre la misère de l'homme'. For him, the performance evoked the memory of Saint Vincent de Paul who had put himself on the side of the common man in his fight against injustice – even setting himself against the hypocrisies of the contemporary church.

> Sous la nef centrale, aux expressions de violence, succédèrent les douces espérances de l'humanité. Certains assistants de ce spectacle étrange ont découvert une autre dimension à leur église plus chaude et plus généreuse ce soir-là.[13]

This comment is valuable for two important reasons: first, it reveals the potential of the play as a means of spiritual unification, and second, it reflects the medieval nature of the event and thus justifies Cousin's manifest attempt to bring theatre into the reach of all, while at the same time encouraging a *prise de conscience* of the social and moral ills of our time.

The development of society in general, and of the more relaxed attitudes towards artistic expression in particular, allowed Cousin to advance the cause of popular theatre with *Vivre en 1968*, and in this new historical context, he was able to achieve more successfully the goals originally intended by Copeau for a theatre approaching in form and spirit that of a circus or public festivity.

ARIANE MNOUCHKINE'S THEATRE DU SOLEIL

Ariane's Mnouchkine's name is synonymous less with revolutionary theatre than with theatrical revolution: she has challenged the traditional notions of the theatre as an institution, as a bourgeois enclave reflecting middle-class values, and she has brought about popular theatre through a determined policy of 'collective creation' and sheer house-style.

Since the creation of the company in 1964 the Théâtre du Soleil has been a workers' co-operative and during its first two years its forty members worked as sheep-farmers while rehearsing for their first production, Gorki's *Les Petits Bourgeois* (Philistines). In Mnouchkine's non-hierarchical troupe, each member receives the same salary and contributes equally to the work of the group:

> On essaie de vivre en commun avec un minimum de règles de solidarité. Tout le monde participe à tous les travaux: ateliers le matin, répétitions l'après-midi. Egalité de salaire pour tous: 7500 francs par mois pour les comédiens, 6200 francs pour les stagiaires. Nous faisons tout sur place: décors, costumes, meubles. Nous fabriquons même des instruments de musique.[14]

Where Mnouchkine has differed from Jacques Copeau's community of actors, Les Copiaus, who toured Burgundy with farces and *divertissements* in the 1920s, is precisely in that area acknowledged by Copeau as essential:

> To create a community of actors. I had felt, from the beginning, that was where the problem lay. People living together, working together, acting together. But I had forgotten that other term, which I should logically have arrived at: creating together, inventing their performances together, drawing their performances from themselves and each other.[15]

Following the experimentation with various acting conventions, the troupe worked on an adaptation of Gautier's *Le Capitaine Fracasse* using *commedia dell'arte* techniques at the Théâtre Récamier in 1965–6. But it was in 1967, with Wesker's *The Kitchen*, that the company met its first success at the Cirque de Montmartre; it attracted 63,400 spectators, ten times the number who saw the first two productions.

The Kitchen introduced the company to their future method of 'collective creation' and, in order to achieve authenticity, they visited several restaurants, invited kitchen staffs to their rehearsals, and over several months elaborated a style that has remained with them ever since. It has been described as 'an ebullient, physical style, achieving its effects by patterns of orchestrated movement that [become] almost acrobatic at times'.[16]

For their first few productions the Théâtre du Soleil had made use of diverse venues, in Maisons des Jeunes and various small halls in the provinces. But the experience of the Cirque Médrano in Montmartre – with the audience seated in a semi-circle before them – resulted in their developing a penchant for large open auditoria and an extravagant theatre of gesture and energetic movement to accompany it. At the same time, the events of 1968 led them to reappraise their political stance within the theatre; they adopted some Brechtian techniques such as the use of mime and a deliberately provocative and political style which they transformed into their first real group-product, *Les Clowns*. This was a collage based on a series of improvisations on clown masks and comic routines; it lacked the coherence of a written play, but it allowed the actors to develop their personal talents, an important step in the subsequent growth of the company's house-style.

The previous winter, a remarkably erotic production of *A Mid-*

summer Night's Dream, also performed in the Cirque Médrano, brought the criticism from Gilles Sandier that it was '*Le Songe* passé à travers Artaud'. The sensual and the subconscious were emphasized, the aesthetic, the banter and frivolity excluded.

After examining its own *raison d'être* during the events of 1968 and concluding that creative unity could only be achieved with a proper sense of collective responsibility, the troupe evolved a style that, thanks to the new demand for artistic self-appraisal and justification, led to a unique theatrical form that set it apart from all other French theatre companies.

> La forme du spectacle marque le départ d'une dramaturgie nouvelle, qui ne s'est pas imposée comme une révélation, mais représente l'aboutissement de notre formation commune.[17]

The actors themselves appreciated the interdependence within the group despite the criticism which they endured as a result: 'Le Théâtre du Soleil, c'est la façon de vivre d'un groupe en accord avec ce qu'il accomplit.'[18] The evolving style of Mnouchkine's group was one of pace and contrast. As in Kabuki theatre, the inspiration was historical and the form episodic, but it was (and is) the pace that lent it uniqueness: actors develop their own feeling for it and sometimes enter the acting area at a sprint and frequently from a great distance, confronting the audience with a directness and intimacy that both astonishes and captures the attention. Comedy contrasts with tragedy, satire with pathos, and scene succeeds scene with dazzling rapidity and panache.

In the winter of 1970, the Théâtre du Soleil acquired a new home, a disused armaments factory on the eastern outskirts of Paris, the Cartoucherie de Vincennes. The company completely rebuilt the vast single-storey hangar-like building measuring 45 metres by 36 metres into an open-plan theatre which they still occupy today. Half of the available floor space was turned into an acting area, the rest was given over to dressing space and props storage – open to the public – and a large concourse which serves as a restaurant, foyer and sales-and-exhibition area. The resulting liberation of the actors, both *vis-à-vis* their acting environment and in their relationship with audiences, has produced the very popularization which their house-style enhances and which had not been seen in France since Vilar's TNP in the 1950s. As if to applaud the move to the Cartoucherie and its concomitant popularity, over a quarter of a million people came to the company's new production, *1789*.

It seemed entirely appropriate, after the events of 1968, that the Théâtre du Soleil should embark on a political interpretation of a historical event and the two productions at the new Cartoucherie theatre, *1789* and *1793*, carried the respective subtitles *La Révolution doit s'arrêter à la perfection du bonheur* and *La Cité révolutionnaire est de ce monde*.

A period of improvisation lasting about six months had preceded the opening of *1789* and to a large extent the actors worked independently during the performance, the whole effect being that of a street carnival. A series of small platforms joined by catwalks around the perimeter of the acting area allowed the audience to gather and stand in the midst of the action; as in a fairground they moved from place to place, listening to the popular orators of the Revolution, watching the re-enactment of historical scenes, or, as if in the streets of contemporary Paris, following the crowds experiencing social upheaval. The audience were thus not only involved in the action of this play, but also swayed by the ideas it transmitted in such a direct fashion; from being mere spectators they became participants in the Revolution itself.

For the next production, *1793*, the stage area was constructed like an assembly hall, with galleries on two adjacent sides and three tables in the inner area around which the players performed. This was the meeting-place of the Mauconseil assembly of 1793 but, although it was a recognizable historical setting, the audience were more objective observers of the action.

Both style and period changed in the company's next production: *L'Age d'or* related the story of an Arab worker's life in France at the time of the play (1975) and, using techniques drawn from both Chinese theatre and *commedia dell'arte*, it sought to satirize contemporary French society. Research and experimentation among students and factory workers, coupled with further improvisations with masks, brought about a final production which presented a stylized and variegated picture of certain types within that society. The stage area was divided into four equal-sized shallow craters over which the audience clambered to follow the moving actors; the whole acting space was lit by thousands of tiny ceiling lights which, as with *1789*, lent a fairground atmosphere to the performance. Without props or scenery, the actors relied for their effect entirely on their relationship – always close – with the spectators, and their use of mime and gesture counted for as much as the spoken text. However, *L'Age d'or* was seen by Mnouchkine more as an experiment than as a definitive work: the play's title contained the rider 'première version' and Mnouchkine herself doubted the group's capacity to succeed with a modern subject without further preparation:

> Qu'on retravaille à fond sur les masques, à fond sur les mots . . . C'est vraiment ce que j'espère, pouvoir travailler un moment comme ça, et voir ce qui se dégage de là. Voir si on peut faire quelque chose sur l'histoire contemporaine, parler de maintenant au théâtre. Mais je ne suis pas sûre que nous soyons prêts.[19]

The Théâtre du Soleil experienced a sort of interlude in the later 1970s – a period of professional reappraisal – during which they abandoned the theatre proper to make a film of Molière's life (neatly emphasizing the difficulties inherent in the life of any closely-knit theatre company) and presenting a stage adaptation of a Klaus Mann novel entitled *Méphisto*, also dealing with the changing lives of a group of actors, this time in Hitler's Germany.

The new, longer-term project for the 1980s became a cycle of Shakespeare plays – *Richard II, Twelfth Night* and the *First Part of Henry IV* – which in total were to attract over a quarter of a million spectators. Ariane Mnouchkine brought some new members into the company in 1979 to work on this set of plays with remarkable oriental – Indian and Japanese – settings.

Mnouchkine's achievement has been constantly to question the hierarchy of theatre workers, the existence of an initial text and the boundaries of the acting area. The company amaze their audiences with their stamina and speed and, by ignoring production risks and theatrical traditions, they have torpedoed their way into theatre history by re-establishing popular drama with its epic scope, its universal appeal and its panache.

THEATRE OUVERT

Lucien Attoun's preoccupation with the promotion of new drama in France stemmed from his work during the 1960s on the France-Culture radio programmes entitled *Le Nouveau Répertoire Dramatique* and his subsequent directorship of the Collection Théâtre Ouvert with the publishers Stock. The Stock venture incorporated three formats:

> A travers des pièces inédites, des textes-programmes, des essais

et documents, *Théâtre Ouvert*, en suscitant un théâtre de création, se propose de participer au théâtre de notre temps, un théâtre qui dérange en refusant l'acquis.[20]

and led naturally to the creation of Attoun's own experimental theatre organization with the identical title of Théâtre Ouvert.

The original proposal by Lucien Attoun for a Théâtre d'Essai et de Création was made to Jean Vilar and Paul Puaux in 1970 and, at the twenty-fifth Avignon Festival in 1971, the Chapelle des Pénitents Blancs was adapted and placed at his disposal. 'L'Association Théâtre Ouvert–Théâtre de Création' was established officially on 30 June 1971. Using the Avignon Festival as its platform, and with grants from the ORTF (French Broadcasting Authority) and the Ministère des Affaires Culturelles, Théâtre Ouvert began to function as a service for new dramatists; the emphasis was on the text itself, with playscripts subjected to experiment and research by a production team consisting of the author, producer and a small group of actors.

Théâtre Ouvert thus became a textual laboratory available to new authors to develop their talent in conjunction with experts in the field; it helped theatre producers to minimize their risks with unknown writers and works; above all, it reaffirmed the philosophy latent throughout French theatre in the 1960s, of collective writing and collaborative production within the theatre movement. This liaison between creators and interpreters was further extended to include the audience themselves who, in the tradition of the Avignon Festival, were invited to participate in discussions with the production team after each performance. This working practice, a formula exclusive to Théâtre Ouvert, became known as a *mise en espace*, while the eventual performance of a play, without scenery or costumes, was called a *présentation*.

Of the twenty *mises en espace* presented at Avignon during the first three years of its existence, Théâtre Ouvert introduced the French public to eight new authors. Among the plays that later achieved greater recognition elsewhere were Roger Planchon's *Le Cochon noir*, and Jean-Claude Grumberg's *En r'venant d'l'Expo*. There were also six playreadings presented by Théâtre Ouvert at Avignon during the years 1971–3, including Armand Gatti's *Rosa Spartakus prend le pouvoir*, Rezvani's *La Colonie* and Michel Deutsch's *Le Château dans la tête*. Many of the plays and debates sponsored by Théâtre Ouvert were broadcast on Attoun's *Le Nouveau Répertoire Dramatique*, and TF1 (a major French television channel) featured a documentary programme on the work of Théâtre Ouvert in the summer of 1972.

Over the following two years Théâtre Ouvert expanded its activities in two ways: *le gueuloir* was introduced in 1974, and *la cellule de création* in 1975. The former offered authors the opportunity to give free, public readings of their works at early-evening sessions in Avignon's Chapelle des Cordeliers, while the latter gave one director *carte blanche* to rehearse a script of his choice before an audience during the whole three-week period of the Festival, without a definitive interpretation or public performance at the end. In both these experimental forms, the audience were to play an active role in the creative process, a phenomenon hitherto unknown in France; the text itself became a medium for the exploration of dramatic devices and individual ingenuity while the end-product merely served as a stage in the developmental process, emphasizing the constant state of flux in all artistic effort.

> J'ai mis sur pied Théâtre Ouvert parce que j'en avais assez des colloques sur les problèmes de la création contemporaine. Il faut être pratique, concret, analyser la situation dans son ensemble, sérier les questions, dégager les manques, voir ce qu'on peut faire, comment, et avec quels moyens.[21]

In giving the initiative back to the authors themselves, Attoun was also attempting to reverse the trend towards state intervention in the arts observed in the expansionist era of decentralization within French theatre during the 1960s.

In 1976 Théâtre Ouvert's grant was increased sufficiently to allow for a further stage in its development: after an unsuccessful attempt to move into a renovated Vieux-Colombier the previous year, a new administrative headquarters was found nearby in the rue Cassette, thus permitting the establishment of a meeting-place for all concerned with contemporary theatre. This state of permanence – albeit temporary until better facilities including theatre space could be found – also allowed arrangements to begin for touring groups to visit the provinces under the general aegis of Théâtre Ouvert which co-ordinated their activities from its new Paris base. By now, Théâtre Ouvert was attracting nationally known directors into its ambit: Jacques Rosner, Patrice Chéreau, Gabriel Garran and Jorge Lavelli had all participated in presentations at Avignon and on tour. It was also promoting the work of new French authors such as Michel Deutsch,

Jean-Claude Grumberg and Jean-Paul Wenzel, thus complementing rather than competing with the work of the decentralization movement. Its socio-political aims may, however, be more analogous to those of some regional theatre managements: its brochure for the 1977 Avignon Festival defines its role as one of 'susciter une dramaturgie d'aujourd'hui qui nous parle d'ici et de maintenant'; the 1978 *Cahiers du Festival* speak of its seeking 'échange et solidarité avec ceux qui, au-delà des frontières, attribuent une fonction sociale élevée au théâtre', and it is no coincidence that there have been close links between Théâtre Ouvert and, say, the Comédie de Caen or the Théâtre de la Commune in Aubervilliers, both enterprisingly experimental in their programming.

In February 1978 Théâtre Ouvert launched five new projects: *tapuscrits* are cheap, sporadically produced playscripts of which 800 copies are duplicated and distributed to the author and to other interested parties; *molécules* are minor extensions of the *cellules*, providing inexperienced dramatists with a week-long apprenticeship in writing techniques in collaboration with a director and a small group of actors, with a view to rewriting or completing a previously unfinished work; *Ecritures* is the information bulletin of Théâtre Ouvert appearing at irregular intervals; Les Mardis de Théâtre Ouvert are social gatherings aimed at bringing together people in the theatrical profession; *rencontres* are occasional debates organized to exchange ideas and elaborate policies on the production of new drama. In these various ways Théâtre Ouvert continues to sponsor a system for the effective production, exchange and distribution of new plays; operating on co-operative lines as a non-profitmaking organization, it ensures the protection of authors from commercialization during their vital formative years while at the same time bringing them into contact with the expertise and experience of accomplished practitioners of the stage.

This progress in the positive contribution to the development of new French drama was suddenly interrupted, however, by the announcement in *Ecritures* no. 6, dated February 1979, to the effect that Paul Puaux, permanent administrator of the Avignon Festival, was not inviting Lucien Attoun's organization to participate in the thirty-third Festival that summer. Despite Jean Vilar's untimely death in May 1971, Théâtre Ouvert might have expected better treatment from Puaux who, after the 1971 Festival, had declared: 'C'est la première fois qu'une expérience nouvelle présentée au Festival d'Avignon rencontre l'adhésion immédiate du public et de la presse.'

However, making a virtue of necessity and refusing to be drawn into a polemical dispute, Lucien Attoun decided to pursue his aims and disregard the loss of his once permanent base.

During the spring of 1979 Théâtre Ouvert diversified its activities: in March it toured extensively with Vinaver's *Les Travaux et les jours*; in April it collaborated with Gabriel Garran in two *mises en espace* at his Théâtre de la Commune in the Paris suburb of Aubervilliers and took a playreading to three local schools; in May the same productions were taken to Nice at the invitation of the Nouveau Théâtre during the Foire du Livre.

Théâtre Ouvert's principal event of the 1980 season was the programme organized at the Centre Georges Pompidou during the month of March; it consisted of one full-length play (Vinaver's *Les Travaux et les jours* was given twenty performances), two *mises en espace*, three *gueuloirs*, two debates, six *auditions* (free public hearings of plays recorded by France-Culture), and three *écritures/lectures* featuring the works of writers who have or could influence contemporary theatre. The eclectic jamboree of drama and related events was the most ambitious project to date – it not only provided a stimulating experience for all concerned with new drama, but it was at the same time a necessary forum for debate among a group of creative people who otherwise rarely see each other or have the opportunity to exchange ideas on common problems.

Théâtre Ouvert celebrated its tenth anniversary in July 1981 by announcing its move to a permanent site at the Jardin d'Hiver in the Cité Véron behind the Moulin Rouge in Paris. The premises comprise two small but flexible theatres holding one hundred and two hundred spectators respectively, dressing-rooms, an entrance foyer with exhibition area, and office space. With its grants from the Ministère de la Culture and the Ville de Paris, it has continued its policy of providing a testing-ground for new work (through the four-phase process of *gueuloir – cellule de création – mise en espace – présentation*), and of helping the incipient dramatist by making professional assistance available, thus diminishing the likelihood of failure. Of the three or four hundred scripts received annually, about fifteen are selected by the six members of the Théâtre Ouvert team for their interest and originality. Lucien Attoun himself has campaigned vigorously to combat the inequitable operation of authors' rights: by setting up the Collection Théâtre Ouvert with the publishing house of Stock, he has controlled the performing rights of a play, for which each director will have to negotiate a contract and pay a fee in advance of any production. Whereas previously authors were paid 10 per cent of box-office receipts (12 per cent in Paris) after performance, Théâtre Ouvert now acts as a kind of agency on behalf of authors and guarantees payments of their dues in advance.

In an area of artistic activity too frequently dominated by the state and stultified by bureaucratic wranglings and professional jealousies, the unique work of Lucien Attoun's organization continues to stimulate interest in new drama and to effect creative contacts between writers, actors, directors and the public. Full recognition of the work done by Théâtre Ouvert since 1971 in the field of research and development was accorded more recently with the promotion of the organization, on 1 January 1988, to France's official and only Centre Dramatique National de Création.

ARMAND GATTI

One of the most original and eclectic minds in the French theatre this century has been that of Armand Gatti. Born in Monaco in 1924, the son of destitute Italian immigrants, his struggle for survival mirrored his father's experiences during and after the First World War.

Auguste Gatti had been one of twenty-one children of whom six died in childhood and a further seven brothers were killed in 1914–18; he himself just managed to escape being buried alive after a bomb explosion in 1917. With his wife Letizia, he emigrated to Chicago after the war, but his anarchistic activities during a strike at the abattoir where he had found work led to his being stabbed and left for dead. Letizia returned to Piedmont, then, hearing the astonishing news that Auguste had survived and left America for Monaco, made her way there to join him. Armand was born shortly afterwards, and the family remained in Monaco's shanty town of Tonkin which housed immigrant workers from all over Europe and North Africa.

At school, Armand soon assimilated his adoptive tongue of French – which he enjoyed and was successful at – but this pleasure was short-lived as he was obliged to leave school at 11 to find work, first as a furniture-remover, then as an undertaker's assistant. When Armand was 15, his father, now a dustman, died after being beaten by the police during a strike. Armand was sent by his ultra-Catholic mother to a seminary from which he was expelled for illicitly reading the works of Rimbaud. By 17, Armand was a maquisard in Occupied France; he was caught, tortured and interned; he was sent to a forced-labour camp in Hamburg, escaped, and after many months of near-death existence, joined up with a parachute commando group in London. He finished the war still as a parachutist. Since the war, Gatti has been a journalist, a legal correspondent, an animal-tamer, part-time revolutionary in Guatemala, film-maker and, during all this time, a novelist, poet and prolific dramatist.

It would be simplistic and erroneous to suggest that Gatti's work is a product of his peregrinations and personal experiences, for his life and creativity are one. His search for the correct theatrical tone – achieved through *le mot juste* for a particular situation – bind language and the event it describes in what he calls 'l'aventure de la parole errante'. What is clearly unique in his output for both the theatre and the cinema is that all his dramatic statements have depended, in the first instance, on his direct association with groups of people in France and elsewhere, and that these experiences have been transmuted into an individualistic political philosophy. The tragic fate of his father is the essence of his play *La Vie imaginaire de l'éboueur Auguste Geai*; his life in the German concentration camp spawned three plays (*L'Enfant Rat, La Deuxième Existence du Camp de Tatenberg* and *Chroniques d'une planète provisoire*) and a film, *L'Enclos*; two plays on China, *Le Poisson noir* and *Un homme seul*, resulted from visits to China in 1955 and 1959.

Equally, the form of Gatti's theatre matches the breadth and depth of his reading and the variety of his foreign experiences. In adolescence, he attached himself to the Symbolists Rimbaud and Mallarmé; when he was a novice journalist it was the Surrealists such as Breton, Desnos and Soupault whom he sought out to read his poems to and who provided him with the notion of the surreal – a fusion of the real and the dream worlds; in the 1950s his China experience taught him a new approach to theatre using single artefacts as symbols and simple gestures to illustrate complex ideas.

While Gatti's theatre obviously demonstrates a clear lineage from Brecht, with its anti-Aristotelian approach, its political commitment and didacticism, and its attempt to change Man while remaining fraternal with him, Gatti's individual stamp is everywhere apparent: it is characterized by the ubiquitous use of simultaneity of character, space and time.

Après avoir été retenu par le thème de la victime, je suis intéressé maintenant par celui de la révolution. Et la révolution appelle une forme révolutionnaire. D'ailleurs, pour moi, chaque sujet commande une forme particulière. Les problèmes que me

pose la traduction en termes de théâtre du sujet choisi, m'amèn-
ent naturellement à déterminer la mise en scène – sur le papier.

Ce qui me paraît essentiel, c'est le temps, un temps où le passé
se recrée avec la force du présent de façon toujours différente.
Planchon dit de mon théâtre qu'il est 'éclaté'. Mais il faut se
méfier du recours au flash; il convient d'arriver à une construction solide.[22]

There may be a paradox here: if time is to be shattered ('éclaté') and
past, present and future psychological states are to be mingled, what
form might the 'construction solide' take? There can be no place for
unity of action or plot either, for an event is seen from many angles
and in many time-periods at once. Solidity, if there is any at all, lies in
the insistence upon wholeness of vision, a cohesion of collectives
wrought by Gatti's own multiple viewpoints. This is not the
outrageous, extravagant outpourings of the adolescent Rimbaud or
the alchemy of Artaudian symbol, but the controlled attempt to
reproduce the mind's natural simultaneity of experience.

A prime example of this technique of simultaneity can be observed
in the early biographical play *La Vie imaginaire de l'éboueur Auguste
Geai*, first produced by Jacques Rosner at the Théâtre de la Cité in
Villeurbanne in 1962. Gatti's father is portrayed at five different
stages of his life, played by five different actors, and moving around
an acting space divided according to the time-periods represented.
The simultaneous interaction of these five characters is like a set of
five superimposed pictures: each bears upon the others, creating an
instantaneous whole rather than a development along a linear
pattern. By this means, Gatti shows the interconnection between the
psychological states of man as well as the indissoluble link between a
man's private life and the public's perception of that life. The 9-year-
old orphan Auguste is terrified by a tramp known locally as 'the black
baron'; as a 30-year-old, Auguste is equally fearful of 'the white
baron', the tyrannical boss of his dust-cart company. The depiction of
a dance marathon brings together in the 46-year-old Auguste's mind
the memories of Pauline, the winner of the marathon, later his wife,
and his son, now competing again for survival in a later world. The
dance marathon thus becomes a metaphor for the struggles of life
itself, its humiliations and its preponderant pressures; at the same
time, it vividly expresses social reality for Gatti – the dance band is
composed of CRS officers (French riot police) dictating the pace of
bourgeois life itself.

Gatti's aim, like that of Gabriel Cousin, was to raise an audience's consciousness about contemporary issues; the *prise de conscience* thus achieved was enhanced through audience part-participation in the action, by subsequent critical reaction or, best of all, through voluntary discussion of the problems raised in a play after its performance. This practice shows parallels with those of Dario Fo and Franca Rame. Gatti's personal style of dramatic technique heightened audience reaction by its constant provocation and suggestivity: in his *V comme Vietnam*, for instance, first performed at the Grenier de Toulouse in 1967, Gatti not only presented the political contrasts between the USA and Vietnam, or the wanton destruction of human life and habitat by the aggressor, but, in characteristic style, opposed the human (Vietnamese peasants) with the robotic (American military might) in the form of caricature. The American President Lyndon Johnson became Megasheriff, and the Pentagon computer La Châtaigne (originally 'The Walnut'), while news from one country to the other was transmitted via fantastical electronic devices distributed around the set. However, far from being a mere spoof Western, this play vividly showed the power struggles, subversion, interrogation procedures, propaganda and guerrilla warfare that characterized the Vietnam conflict.

The bombing of Hiroshima and Nagasaki, the dawn of the atomic era, its morality and consequences had provided many post-war French dramatists with stage material, and Michel Parent, Jean Vilar and Gabriel Cousin had already completed their works on the subject before Gatti's *La Cigogne* was produced in Strasbourg in 1968. This play demonstrates the effects of the bomb on the population of Nagasaki, but from this catastrophe Gatti draws the conclusion that a new vision of life is now necessary: a philosophy of optimism must somehow be summoned up to overcome the desperate resignation felt by the inhabitants of the city. Thus Gatti's play, while condemning American technology and aggression which have made guinea-pigs of the people of Nagasaki, is an attempt to persuade people of the futility of stagnant anguish. *La Cigogne* thus belongs to the literature of remorse and bears close affinities in this respect to Sartre's *Les Mouches* – Enemon being the new Oreste – and, although Gabriel Cousin is also trying to awaken people from their post-nuclear physical and mental sterility in his *Le Drame du Fukuryu-Maru*, Gatti's call for a new way of thinking has more of an intellectual appeal than Cousin's. Gatti explores the psychology of abandoned beings more thoroughly, and creates greater complexity by reanimating the objects affected by the atomic blast, thereby lending their owners a dual personality and making them fulfil a double role in the plot.

> A chaque déblayeur va correspondre un objet, lequel va enfanter le personnage de son quotidien (auquel il appartenait autrefois). Chaque déblayeur joue en principe l'objet de son personnage (désigné ici par sa profession). La ligne de partage sera tracée par la mise en scène.[23]

Japanese paper-screen walls (*shoji*) define the acting areas, but they also symbolize the objects in a different form, as the silhouette of each object is cut out in the screens behind which the characters speak, thus animating the objects themselves.

The title of the play is drawn from a Japanese legend that states that a dying person may survive if he can make a thousand storks; however, there is pessimism and optimism present at the end of the play: while Kawaguchi burns the thousandth stork in despair, Tomiko snatches it from him, claiming that there are other kinds of stork – less ethereal – which exist to save us. In a final exhortation directed at the audience, Tomiko reminds us that, unlike the scenes we have witnessed of suicidal depression, we must learn to recognize the ruins within our lives and be alert to the possibility of ignoring them to create a new existence. As in other plays by Gatti, the future is present in time past, but past associations should not cloud our vision of a better future.

So far, little mention has been made of the role of the audience at performances of Gatti's plays. Gatti's own experience of political censorship while preparing his 1968 version of *La Passion du Général Franco* for the TNP gave him ample grounds for rejecting formalized theatre subsequently, and the second version of the play, re-titled *La Passion du Général Franco par les émigrés eux-mêmes*, not only presented him with an opportunity of incorporating Spanish emigrants' views into the work, but enabled Gatti to produce a new production format closer to his vision of the theatre as a 'spectacle without spectators'.

The second play was premièred in March 1976 in the transport depot of the firm Ney Calberson on the outskirts of Paris. The audience (or rather, participants) followed the actors around the vast warehouse as the play proceeded from scene to scene. When more than one scene took place simultaneously, they had to choose which to watch. Around the acting area, bookstalls provided information on the various political groups involved in the action, thus complementing Gatti's piece and explaining some of the subtleties of its intricate political background. The play itself consists of the depiction of a series of journeys undertaken throughout the world by exiles from Francoist Spain, showing their reasons for leaving their native country, their experiences while abroad, and their consequent political outlook from their detached position as exiles. The resultant collective image of Spain and its detractors during the Francoist era – enhanced by the occasional (hypothetical) meeting of the various groups – presented in a very direct way the conflicts and preoccupations of Spaniards during the dictatorship. The 'Passion' was not that of Franco himself, but the one which he created for these exiles and, in a sense, of those who came to watch and share the experience. The piece is described as

> La mise à mort d'un tyran par ses victimes sur les différentes trajectoires de leur calvaire. C'est aussi un acte de solidarité avec ceux qui récemment sont tombés ou sont imprisonnés.[24]

The spectators at *La Passion du Général Franco par les émigrés eux-mêmes* were therefore fulfilling Gatti's aim of having his audience live his presentation.

Despite its complexity, its abundance of images, its political intricacy, the theatre of Armand Gatti speaks out loudly to its audiences: the reactions of two hundred dustmen to the Paris production of *Auguste Geai*, the involvement of Spanish émigrés in their own history in *La Passion du Général Franco*, and the numerous real-life experiences witnessed at first hand by Gatti when researching his material all testify to the immediacy and the dynamism of his work. This dynamism is expressed in his perpetual search for new subjects through which he can project a particular and passionate stance towards an issue. Thus, at the Peugeot works in Montbéliard in 1975, he persuaded the (mainly immigrant) workers to write about their experiences of the conflicts between their native culture and that of the French community in which they had settled. The resulting scenarios were collated into a film entitled *Le Lion, sa cage et ses ailes*, derived from the Peugeot symbol of a lion. At Saint-Nazaire the following year, Gatti and his troupe, 'the Tribe', brought together shipyard workers from the town to enact the fate of dissidents imprisoned in psychiatric hospitals in the Soviet Union. This experiment resulted in the publication of a broadsheet and some videos, an exhibition, and the eventual release of Vladimir Bukovsky, one of the most celebrated detainees in Soviet asylums. Gatti's work with other marginalized groups of people – delinquents, drug addicts and prostitutes – became a sort of remedial exercise. This collective creation, developed between 1983 and 1985 in Toulouse, on the subject of the anarchistic activities of the Ukrainian Makhno, allowed the participants to identify with Makhno's predicament and to find their own liberation through an examination of his story.

This emphasis on collective creation – a common form in French theatre in the 1970s and 1980s practised always by the Théâtre du Soleil and generally encouraged by Théâtre Ouvert – suited Gatti's purposes well. It enabled him to reach many groups – especially those on the fringe of society – for whom theatre was an alien art; Gatti, in these circumstances the *animateur* rather than the director, taught these groups to express their struggles in an articulate and novel way, so creating a new dramatic reality for them and for the spectators who came to witness their creations.

What is particular about Gatti's style of collective creation, and about his theatre in general, is his obsession with the simultaneity of time, place and action. Deriving from his observations of Chinese theatre during a visit to China in 1955, this obsession freed conventional theatre from its traditional limitations by situating stage action on several different planes and time-scales simultaneously and by presenting characters in multiple guises within a single plot. More recently, Gatti has developed this notion of simultaneity in his *selmaires*, roughly defined as the parallel observations by actor-spectators of the action currently being performed on the stage. They may be used to indicate the multiple aspects of a personality, to relate different versions of an event or to present the supposed viewpoint of a spectator while the action is proceeding. Both the form and effect of the *selmaires* are similar to the interventions and interruptions of Brechtian theatre and, as such, distance us, the real audience, from the performance as performance.

Gatti continues to experiment with participatory theatre: during the bicentenary year of the French Revolution he produced a play and a film on the rights of man in the prison of Fleury-Mérogis, and a play entitled *Le Métro Robespierre répète la Révolution (Française)* in the station itself.

If there is one anomaly in his work to date, it is that his working-class origins have become obscured by his intense intellectualism and this risks making him inaccessible to those audiences he might wish to cultivate. Indeed, Gatti makes no concessions to easy intelligibility: in

1962, in a Preface to a volume of his plays, he was already giving indications to potential directors of his work:

> Un tiret marque une rupture de pensée; un changement de vitesse vers l'extériorisation; un crochet marque un changement de vitesse vers l'intériorisation. C'est en quelque sorte une écriture à trois tons où les différentes hauteurs ne sont pas données une fois pour toutes mais s'établissent continuellement les unes par rapport aux autres.[25]

It has been by means of such theoretical positions, precisely, that Gatti has created a new dramatic style which is at once unique, direct and intellectually invigorating.

NOTES

1 Raymonde Temkine, *L'Entreprise théâtre*, Paris, Editions Cujas, 1967: 184.
2 ibid., 197–8.
3 David Bradby and John McCormick, *People's Theatre*, London, Croom Helm, 1978: 25.
4 Maurice Sarrazin, *Comédien dans une troupe*, Toulouse, Grenier de Toulouse, 1970: 63.
5 Paul Surer, *50 ans de Théâtre*, Paris, Société d'édition d'enseignement supérieur, 1969: 211.
6 Jean Dasté, *Voyage d'un comédien*, Paris, Editions Stock, 1977: 71.
7 Jean-Luc Dejean, *Le Théâtre français d'aujourd'hui*, Paris, Nathan, 1971: 126.
8 Françoise Kourilsky, *Le Bread and Puppet Theater*, Lausanne, La Cité, 1971.
9 *Théâtre Populaire*, 51, 1963.
10 Quoted in *Avignon, 40 ans de Festival*, Paris, Hachette, 1987: 106.
11 *Trévoux-Libre*, 9 Aug. 1968.
12 *Art et Education*, 19–20, 1969: 4.
13 Claude Garbit, *Le Dauphiné libéré*, 29 July 1968.
14 Ariane Mnouchkine, *Le Nouvel Observateur*, 25 Sept.–1 Oct. 1987: 112.
15 Jacques Copeau, quoted in 'Confronting history' by Adrian Kiernander in *The Times Higher Education Supplement*, 1 Nov. 1985.
16 David Bradby, *Modern French Drama 1940–1980*, Cambridge, Cambridge University Press, 1984: 193.
17 Ariane Mnouchkine and Jean-Claude Penchenet, *Preuves*, 7, 1971, quoted in Judith Graves Miller, *Theater and Revolution in France since 1968*, Lexington, Ky, French Forum, 1977.
18 Françoise Descotils, *Où est la différence?, Travail Théâtral* (special issue), Feb. 1976: 19.
19 Ariane Mnouchkine, interviewed by Françoise Kourilsky, quoted in *Où est la différence?, Travail Théâtral* (special issue), Feb. 1976: 91.

20 Publisher's Frontispiece, *Collection Théâtre Ouvert*, Paris, Editions Stock, 1970-9.
21 Lucien Attoun, in 'Agir sur la Création', *Le Monde*, 10 Jan. 1976.
22 Armand Gatti, in *L'Avant-Scène*, 272, 15 Sept. 1962: 17.
23 Armand Gatti, *La Cigogne*, Paris, Seuil, 1971: 7.
24 Programme of production by the Centre de Création Contemporaine at the Entrepôts Ney-Calberson, 1976.
25 Quoted in Seuil editions to Gatti's works.

BIBLIOGRAPHY

Avignon, 40 ans de Festival, Paris, Hachette, 1987.

David Bradby, *Modern French Drama 1940-1980*, Cambridge, Cambridge University Press, 1984.

David Bradby and John McCormick, *People's Theatre*, London, Croom Helm, 1978.

Différent: Le Théâtre du Soleil, Travail Théâtral (special issue), Feb. 1976.

David Jeffery, *Evolution in the Theatre of Gabriel Cousin*, Paris, Theatre Research International, 1976.

David Jeffery, *Théâtre ouvert*, Paris, Theatre Research International, 1984.

Dorothy Knowles, *Armand Gatti in the Theatre*, London, The Athlone Press, 1989.

Guy Leclerc, *Le TNP de Jean Vilar*, Paris: Union Générale d'Editions, 1971.

Judith Graves Miller, *Theater and Revolution in France since 1968*, Lexington, Ky, French Forum, 1977.

Raymonde Temkine, *L'Entreprise théâtre*, Paris, Editions Cujas, 1967.

Jean Vilar, *Le Théâtre, service public*, Paris, Gallimard, 1975.

3

FRANCE

Jérôme Savary, the 'ordinary magician' of French theatre

Martin Sorrell

In 1988 after the late Antoine Vitez had left to take up his appointment at the Comédie Française, the choice of his successor as director of the Théâtre National de Chaillot, the old Théâtre National Populaire of Jean Vilar and others, caused many eyebrows to be raised rather high. Jérôme Savary was and still is the epitome of post-1968 subversion, a ringleader of the anti-establishment fun-and-games school. This brilliant but 'unsolid' *enfant terrible* of the psychedelic counter-culture was now apparently coming off the streets, stopping his hippy wanderings and taking charge of one of France's best-known institutions. To be fair, the great anarchic days of his Grand Magic Circus were effectively over well before 1988, but Savary had scarcely become 'respectable' for all that, and placing him in the vast and monumental Palais de Chaillot, with its marble solemnity, was most certainly controversial. For in Savary's theatre, however well-heeled and well-scrubbed it may have become recently, there still lurks, in the words of David Whitton, 'a theatre of greasepaint, false noses, trapeze artistes, percussion instruments and fireworks'.[1]

Savary's origins and background are colourful, even exotic. If his personality seems to be that of a thoroughgoing Rabelaisian Frenchman and Parisian, the fact is that he arrived on the French stage via Buenos Aires. In 1938 the Savary family had left France and the farm they had tried to run near Cahors, and after a spell in Mexico they took root in Argentina. Jérôme was born in Buenos Aires in 1942, the third son of a chaotic ménage run by his long-suffering mother, who was abandoned at about this time by her bohemian failed-novelist husband. To add to the cosmopolitanism of Jérôme Savary's world, his maternal great-grandfather, by the name of Higgins, had been a Governor of New York City. Savary speaks very good English, he has a kind of nostalgic love for the culture of the United States, and it appears that his early years predisposed him to the kind of internationalism that has been a characteristic of his work. In his autobiography Savary lets us see what a crucial formative experience was his stay in the United States during his late teens. He also tells us that another major influence came from the gaudy and in some ways distasteful Argentinian street carnivals which clearly have helped shape the distinctive theatrical orientation from which he has never really veered.[2]

At the age of 6, Savary returned with his mother and brothers to France. Eventually Jérôme wound up in the south, in a school in the Cévennes. During his time there, he saw and was impressed by the regular visits of Jean Dasté's travelling company, the forerunner of decentralized theatre in France. Savary writes of the fascination and excitement engendered by the arrival in his village of Dasté's old bus laden with stage décor and machinery, and it is clearly from that time that his enchantment with the magic of spectacle, learned in the streets of Argentina, became focused on the theatre.

Savary's entry into a theatrical career was mildly unorthodox. He received no formal training, but went instead to the Ecole des Arts Décoratifs in Paris. He also studied music, in particular, harmony, percussion, the piano and the trumpet. What really launched him, however, was the experience of joining the Université du Théâtre des Nations in 1964. This 'University', a sort of informal and continuous seminar, made Savary truly passionate about theatre, thanks in good measure to his meetings with such people as Lavelli, García and Serreau. He began to work with the last-named as a set designer, but came to realize that his real desire was to be a director. In fact, Savary has said in an interview with Bettina Knapp that he found the whole business of stage design 'absurd'.[3] His idea instead was that a modern person of the contemporary theatre had to be complete, that specializations and divisions were no longer valid. Nor did he seem to believe in dramatists: he was interested in productions devised by a company or group. In other words, Savary quickly and rather instinctively nailed his colours to the mast of the 'total' theatre movement that gained enormous ground in the 1960s and after. From 1965, when the Compagnie J. Savary was founded, the majority of the productions which he put on were devised either by himself or collectively by a group. In this way he laid down a principle which was to sustain his work for a good many years after. In 1965 *Les Boîtes*, which he scripted jointly with Fernando Arrabal, was produced at the

Comédie de Paris. This was a loosely constructed piece, and it made use of film and two other elements which are very much Savary hallmarks – namely, on-stage music and animals. The collaboration with Arrabal arose out of Savary's association with this playwright and with Topor and Jodorowsky, who together formed the so-called 'Théâtre Panique', named after the deity Pan and intended (by Arrabal at least) to represent a distancing from Absurdist theatre. What exactly 'Panic theatre' amounted to remained confused and confusing, but it incorporated the notions of *fête*, contradiction and chance, and it led Savary to change the name of his company in 1966 to Grand Panic Circus. The *panique* 'anti-movement' was short-lived, however, and influenced only one of Savary's productions, *Le Labyrinthe*.

Les Boîtes was a commercial failure, as was in the following year Savary's adventurous *Le Radeau de la Méduse*, whose most interesting aspect probably was the use as the playing area of a raft suspended high above the stage, visible to the audience below through a stretched-out net. With its emphasis on filth, physical misery and extreme violence, *Le Radeau de la Méduse* was arguably an embodiment of a certain notion of cruel theatre. The year 1966 also saw the staging of Savary's production of Arrabal's *Le Labyrinthe*, at the Théâtre Daniel Sorano, Vincennes. The fact that he was working from a text did not embarrass Savary, who doubled the original cast of five by adding a goat and chickens. He brought to Arrabal's grim and wordy play a fresh and unorthodox circus element. By the time this show went to New York, via an acclaimed production at the Mercury Theatre, London, in June 1968, the original play had been drastically altered and Arrabal's name taken off the programme. Actors were constantly changed, and the final cast was a multi-national one whose members by all accounts randomly delivered their lines in French, Spanish or English. The often improvised action took place on several different platforms, sequentially or simultaneously, and Savary himself acted as a kind of ringmaster, directing the proceedings from a raised platform, banging a drum, playing his trumpet or addressing the actors through a megaphone. With *Le Labyrinthe* Savary moved towards that festive, carnivalesque circus that in his next productions was to make him well-known to large and often astonished audiences in France and abroad. For David Whitton, *Le Labyrinthe* amounted to Savary's rejection of theatre.[4] To be tied to a text was to be tied to literature and thus to the Establishment. And as France careered towards the momentous and revolutionary days of May 1968, Savary identified orthodox theatre with the repressive forces of bourgeois high culture, and placed himself firmly in the camp of revolt. Indeed, so uncompromising was Savary's condemnation of high-culture elitism that he was inimical even to such un-mainstream practitioners as Grotowski and Julian Beck, whom he saw only as disguised elitists, not genuinely providing theatre for the people.

And so, in 1968, in the service of a real people's audience, Savary's troupe took on its final and most celebrated name, Le Grand Magic Circus et Ses Animaux Tristes. The sad animals were human beings, sad because they are animals who have lost the ability to express their animality in any joyous way. There followed a series of amazing productions over the next few years which for many theatre devotees and critics alike represent the peak of Savary's achievement. The 'classic' Magic Circus productions were *Zartan, frère mal-aimé de Tarzan*, first given in Toronto in 1970, then in New York, and then at the Cité Universitaire in Paris in 1971; *Les Derniers Jours de solitude de Robinson Crusoe*, Cité Universitaire, Paris, and the Roundhouse, London, 1972; *De Moïse à Mao, 5000 ans d'aventures et d'amour*, Théâtre National de Strasbourg, then Théâtre d'Orsay, Paris, 1974; and *Good Bye Mister Freud*, Théâtre de la Porte-Saint-Martin, Paris, also 1974.

The distinctive nature of these productions was apparent at every level. The choice of venue, to begin with, was as non-theatrical as possible. Sometimes huge tents were used, or sports halls, or the friendly, rough-and-ready space of the Cité Universitaire, which is where the Magic Circus gained major fame with *Zartan*. Then, in the pre-performance period of a show, the arriving audience would be entertained by a circus-like build-up, involving loud, brassy music, the play of strongly coloured lights, and the chatter and activity of the troupe itself (a style developed in a more refined way by Le Théâtre du Soleil in the Cartoucherie at Vincennes). The printed publicity outside the venue as well as the hand-outs for the audience were visual, full of illustrations and cartoons, and devoid of verbal exegesis. The plays themselves took the form of loosely linked tableaux performed in several areas of the space. In *Zartan*, for example, there were eight such areas. Besides this, the company constantly moved among the spectators, creating yet another performance area, and coming as close as possible to abolishing the distinction between players and audience. For those not used to it, this was certainly a theatre of assault and embarrassment, at least in the early stages of the evening – by the end, audiences tended to be won over and to lose any residual inhibitions. In *Zartan* the joy and exuberance of performance tended to eclipse the darker potential inherent in its subject, the history of colonialism.

The rambling plot and action of the classic Magic Circus shows never quite lost coherence, thanks in part to the familiarity of the original stories to most of the audience, in part to the largely self-contained nature of the episodic tableaux, and in part to the control-ling, ringmaster presence of Savary himself, guiding and shifting the action with a flourish of his trumpet and some rudimentary commen-tary on the action for the spectators' benefit. The dominant aesthetic was exactly that suggested by the company's apt name, the wide-eyed and intoxicating magic of the circus. And so the action was fast and acrobatic, the players' make-up clownishly garish, the costumes extravagant and glittering, the lighting powerful and rich in simple colours and the whole spectacle propelled by loud music, often with a Latin beat. If all this sounds innocent enough, the spice and the controversy lay in the deliberate offence to good taste that ran like a vein through the whole of these shows. The most obvious form of this 'offensiveness' was the sexual near-explicitness, the very frequent nudity of performers of both sexes, who were never shy of keeping themselves at an indelicate distance from the audience, and the creation of well-known characters from real life who were then made to behave in 'outrageous' fashion. For example, in *Zartan* there was a moment when an actress looking startlingly like the Queen of England arrived on stage piggy-back on a man's shoulders, a cigarette in the corner of her mouth, tiara on head, royal blue sash awry and one regal breast exposed for our close inspection. A small detail perhaps, but one which caused mutterings on the night the present writer saw the show at the Cité Universitaire. The real danger to society (one must remember that these shows were being given not long after the 'événements' of May 1968) resided really in the visceral message of physical and mental joy that the Magic Circus imparted to all their spectators. In a real sense, these shows were subversive. Everything about them explicitly or implicitly questioned how we live, asked why a society so much flushes away its life that it comes to accept as natural a kind of collective depression (a theme which regularly surfaces, incidentally, in the French cinema: think of such films as *Bof* and *Themroc* and so on). There was obviously nothing original in the Magic Circus's naïve political message of the late 1960s and early 1970s, but its potency on the stage was very persuasive. By the time shows such as *Zartan* reached their last tableaux, the audiences were enchanted, they had come to life more and more as the evening went on, there was a heady feeling of liberation in the air, and the evening closed with a long sequence of Latin music played by the actors, who invited the audience to get up and dance. This they did, and the players gradually withdrew, leaving the floor to the spectators who by now were very much the protagonists, as it were. On the day this writer saw *Zartan*, the evening's unforgettable events culminated in a huge dance in which every single member of the audience participated, young hippies in purple flares sambaing with stately OAPs, until the whole thing spilled out into the drizzly street where a cordon of glistening black CRS riot police, truncheons at the ready, were waiting to make sure that the party was over, and that everyone vanished quickly, quietly and separately. This image says a great deal about post-1968 France and the collision of two philosophies of social life.

Savary's own note to the production of *Zartan* probably gives as good a flavour of what these famous Magic Circus shows of the early 1970s were like.

> Zartan, sporting his leopard skin, stars in this marvellous story of colonialism from the Middle Ages to the present. The production, though full of atrocities, employs fairy-tale techniques: tricks, magic, the simple dialogue of a children's story. Ropes, pulleys and tunnels allow continual movement of men and materials; fireworks, smoke and artificial fog provide a permanent atmosphere of war and battle, interspersed with touching little love scenes and a charming aquatic ballet in an inflatable swimming-pool. . . . Three small hills [are] connected by tunnels or ditches. The hill on the left is Zartan's Domain: here, in the shadow of an odd Statue of Liberty, Zartan wages war against everyone else. The hill in the centre is occupied by the Silent Majority (the spectators): a cloud occasionally rains on them (umbrellas are provided) but their situation, though precarious, permits them to watch with pleasurable emotion the surrounding cataclysm. (Next to this hill a businessman, indifferent to the noise around him, calmly sells hot dogs and root beer to the enchanted audience.) The hill on the right is a peaceful, idyllic corner anywhere in the world: here actors sing and dance, make love and grow cabbages. Zartan tries unsuccessfully to exterminate this last group, but each time he blows up a palm tree, another blooms in its place; each time he stabs a

woman, a baby is born. The show ends with Zartan's invasion of Cambodia – or the country most recently invaded – in a magnificent emotion-packed scene certain to bring tears to your eyes. . . . The audience participation is unique. The spectators, in their customary passivity and in their geographical place-ment between the two poles of action, incarnate – and oh how actively – the role of the 'silent majority'. Most 'active' in their passivity are those seated on the hill at the centre: each spectator must witness the horrible massacre surrounding him, without moving (unless, of course, a tunnel should be dug under his chair, causing him to fall into the hole – and there is always the possibility of a stray bullet). Other spectators are standing and can play 'war correspondent' in the battlefield. They may even, if they wish, take sides. The actors do in fact need people to help reconstruct the palm tree Zartan destroys, and Zartan needs help in operating the enormous bazooka he uses to destroy this same palm tree. Other opportunities arise, and it is not impossible that the spectacle end in mass confrontation, with a barrage of bananas.[5]

From the mid-1970s, the character of Le Grand Magic Circus began to change. For one thing, the 'swinging sixties' (which swung in the early 1970s too) gave way to something else, and the Magic Circus, whatever else, was a product of the flower-power years. The company carried on working, and put on a considerable number of shows which were toured a good deal, frequently in Germany, a country with whose theatre Savary has always had a special rapport. There was, for example, a production of the original Grimmelhausen story of Mother Courage, done jointly in 1977 by the Magic Circus and a German troupe. There was a handful of productions before the 1980 staging of Savary's interesting interpretation of *Le Bourgeois Gentilhomme*, seen at Aulnay-sous-Bois, and then at the Théâtre de l'Est Parisien. Savary's view of Monsieur Jourdain as a naïve but sympathetic man whose genuine search for knowledge and culture is triumphantly vindicated in the play's final scene has been described by one critic as 'the defeat of high culture by low', a recognizably Savary theme.[6] (Savary's 1989 production of the same play will be discussed later.)

Also in the late 1970s, as part of his increasing workload as a director independent of the Magic Circus, Savary began to be involved in the staging of opera. In 1978 his productions of Offenbach's *La Périchole* and *La Vie parisienne* were staged in Hamburg and

Frankfurt respectively. In broad terms, Savary's opera productions have always been obviously his – kaleidoscopic gaiety, visual jokes wherever possible, on-stage animals; but necessarily constrained by the technical requirements of singing in performance – reduced movement, the need to see the conductor, and so on.

The choice of Offenbach is perhaps indicative of Savary's theatrical taste since the late 1970s. True, he has put on Mozart (*The Magic Flute, Don Giovanni*) and Molière, but his efforts to create the genuinely popular theatre he has always wanted led him away from the unscripted, partially improvised productions of the 'classic' Magic Circus, to the somewhat lightweight repertoire of Dumas (*Les Trois Mousquetaires*), Verne (*Le Tour du monde en 80 jours*), Rostand (*Cyrano de Bergerac*), Pagnol (*La Femme du boulanger*). Predictably and happily, Savary's productions of these 'family favourites' were done with his usual verve and sparkle. They were rich in visual and aural spectacle, and full of surprise and surprises. Undoubtedly, too, he was achieving a popular theatre, to judge by the criterion of seats sold. What can be said is that the impetus that gave rise to the controversial, anarchic and innovatory type of drama of the early Magic Circus persisted into the 1980s as energetically as ever, though it spawned something 'safer', based very much on Savary's attachment to showbiz. Indeed, one of his most popular productions of the 1980s was *Bye Bye Showbiz*, given at the Venice Carnival of 1984, and then at the Théâtre Mogador, Paris, in the following year. This was a glittery affair, a choreographed musical, easy on the eye and ear, and a foretaste of one of Savary's major successes of recent years, his re-working of *Cabaret. Bye Bye Showbiz*, as well as the charming piece *L'Histoire du cochon qui voulait maigrir* ('rock musical for people of all ages'), its sequel *Les Aventures inédites du cochon en Amazonie*, and an ill-received strip-cartoon satire called *Superdupont*, all from the early 1980s, were nominally Magic Circus productions. Indeed, the company was still in existence during those years, but only just, and Savary's peripatetic life took it to the south (Béziers and Montpellier) and to Lyons, places where he had been appointed as director of state-run regional theatres. In effect, in recent years the Magic Circus has existed only as a name and has sprung into action just on those occasions when Savary has decided that it should. Increasingly, he has grown in stature and prestige as an independent director, a 'name', but he has kept faith with some of the old members of the Magic Circus, who act in his productions at Chaillot.

The mention of Chaillot brings the Savary story more or less up to date. Since his arrival there, he has been successful in attracting audiences and filling his vast auditorium. Whether the clientele is drawn from all social classes, as has always been the avowed aim of the national popular theatre, is not so sure. Savary launched his reign with a swashbuckling *D'Artagnan*, scripted by Jean-Loup Dabadie, which ran in the autumn of 1988. It was a virtuoso production, lavish, energetic, flamboyant, and the audiences loved it. But for anyone hoping for the mixture of inventiveness and hard-hitting content as in the old Magic Circus shows, it was disappointing. Savary is alive to the criticism that he was a sharper, less commercial director twenty years ago. He counters that he has kept pace with his public, with the demands of ordinary spectators whom he wants to enchant; his box-office receipts speak for themselves. He claims that nostalgia for a twenty-year-old fashion is rearguard and out of touch, and perhaps one can see what he means. With his new version of *Le Bourgeois Gentilhomme* in the autumn 1989 season, Savary nevertheless looked over his shoulder at the Magic Circus days. Some ten years after his exciting first version in which the conventional view of Jourdain was stood on its head, Savary offered a reading of Molière's text that preserved the sense of fun and simple-hearted enjoyment of life available to ordinary folk if they abandon themselves to low culture. But the message seemed diluted by the very circumstances of the play's production. It seemed 'high culture' in that a hugely lavish and expensive piece of technical wizardry was being applauded by a well-heeled, literate audience seated in plush armchairs within the gran-diloquent splendour of the Chaillot palace in one of the most fashionable districts of Paris. This of course was not entirely Savary's fault, but the tone of the production did not lend itself to pointed statements about high and low cultures. Say what one will, Savary's exuberant productions of twenty years ago inescapably were harder-centred.

In the summer of 1990, Savary had his first ever production at the Avignon Festival, a lively and colourful account of *A Midsummer Night's Dream*, a play which he himself has described as an 'anarchie amoureuse'. It transferred later in the year to Chaillot, where the autumn season opened with a reprise of *Zazou*, a musical on the subject of the 1940s and 1950s Parisian 'swingers'. Savary both wrote and directed this charming – if in the end not very memorable – piece of nostalgia for an era of good jazz, ostentatious style and Citroën 'traction avant' cars. *Zazou*'s apparent toughness of theme, its bitter-sweet quality, in no way disguised a core of sentimentality. And roughly the same may be said about Savary's latest venture at the time of writing, a rock opera entitled *La Légende de Jimmy*, scripted by Michel Berger and Luc Plamondon, which opened in late September 1990 at the Mogador. But, however dubious James Dean's claims to great hero status may be, this production was strong, even moving at times, with some excellent numbers excellently sung. Savary, of course, was and still is a musician, and there is no doubt that whether he is tackling a musical, a rock opera or a classical opera, he has a real gift for putting music on the stage. *La Légende de Jimmy* was produced with warmth and a delicacy not always found in his productions. At certain moments the flavour of the United States in the immediate post-war years was wonderfully captured, and there were striking tableaux that called to mind the paintings of Hopper and particularly of Sheeler. Savary's predictable technical virtuosity only occasionally drew too much attention to itself and became intrusive. The first-night audience at the Mogador was wildly enthusiastic, and there were quite a few high-decibel curtain-calls.

As for the production of *A Midsummer Night's Dream*, it was yet another of those more recent offerings in which the good was very good and the bad infuriating. The good was the stunning set which included a deep pond into which various characters fell (though rather too regularly), sometimes disappearing altogether; effects of magical lighting and sound; the beauty of some of the actors, notably those playing Helena, Hippolyta and Demetrius; and the up-tempo rhythm of the production (2 hours 15 minutes, without interval), which sped by as if it were all a cat-nap. The bad, however, was fundamental and serious. The Athens court scenes were set in a gypsy encampment in modern Andalucia. The reason for this anachronistic displacement remained unclear. The effect created by flamenco singers sitting outside their beat-up caravans hitched to flashy 1950s convertible cars was pleasing (though not so the tackiness of closing the play with the flamenco dancing of a 6-year-old girl in all her chintzy regalia), but none of this tallied with the Greek temple set on a cliff behind the encampment nor with the faithfully delivered textual references to Athens. Similarly, the distraction, for the on-stage court audience watching the Pyramus and Thisbe play, of passing jets and high-speed trains was either gratuitous or making a point that a lot of spectators in the auditorium were unable to grasp. However, the most basic problem was one for which Savary cannot carry all of the blame. Shakespeare is not easy to do in French. A wonderful translation is needed, of course, and there are few of them. The best French translator of Shakespeare probably is Yves Bonnefoy. The translation used by Savary was by Jean-Michel Déprats. It sounded pleasing at times, especially in the rude mechanicals' scenes. But much of it sounded ordinary. On top of that, any poetry it might have contained was too often crushed in the loud mêlée of over-excited acting. (It should be said, however, that there were two wonderfully judged performances from Maxime Lombard as Puck and Alain Trétout as Bottom.)

Savary's *Dream* was as colourful and assertive as any of his productions, and also as free of a unifying idea. But it was enthusiastically received, and the distinctive Savary style at Chaillot is obviously paying dividends. The performance was preceded by half an hour of flamenco singing and dancing in the foyer, though the acoustics of that vast place were quite wrong. In addition, Savary has introduced (and this is the first time it has happened in Europe) an 'audiovision' system, defined in the programme notes as

a method of describing simultaneously with the action on stage all those aspects of the production that are inaccessible to the visually disadvantaged. A commentator selects the significant detail and relays it to the spectator by means of a cordless head-set.

This application of Savary's philosophy of theatre for everyone is to be applauded, as is his declared intention of investigating other similar possibilities for spectators with hearing and mobility problems.

Savary has enthusiastic plans for his theatre. A glance at the 1990–1 programme shows a Victor Hugo, a children's show and a piece about tailors' dummies in the Salle Gémier, whilst in the main space, the Salle Jean Vilar, there will be two Shakespeares, one Molière and three productions whose theme broadly is the circus. Obviously, Savary intends to go on as he has so far, bringing his distinctive physical, circus-inspired type of theatre to as wide a public as possible, including children. And the policy seems to be working. *Zazou*, for example, was playing to substantial and enthusiastic houses in the autumn of 1990. Savary has told this writer that he would like to increase the seating capacity of the main auditorium by 200 seats, and that he hopes to put on some interesting and more experimental work in the Salle Gémier studio.[7] He would like to establish a resident company of some 25 artists, as well as a small theatre school. He would also like Chaillot to have something on offer to the public for ten months out of every twelve, with some 400 events per annum. He has ideas too about bursaries for hopeful actors and actresses and for authors, about taking Chaillot productions into privately run theatres in Paris and abroad, and about hiring out his premises. He would like to attract sponsorship, and to introduce a subscription system targeting in particular people in the provinces. One of his ideas which has already been implemented is the re-introduction of *apéritif-concerts* in the foyers.

There is no doubt that Savary has made a distinctive mark on the Théâtre National de Chaillot, and this in itself is no small achievement. He has done his best to take the chill off that too-imposing building. The pre-performance part of an evening there smacks of the old Magic Circus days. For example, as part of his production of *Le Bourgeois Gentilhomme*, he had jazz musicians and circus trapeze artistes performing in the foyer area, creating an easy and playful atmosphere which was the right prelude for the evening's main event. And he has used self-publicity to make his theatre and its wares better known. There is something just a little larger than life about the hard-living and hedonistic Savary, a Havana cigar permanently between his lips. Not too many serious critics have liked his work over the years (with the notable exception of Colette Godard of *Le Monde*), and for many he has remained simply the unreformed and undisciplined champion of a post-1960s theatre of sex, drugs, rock and the rest. His history has shown, however, that this is not quite the case. A showman undoubtedly he is; a sentimentalist as well, to an extent. But he is a disciplined artist, an actor as well as a musician, a ringmaster, a director. In a way his view of the world and his aesthetic sense are reminiscent, in the field of poetry, of Jacques Prévert. The comparison may be particularly apt, for it will be remembered that Prévert was closely involved in the 1930s with the Groupe Octobre, that small, anti-elitist company which mounted colourful productions of plays with a simple, left-wing content, for the benefit of ordinary people. It is a nice coincidence that Prévert, and Savary some thirty years later, were both involved in separate productions of Cervantes's rarely performed *entremés* (interlude), *Le Tableau des merveilles*. Again like Prévert, Savary is an outsider on the inside. It is not easy to place him in a particular theatrical tradition. His career seems inescapably to fall into two parts. In the first, the era of the major Magic Circus shows, he was at the smiling and largely optimistic end of the Latin American group that included García, Lavelli and Arrabal. He and his company had a unique power to enchant, to create 'magic'. There has been nothing quite like the early Magic Circus ever since. If anyone is carrying that torch forward now, it is probably the various 'circuses' that have come into being recently, such as the currently fashionable Archaos (who toured the United Kingdom with a clever and flashy show in 1990), the more gentle Cirque du Soleil (a French Canadian outfit), and even – but the link is tenuous indeed – the dreamy, much-missed Cirque Imaginaire of Jean-Baptiste Thierry and Victoria Chaplin. Yet none of these is quite the same as the Magic Circus, which surely was as instrumental as any other company in freeing theatre from its old orthodoxies of taste. It might be argued that Savary and Mnouchkine (with her Théâtre du Soleil) simultaneously did the most in France to challenge all presuppositions about what constitutes a theatrical event. Both these people almost literally exploded theatre in the late 1960s and the 1970s. Mnouchkine has maintained her vision in a rigorous, impressive but largely unsmiling way. Savary, in that second, post-Magic Circus part of his career, has gone on smiling from behind his glittering theatrical stall which abounds in magical objects, tricks and delights, but now when the magician waves his wand it is not always clear what artistic vision is being conjured up from what artistic principles. Nevertheless, you never see long faces on stage or in the audience at the end of a Savary show. This magician still spells success.

NOTES

Grateful acknowledgement is made to the British Academy for the award of a grant that allowed a substantial part of the research for this chapter to be undertaken.

1 David Whitton, *Stage Directors in Modern France*, Manchester, Manchester University Press, 1987: 180.
2 Jérôme Savary, *La Vie privée d'un magicien ordinaire*, Paris, Editions Ramsay, 1985: 23.
3 Bettina Knapp, *Off-stage Voices*, New York, Whitston, 1975: 64.
4 Whitton, *Stage Directors*: 183.
5 The scenario of *Zartan* plus Savary's accompanying note are reproduced in *The Drama Review*, 15/1, Autumn 1970: 88–92, from which this extract is taken.
6 David Bradby, *Modern French Drama 1940–1980*, Cambridge, Cambridge University Press, 1984: 220.
7 Martin Sorrell, 'An interview with Jérôme Savary', *Studies in Theatre Production*, 1, Jan. 1990: 45–51.

BIBLIOGRAPHY

By Savary

'Nos fêtes', in *Le Théâtre 1968-1*, Paris, Bourgois, 1968: 81-6.

'*Zartan*, a scenario', *Drama Review*, 15/1, 1970: 88-91.

'*Zartan ou le frère mal-aimé de Tarzan* and *Les Derniers Jours de solitude de Robinson Crusoe*', *L'Avant-Scène*, 496, June 1972 (this issue is devoted to Le Grand Magic Circus).

'Une grande fête pour adultes tristes', *Preuves*, X1, 1972: 137-45.

'*De Moïse à Mao*', *L'Avant-Scène*, 539, Apr. 1974; 3-42 (playtext plus illustrations).

Album du Grand Magic Circus, Paris, Belfond, 1974.

La Vie privée d'un magicien ordinaire, Paris, Editions Ramsay, 1985.

About Savary

Bradby, David, *Modern French Drama 1940-1980*, Cambridge, Cambridge University Press, 1984: 189-90 and 220.

Knapp, Bettina, *Off-Stage Voices: Interviews with Modern French Dramatists*, New York, Whitston, 1975; 63-70.

Knowles, Dorothy, 'Ritual theatre: Fernando Arrabal and the Latin-Americans', *The Modern Language Review*, 70/3, 1975; 526-38.

Sorrell, Martin, 'An interview with Jérôme Savary', *Studies in Theatre Production*, 1, Jan. 1990: 45-51.

——(Essay review), '*Le Bourgeois Gentilhomme* at the TNP', *French Cultural Studies*, 1/1/2, 1990: 161-6.

Webb, Richard, C., 'Towards a popular theatre: *Le Grand Magic Circus*', *Journal of Popular Culture*, 9/4: 840-50.

Whitton, David, *Stage Directors in Modern France*, Manchester, Manchester University Press, 1987: 180-90.

APPENDIX

Productions by Savary with Le Grand Magic Circus

1970 *Zartan, frère mal-aimé de Tarzan*, Toronto, New York and Paris.

1972 *Les Derniers Jours de solitude de Robinson Crusoe*, Paris and London.

1973 *Cendrillon ou La Lutte des classes*, La Rochelle.

1974 *De Moise à Mao, 5000 ans d'aventure et d'amour*, Strasbourg and Paris.
    Good Bye Mister Freud, Paris.

1975 *Les Grands Sentiments*, Villeneuve-sur-Lot and Paris.

1976 *Les Grands Sentiments*, on tour.

1977 *Courage*, Bochum, and on tour.

1978 *Les Mille et une nuits*, Freibourg, Rotterdam and Paris.

1979 *Les Mélodies du malheur*, Istres and Paris.
    Noël au Front, Hamburg.

1980 *Le Bourgeois Gentilhomme*, Aulnay-sous-Bois and Paris.

1982 *Superdupont*, Béziers and Paris.

1983 *L'Histoire du cochon qui voulait maigrir,* Paris and Vienna.
1984 *Bye Bye Showbiz,* Venice, on tour, and Paris.
1985 *Les Aventures inédites du cochon en Amazonie,* Paris.

Other productions

1965 *Les Boîtes* and *L'Invasion du vert olive,* Paris.
1966 *Le Labyrinthe,* Vincennes.
      Le Radeau de la Méduse, Vincennes.
1968 New version of *Le Labyrinthe,* London and New York.
1969 *Os Montros,* São Paulo.
1977 *Léonce et Léna,* Hamburg.
      Les Trois Mousquetaires, Mannheim.
1978 *La Périchole,* Hamburg.
      La Vie parisienne, Frankfurt.
      Le Tour du monde en 80 jours, Hamburg.
1979 *Le Voyage dans la lune,* East Berlin.
      Jeder stirbt für sich allein, Berlin.
1980 *Dommage qu'elle soit une putain,* Bonn.
1982 *L'Histoire du soldat,* Milan.
      La Périchole, Geneva.
1983 *Anacréon,* Milan.
      La Belle Hélène, Paris.
      Cyrano de Bergerac, Paris.
1984 *La Périchole,* Paris.
      Don Giovanni, Rome.
      La Vie parisienne, Montpellier.
1985 *La Flûte enchantée,* Bregenz.
      La Femme du boulanger, Paris.
1986 *Cabaret,* Lyon and international tour.
      Le Voyage dans la lune, Geneva.
      Don Juan Tango, Barcelona.
1987 *Cabaret,* Paris.
      Cocu and co, Hamburg.
      Le Barbier de Séville, Strasbourg.
      Les Contes d'Hoffmann, Bregenz.
      La Veuve joyeuse, Vienna.
      Le Comte Ory, Lyon.
1988 *Cabaret,* Paris and Geneva.
      L'Italienne à Alger, Strasbourg.
      Les Contes d'Hoffmann, Bregenz.
      Astérix, Paris.
      Le Barbier de Séville, Lyon.
      D'Artagnan, Paris.
1989 *Metropolis,* London.
      La Flûte enchantée, Vienna.
      Cabaret, Tel Aviv.
      D'Artagnan, Berlin.

Zazou, Paris.
Le Bourgeois Gentilhomme, Paris.
1990 *Blimunda*, Milan.
Le Songe d'une nuit d'été, Avignon and Paris.
Zazou, Paris.
La Légende de Jimmy, Paris.

4

WEST GERMANY

*Theo Girshausen**

WHY THIS CHRONOLOGICAL DIVIDE?

Apart from purely chronological considerations, where decades function as convenient units of time, on what basis can an analysis of
contemporary West German theatre begin with the 1960s? Why is it
possible to look at this period as different from the last, and how far
does this period characterize a turning-point, whose effects are still
felt today?

These questions are clearly of some importance, because at first
sight it seems illogical to choose the 1960s as a starting-point in the
light of other conventions of dating in the history of the theatre: as
far as both the participants and the institutions are concerned, a
concrete turning-point in West German theatre only became apparent in the years 1971 and 1972. It was then that names connected with
the post-war theatre movement began to disappear. Boleslaw Barlog
(Berlin Staatstheater), Karlheinz Stroux (Düsseldorf Schauspielhaus),
Helmut Henrichs (Munich Staatsschauspiel), Hans Schalla (Bochum),
Walter Erich Schäfer (Stuttgart), Gerhard F. Hering (Darmstadt) and
Gustav Rudolf Sellner (German Opera House, Berlin), the long-
serving precursor of Hering in Darmstadt, all left their posts. Even if
not all these managers had been around for as long as Barlog (since
1948), Schalla (since 1949) or Schäfer (since 1951), they had none the
less been equally influential throughout the 1950s and 1960s. It is
clear in any case that only with the retirement of these theatre
managers did the first era of West German theatre come to an end.

Of course, we are not merely talking here of a sudden transition to a
new generation. The departure of these personalities precipitated a
simultaneous shift in focus in West German theatre from every

* Translated by Judith Grayston and Ralph Yarrow

perspective, the institutional as well as the aesthetic. New aesthetic concepts, a new way of looking at production, a new dramaturgy and an extensively restructured theatre language replaced the old conventions. New methods of organizing work within the theatre replaced the old. In the face of these radical changes, a change of central personalities takes on less significance.

But such a far-reaching transformation of the theatre could not take place overnight. It necessitated preparation and groundwork – and this is where the 1960s gains in import, with its dramatists and other members of the theatrical profession still working in the provinces at this point. Together they had pushed, throughout this decade, for a careful modification of the whole theatre system. Thus the radical structural transformation set in motion by the departure of the managers can only be understood as a consequence of these internal changes which took place in the space of ten years.

This is why the 1960s can and must be included in an analysis of the processes of change. While the visible break occurred at the beginning of the 1970s, it was the developments of the previous decade that were responsible for the disintegration of a whole tradition of theatre, namely the disintegration of *Intendantentheater** itself, with the departure of the old *Intendanten*.

INTENDANTENTHEATER

Intendantentheater, the term used to denote the prevailing state of this institution during the first twenty-five years following the war, is also used with reference to a long-standing tradition in German theatre. The title of *Intendant* has in fact been borrowed from that of an administrative post in royal German courts of the eighteenth and nineteenth centuries, and the name as well as the idea it denotes (sole responsibility, but also the exclusive decision-making power of a theatre manager who has the last word in all organizational and artistic matters) has unquestionably outlasted not only the conversion of the courts into state theatres but also all subsequent transformations. Even in the years immediately following the Second World War there were no significant changes. In 1949 the status of the *Intendant* was newly defined and finally confirmed in the *Intendanten-Mustervertrag*, published by the *Deutscher Bühnenverein*, the organization of theatre sponsors and managers. This contract

* The term *Intendant* loosely equates to the English 'theatre manager', but the German function is more administrative as opposed to the actor-managers of nineteenth-century British theatre.

ensured the sole right of the *Intendant* to engage acts and arrange the programme, ensured, in other words, the artistic freedom of the *Intendant* from any restrictions imposed by the sponsors, and by the *Länder* or town administrations, and cemented the internal hierarchical structure of the theatre business, the absolute supremacy of the *Intendant* over anyone else involved with the theatre.[1]

Freedoms and rights of this kind allowed the *Intendanten* to practise 'a process of identifying themselves and the theatre they managed as one and the same',[2] and this had a significant effect on the prestige a theatre could achieve in this period. The *Intendant* saw to it (using his name as a guarantee) that 'his' theatre presented itself as a *Stadttheater* in the true sense of the word, that is, as a theatre that was not only financed by municipal funds, but simultaneously took on the hallmark of a municipal institution representing a cosmopolitan tradition of education and urban culture, and therefore exercising a certain power of attraction over that small section of the population who actually attended the performances. It was on such a solid base that *Intendantentheater* became one of the most highly regarded and most attended in the whole history of the Federal Republic: the audiences attracted by the national, regional and local theatres reached a peak of 20 million in the 1956/7 season (filling 90 per cent of seats in city theatres) and were maintained for a period of 10 years until the great collapse of 1966/7.

CULTURAL THEATRE IN CRISIS

But where was the weak spot in such a tightly knit system? With the benefit of hindsight, the answer comes easily enough – the weaknesses of *Intendantentheater* consisted in the eclectic and arbitrary nature of the programmes[3] as well as in the vague and non-committal style of the productions, which seemed intent only on doing justice to the 'work' being presented at that point.[4] They lacked the courage to tackle anything unusual, anything not immediately comprehensible; definite ideas, opinions, contemporary interest were all missing from the productions. In short, it can be said that the aesthetic hallmark of this type of theatre is an all-embracing formalism.

This characteristic needs to be explored in more detail, as it concerns more than the purely aesthetic aspect. On closer examination it sheds light on the real function of theatre and thus its unequalled success, and it was against this social function that the reforming figures of the 1960s made a decisive stand; it seems appropriate to describe it briefly, in order to understand that the younger generation's growing opposition to the omnipresent *Intendantentheater* was not merely a question of the generation gap, but one of principle, concerned with a critical attitude towards society.

In effect, the formalism of *Intendantentheater* corresponded exactly to the experiences and needs of the West Germans in a postwar period entailing such comprehensive and energetic reconstruction. The war and the 'collapse', not only of a state, but also of all normal social conditions and everyday trivia, had bred in the German population a profound mistrust of ideology. 'Thousand-year-long' (so-called) values, ideas and goals, which Hitler used to mobilize the nation, collapsed, even before the end of the war, in the face of urban destruction and the ruin of the majority of private lives, and this aroused in most a hatred of even the mildest forms of values, goals and ideas.

The mood of the Germans after the war was epitomized in the formula 'the ideology of non-ideology'.[5] There was little to be done with the nineteenth-century concept that theatre was essentially concerned with 'culture' and 'education', with developing 'sensibility' and 'morality'. *Intendanten* and politicians did make speeches attempting to promote a belief in the aesthetic value of theatre, but they failed to persuade an audience that was predisposed to reject *all* ideological claims.

However, the cause was not abandoned. What people really wanted was the essentially idealistic old myth of the 'complete person', not merely as empty ideological rhetoric but demonstrated in practice in terms of commitment to 'reconstruction'. There was an unconditional totally demanding and all-consuming desire for a framework for meaning, for culture, for spiritual justification.

The culture which was so desperately needed for social reasons quickly started to spread after 1945. It was supported – not only in the realm of theatre – by a broad and unanimous consensus, of a kind never seen subsequently in West Germany. The belief in binding values had disintegrated, but as it is impossible to live without values this culture resorted to a shift in interpretation: the values survived, but as formal principles, free from any meaningful content. No one believed in anything, but at the same time people demanded 'devoutness'; no one saw themselves as bound to anything any longer, but all the same, people demanded 'bonds' as a prerequisite to all human existence; no one viewed the endeavour to found a new society as a spiritual target, but people demanded qualities of intellect and determination while working towards a functioning form of society. Theodor W. Adorno, who returned from exile in the United States to Frankfurt University, registered this 'resurrection of culture' in Germany with a certain dismay. As early as the beginning of the 1950s he was struck by the transformation of the value system from content- to form-orientation and later criticized it, in a radical analysis, as characterizing a conservative mode of thought. He called the jargon of the educated and cultivated, which negated the whole value system, while unquestioningly assigning old values the status of formal principles, the 'jargon of essentiality'.[6]

The vagueness and eclecticism – that is, the formalism of the pluralistic programmes, and the faithful productions of original works – exactly suited the cultural requirements of the immediate post-war years. The theatre regarded itself as an exclusive venue of gravity, as 'spiritual space' overflowing with the 'magic', 'embodiment' and 'symbolic representations' of life, but far removed from its real conditions. It was intentionally 'outside the workaday arena'.[7] That is – to overstate the case for the sake of clarity – the reality of the 'workaday' offered nothing but work and hardship and created a desire to find, in the theatre, an assurance that there was after all something higher, something more tangible than the feeling of total failure in, and in face of, the most recent past and the mere material concerns of 'reconstruction' and the assurance of continued personal existence. In the theatre you could escape from time and participate in something really valuable and meaningful. Only here did the 'classics' still have a message, and in the 'modern theatre of the world', the world and everything in it of value and meaning were open. But no one would or could say what the 'real', the 'valuable' or the 'meaningful', supposedly preserved in this culture, consisted of. They were confined to a lofty and, for a short time, uplifting theatrical experience, after which, however, people had to re-emerge into their own day and age.

The account above is very brief and is, moreover, written from the point of view of those who made a stand against *Intendantentheater* in the 1960s. But formalism and a lack of content as a mark of this theatre had already been recognized and criticized at an earlier date, and not only by those who saw themselves as political opponents of 'cultural theatre' as a blind and thoughtlessly pursued restoration. As early as 1956 Egon Vietta, the long-serving dramaturge under Sellner in Darmstadt, had made a stand against these weaknesses in the theatre that he himself helped to shape, in his book *Katastrophe oder Wende des deutschen Theaters* (Catastrophe or Change in German Theatre). This book is not written from a leftist perspective, from the perspective of people involved in the theatre who were driven into exile and then returned to Germany to be greeted, in their eyes, by the hollow pathos and empty rhetoric that represented the remains of the pompous Nazi theatre and its 'state chancellery style' (in the words of the director Bertholt Viertel). Vietta's book is more of a precise document describing the cultural requirements of the time. It approves in many places the 'jargon of essentiality'. Vietta too demands 'bonds', 'spirituality' and 'devoutness' from the experience of theatre, and his stipulation that theatres should become secularized 'city cathedrals' is less a hope for the future than a reflection of the actual status of theatres as representative institutions and objects of prestige in the towns.

But although Vietta adopts the vocabulary of the period he manages to specify the symptoms that led to the crisis, and he can thus be brought in as an impartial witness. He attacks the waste, the arbitrariness, the conformism of the theatre. Vietta's charge that current programmes were the 'most characterless that Germany has ever seen' is levelled at the lack of discrimination which resulted in anything that appeared either 'spiritually meaningful' or 'sophisticated and modern' getting put on. His summary, 'there is no form of theatre that pleases all', is a criticism of the pluralism practised by the *Intendanten*, which in reality meant a lack of standards in programming and vagueness in production.

When Vietta in this way demands from the theatre what everyone else is demanding from him, but then asks if it in fact satisfies this desire and then arrives at a negative answer, he exposes the crisis affecting *Intendantentheater*. He sees that this kind of theatre is of enormous importance, but has almost never worked – is really a non-event. Theatre only repeats what everyone thinks, illustrates what everyone desires and thus offers only tautologies of the prevailing state of consciousness. Vietta's fundamental demand targets this situation and its aimless free-wheeling: theatre must 'return to the catacombs' and free itself from the pressure exerted on it by audience expectations. This necessitates an act of self-assurance and concentration, whereby theatre once again has to set itself its own goals and tasks.

It is this need for theatre to rethink its aims and methods which gave impetus to the growing opposition to *Intendantentheater* at the beginning of the 1960s. Of course, the new goals were not the same ones Vietta had imagined: both the new tasks ahead of the theatre and the means to complete them successfully were from now on to conform to a programme of 'political theatre'.

OPPOSITION IN THE 1960s: POLITICAL THEATRE

At the very beginning of the 1960s a new term was in circulation that indicated the new political standpoint of theatre and the aesthetic resources that were to fulfil its new aims. 'Documentary theatre' became a widely used term, despite its misleading nature. It would be better to speak of 'documentary drama' because the intended programme was and remained just an ideal for writers, and its effect was felt in the following years principally by dramatists, who were experimenting with new concepts and variations of political dramaturgy. Ultimately, these documentary works had as little success in the theatre as the other forms of political drama that followed in their wake. Throughout the whole of the 1960s *Intendantentheater* still held the limelight; it merely acquired a new colour from the political plays, and discovered a further pluralistic nuance for its own purposes.

What, however, about the intentions and programme of such documentary theatre? The most valid ones were presented when this type of drama was already on its last legs. At the 1968 Brecht Congress in the Berliner Ensemble Peter Weiss presented his 'Notizen zum dokumentarischen Theater' (Notes on Documentary Theatre),[8] which was in effect a résumé of five years of continuous development. These notes treat the term 'theatre' in a manner radically different from its prevailing use in the 1950s. Weiss strongly denies the theatre any special place in society, and disputes its status as a place higher than and distinct from the 'everyday'. He sees it rather as comparable to the other media which form the public face of modern society, akin to cinema, and even closer to radio and television. While others had earlier used these 'technical media' to account for the impending disintegration of theatre, Weiss takes the opposite view. He sees these media as legitimizing the need for contemporary theatre. He tries to prove that theatre can compete against other media, and indeed, in terms of presenting a picture of the world, may be superior to them.

Weiss admits that radio and television could be unsurpassable in the context of pure information, if this had remained the main aim. They could spread more up-to-date and complete information far quicker than any other medium, but the methods of 'mass media' have served to alienate the aims. Instead of concentrating on news, they concentrate on the speed of delivery, which has resulted in the construction of a false reality. The technical possibilities marginalize the significance of reports and information and become a means of distortion, lies and forgery, because the important thing is the briefly presented and attractive picture of a superficial reality, not the indirectly accessible links, the underlying causes, which the microphone and the camera miss. Reasons and causes of a historical kind are left out because of the greater emphasis placed on superficial, quickly transmitted and live reality. Television exists in an eternal present. Yesterday's events belong to the past and are therefore of no interest. This means that the new present given to us every day remains out of reach and irrational. If then the technical media are used for the objective criticism of the presentation and explanation of the state of the world, and omit the causes, the theatre takes on a new meaning for Weiss. It can become an effective instrument of criticism, a critique of lies, forgery and distortion, and can report things as they really are. Theatre should therefore regard itself as a democratic public institution, as a forum for publicizing those truths that are suppressed by the pseudo-objectivity of the mass media and thus for making them more generally accessible.[9]

Weiss's polemic is obviously aimed at the directors of *Intendanten-theater* and their insistence on 'cultural theatre' as a higher form of life. The programme therefore ventured into new areas which, if they had appeared at all in 'cultural theatre', did so in the form of elevated symbols of eternal human truths. The majority of documentary plays deal with Nazi Germany and the guilt of the Germans for systematic mass murder (Rolf Hochhuth's *Der Stellvertreter* (The Deputy), which counts the Pope among the guilty; Peter Weiss's *Die Ermittlung* (The Investigation), partly based on reports of the Frankfurt Auschwitz trial; Heinar Kipphardt's *Joel Brandt* which treats a cynical business deal between the SS and a Jewish aid organization – a million Jews heading for the gas chamber are offered in exchange for 10,000 lorries); others are concerned with the present political situation in the world (Weiss's *Gesang vom Lusitanischen Popanz* (Song of the Lusitanian Bogeyman) about colonialism, exploitation and the freedom movement in the Third World, using Angola as an example) and the social and political reality of the Federal Republic (Michael Hatry's

Notstandsübung (Emergency Drill) and Günther Wallraff's *Nachspiele* (Afterpieces) both of which deal with the tightening of laws for the sake of 'national security', the so-called 'emergency laws'). Topics of this kind serve to confirm that documentary theatre was primarily engaged in exposing the connections between the immediate past and the present and thus dissolving the suppression that was corroborated and reinforced by both the mass media and the theatre. Weiss names the tradition from which this commitment was taken, namely the 'theatre of contemporary realism which has undergone many changes since the Proletarian Cultural Movement, agitprop, Piscator's experiments and the didactic plays of Brecht'.[10]

LINKING UP TO THE TRADITION OF 'POLITICAL THEATRE'

Weiss's reference to a tradition is important, because political theatre of the 1960s is not confined just to documentary theatre and to authors such as Hochhuth, Kipphardt and Weiss. They were rather the initiators of a politicization that had far-reaching effects, of which the most important for the theatre was the rediscovery of the tradition of political theatre as it existed during the Weimar Republic, a tradition that had been tirelessly eroded under National Socialism and during the period of restoration in the 1950s when the 'ideology of non-ideology' prevailed.

Thus it is characteristic that Erwin Piscator was the first to produce a documentary play – Hochhuth's 'scandalous' *Der Stellvertreter* – in 1963, and initiate the first sweeping success of a German-speaking post-war dramatist since Dürrenmatt. Piscator had, since his return from exile in the United States, been forced to spend many years as an obscure producer. Following the success of *Der Stellvertreter*, however, which he had achieved as *Intendant* of the Berlin 'Freie Volksbühne' and as producer, both he and the role he had played in theatre in the Weimar Republic were once again taken note of. Six months after the première of this play a revised edition of his book *Das politische Theater* (1929) was published. The comeback of a major producer meant that the memory of a concept of theatre rich in tradition and an alternative to a popular understanding of theatre could be evoked.

The second most influential member of the theatrical profession during the Weimar Republic found himself in a similar situation on his return from exile. He worked in several West German theatres on a temporary basis, was unerringly logical and often fought furiously for controversial productions as against other more ordinary ones. He was Fritz Kortner. He was strongly opposed to the consensual dogma of 'faithful direction'. 'He took Molière, Shakespeare, and German classics, changed the wording of the translations, in short altered them.'[11] He was concerned with the discovery and unfolding of the reality embedded in the play. Without any intention of relating the plots, themes or motives of the classicists to his own time he sought for individual motivation behind and beneath the action. The truths that came to the surface in his performances were psychological truths. But in the forms of presentation to which Kortner (who himself had been a well-known actor, and who even in the 1960s often took to the stage) urged his protagonists – exaggerated gestures, hyperbolic mimicry, unfamiliar tone and rhythm of speech, intensity, severity and passion of acting – the individual psychic facets multiplied and resulted in supra-individual disclosures. The results were never eternal human truths, but concrete human insights which had revealed themselves to intensive contemplation and empathy. After the press's initial interest in the scandal he caused, in Kortner's last decade his work was once again understood – against a background of political tendencies – as a genuine and promising alternative to the bloodless representative 'cultural theatre' of the *Intendanten*.

The politicization that resulted from documentary theatre led to a renewed interest in Brecht, who had previously been subjected to a boycott (most recently after the erection of the Berlin Wall in August 1961). In the following years Brecht was performed not only at the Munich Kammerspiele and the Frankfurt Schauspielhaus – two houses which had already put on his plays under Hans Schweikart and Harry Buckwitz respectively – but also at other city theatres. The previous policy of toning down Brecht's drama by separating the 'poetic' from the 'Marxist' featured less and less. For example, Gründgen's 1959 production of *Die Heilige Johanna der Schlachthöfe* (St Joan of the Stockyards) in Hamburg emphasized Johanna's personal drama while ignoring the model of capitalism implicit in the text. The Marxist methods and socialist perspectives were now perceived as essential parts of the play, which had to be included in the production.

While Brecht was now being performed more regularly and authentically, dramatists in general began a move away from the Brechtian model. They realized that it was based on the class-war situation of the 1920s and the later political reality of fascism and exile, and tried to develop new forms of drama to express their own contemporary reality.

Even Peter Weiss during his period of politicization started from Brechtian positions. He achieved international success in 1964 with the *Marat/Sade* play in which he pits the antithesis of extreme individualism against revolutionary engagement. Both positions are represented by equally strong characters, and become therefore equally doubtful in their validity, without offering any solutions to the ambivalences portrayed. In this work he found a theme that was to characterize the rest of his work – the precarious situation of an author, of a radical individual, in a world divided into power blocs, a world in need of change where political commitment is a requirement, yet where the only option is a radical but cautious and doubt-ridden support for socialism.

Others who had until this point concentrated on epic theatre and parable dramaturgy (such as Max Frisch with *Andorra*, or Martin Walser with *Eiche und Angora*) sought for political connections in the private sphere of life (Frisch's *Biografie*) and familiar situations (Walser's *Kinderspiel* and *Zimmerschlacht*). A new generation of writers, born in the 1940s, such as Fassbinder, Kroetz and Sperr, came forward at last with topical and critical 'dialect folk-plays', but even these young dramatists sought for links with the 1920s and their models were the modes of thought and behaviour of the lower middle class revealed in the dramas of Ödön von Horváth and Marieluise Fleisser, which described the closed society of the Bavarian Catholic province – fatal for outsiders.[12] But despite appearances, it was only one part of West German theatre that became politicized at that time, and seen from an overall perspective it was only a very small part. It was still the *Intendanten* who were putting on the 'big' productions. Political theatre was merely tolerated by them, although with growing tolerance as time passed. It remained a fringe event. The most important effect of the fringe nature of this theatre was that it remained impossible to change the structure of the theatre as an institution, to change it from a 'cultural event' to a critical forum for public discussion and growth in awareness. And this, as we can see from Weiss's *Notizen*, was what mattered to the supporters of political theatre, not the mere inclusion of plays with a certain political content in the all-consuming 'pluralistic' programmes.

TOLLER AND *TASSO*:
DOUBTS ABOUT POLITICAL THEATRE

It was the experience of the assimilation of political drama by a pluralist theatre, and therefore of its impotence in a cultural institution which had not significantly changed, that the younger generation working in theatre at the end of the 1960s had to undergo. This led in the 1970s to a desire to reshape the institution of theatre which, at least at its leading edge, was to result in radical changes in the theatre scene in West Germany.

Doubts about the possibility of direct political intervention through theatre were frequently expressed at the end of the decade, as for example by Tankred Dorst in his play *Toller*.[13] In spite of his historical subject, Dorst had not written a documentary in the same sense as Weiss; he did not intend to instruct people about the failed revolution at the end of the First World War. He was not primarily interested in a historically accurate account of the participation of the Expressionist playwright Ernst Toller in the foundation of the Socialist Republic in Munich in 1919, which had led to Toller, even more than Brecht, being identified as the symbol of the political artist. Dorst was more interested in Toller as a symbol of theatrical, rather than just political, revolution. Dorst was concerned with the way the writer had adopted the role of the politician and had played it for four weeks; he showed how and why. Precisely because Toller adopted it so earnestly and with such pathos, it revealed itself as a ready-made pose. In contrast to the pragmatism of *realpolitik*, in a situation dominated by a mixture of ideology, self-interest and force, it inevitably made the figure of the political artist and the artistic politician highly questionable. Toller was presented as a living contradiction, and this brought into question the whole issue of political theatre.

Theatre as a whole had to come to terms with the problematic nature of committed art; it began to see it as illusory and ineffectual. This occurred above all where there was painful contact with the real limits of political commitment, limits inscribed in a view of art which did not match its new subject-matter. It became evident that theatre had not changed along with the change in content. This recognition and the resulting consequences are best exemplified in the important and influential failure of an attempt to transcend the limits of artistic practice through political action, and to present this as an artistic statement in an epoch-making *mise-en-scène*. Peter Stein, formerly assistant to Kortner, directed his Munich Kammerspiele company in a provocative attempt to shatter the existing boundaries of political art. They produced a new documentary play by Peter Weiss, *Vietnam-Diskurs* (The Vietnam Debate). The play concerns the history of the Vietnamese people and hence reflected the most urgent theme of the year of its first performance, 1968 – the Vietnam War, which had finally radicalized the rumblings of student protest.

Stein attempted to link up with this movement and with the public disquiet caused by it. The idea was not to present another politically committed play. That was left in no doubt: written on the backdrop and clearly visible throughout the performance were the words 'Documentary theatre is shit'. In addition, the cabaret artist Wolfgang Neuss appeared in a specially inserted role as clown, mocking theatrical commitment as an expression of helplessness – as merely a well-intentioned, but ineffectual, substitute for real solidarity with the Vietnamese.

Relativizing one's own (artistic) effort in this way was a means of taking up a position *vis-à-vis* student activism and its political goals. In the preceding weeks several performances in West German theatres had been interrupted or even broken up by student action; and after the Frankfurt première of *Vietnam-Diskurs* a call by students for donations for the Vietcong had ensured a scandal. Stein's troupe reaped the consequences. At the end of the performance, director and actors intended to collect for the Vietcong in the foyer. The management of the Munich Kammerspiele had been able to accept the choice of a play about Vietnam; that could be accommodated in its experimental space, the 'workshop theatre'. But employing actors as contemporary political activists, rather than as players of roles and wearers of masks, was going too far. This was a deliberate and forbidden rupturing of the demarcation lines of Art – the only framework in which political commitment could be tolerated. The production was taken off; Stein and the company left the Kammerspiele.

Peter Stein's next production, Goethe's *Torquato Tasso*, a year later, can be understood as an artistic response to the disappointment over political theatre.[14] It is also relevant that the play was not presented at one of the 'big houses', but in the provinces, in the theatre in Bremen, where the Intendant Karl Hübner (in post since 1962) had entrusted the most unconventional of new directors, Peter Zadek, with responsibility.[15] A major feature of the work which went on in Bremen – soon referred to by the press as the 'Bremen style' –

were the set designs of Wilfried Minks, who constructed clear, functional sets for Zadek's classical productions: on the one hand they served the needs of the play, on the other hand they enriched the productions by signalling an extra, visual level of expression.

Minks built the set for Stein's *Tasso* too, an entirely artificial space enclosed within shimmering flexiglass walls, with a grass-green floor, containing a minimum of furnishings – a desk, a bust of Goethe in the foreground – a space almost continuously occupied by all the players. Stein had done his homework, and freed up the lines of Goethe's text by transposing sections, achieving an unbroken flow of action, one event merging seamlessly into the next and frequently emerging from scenes played simultaneously. The overall impression was of a courtly society governed by unspoken and therefore even more rigid norms and conventions, adopting puppet-like poses and playing out roles with a dream-like, ultimately traumatic, appearance of security.

Tasso, as part of this playing within the rules of court etiquette, poses as the genius intoxicated with his own self-importance, and is accepted as such as long as he does not overstep the limits of his position as Court poet. But as soon as the mask slips and Tasso cracks open the boundaries of formality and restraint – by offering the courtier Antonio not merely courtly respect but genuine friendship, or by giving the princess to understand that his honour and love for her has a down-to-earth basis in physical desire – he is repulsed and returned to the confines of what is permitted to the artist, that is, what is thought seemly. To want more would destroy his whole existence, so Tasso accommodates with the only way of life he, as a dependent entity, can aspire to: at the end he cowers on Antonio's shoulders, 'an ape being carried out of the ring by his trainer after performing his number splendidly'.[16]

Stein succeeded admirably in expressing what he himself had experienced – the situation of the artist tolerated only in narrowly defined limits – through this distanced view of Court society, not by approaching the play from the outside and attempting to inject contemporary content, but rather the reverse – by taking its elevated hermetic form seriously and using it as the structuring principle of the play. The preciosity and artiness of speech and action materialized the formal rigidity and conventionality of Court life as Goethe had described it from his own experience, and served also to reveal the limitations, dependencies and consequent deformities of the human figures. Out of this precise depiction of Goethe's artistic world emerged the artist as 'emotional clown', allowed then as now to play his role so long as he does not try to be himself and to represent his own responsibilities.

THE LIMITS OF POLITICAL THEATRE:
SOME CONSEQUENCES

Before considering the aesthetic positions implied by the Bremen production of *Tasso*, we need to be clear about its historical significance in respect of the situation of theatre at the end of the 1960s.[17] This is particularly exemplified by the argument between two young actors, published in the periodical *Theater heute* almost exactly a year before the *Tasso* première, which provoked a public debate about the 'authoritarian spirit in German theatre'.[18]

The polemic was clearly inspired by the anti-authoritarian tendency in the student movement, strongly coloured by the cultural critique of Herbert Marcuse. Basic working practices common in theatre were criticized along Marcusian and student lines for their outdated and alienating power structures, which prevented genuine identification with the products of labour and turned what should have been unrestrained self-expression into mere artefacts. The authors wrote from this stance:

> Even political commitment, which young playwrights demand from theatre, only *appears* to bring life to the boards. Old-fashioned working methods inevitably rob revolutionary plays of their sting, making them merely dutiful acknowledgements. Theatre can only reflect its inner condition externally.[19]

And that should mean that the first step is to change the working situation *in* theatre, before any political commitment *through* theatre can be effective.

It was a question then of dismantling stagnant hierarchies and authoritarian ways of thinking and behaving, which were stifling liveliness and productivity throughout the whole institution as well as in individual productions. The demand was for a direct link between performers and their work. They should all be in a position to know what they were doing and why, and should be equally entitled to participate in all decisions affecting the work. The goal was to remove all outside influence and to institute a comprehensive system which would make the product authentic, in the political sense as well. To this end concrete proposals were made and directions indicated: 'The theatre should be run collectively', 'The company should meet regularly and take decisions, it should elect the collective leadership from amongst its members, it should have a say in drawing up the programme for the season as well as in the allocation of parts.'[20]

In this way *Intendantentheater* was radically challenged, admittedly from a utopian perspective, but no longer just out of a feeling of unease, but on the basis of close analysis supported by concrete alternative proposals.

EXPERIMENTATION IN THE 1970s

However utopian the demand for fundamentally different, democratized work structures may have appeared to most people at the time the debate was published, attempts to realize it in a modified form soon followed. As the example of Stein and his company has shown, the restriction imposed by the old order had the effect of making theatre people more interested in change. But theatre criticism too became more sympathetic to the arguments of the reformers; and civic authorities showed themselves (naturally in different degrees) prepared to listen and to accept some of the consequences.

It was possible for the impulse to change work structures to take effect in virtually every city where posts in theatre management fell vacant. That is why the change-over of managers in the 1971–2 season, which has already been mentioned, is not just about personalities or a new generation, but also marks a change of system in West German theatre, a breakthrough to a new beginning on a broad front. Whereas other city theatres only got as far as internal discussions about company participation, in Frankfurt, uniquely, a decisively new, legally enforceable situation was achieved. The opportunity for radical change arose from the retirement of the general manager in 1973. It was not just a case of change of personnel at the head; the managerial structure itself was reformed. Peter Palitzsch, from Stuttgart, did not just take over as manager, but became a member of a directorate along with two others, a set designer and an actor, who were to take decisions collectively.[21]

The Frankfurt experiment was made easier by the fact that there had already been one highly successful experiment in 'participatory theatre'. From 1 August 1970 a democratic set-up had been operating, with the support of the City Senate and significantly increased public subsidy, at the Berlin Schaubühne am Halleschen Ufer – a private theatre founded eight years previously with a political commitment right from the start. Here too the company was involved in all decisions through a leading caucus consisting of its representatives, along with directors Peter Stein and Claus Peymann and the dramaturge Dieter Sturm.[22]

The story of developments in West German theatre in the 1970s can be told through an account of the similarities of the two 'participatory theatres',[23] since aims and achievements can be clearly observed. The successes fall chiefly under two headings: the different perception of the role of director and the development of a theatrical language that brings out the physicality and visual quality of theatre anew.

THE NEW DIRECTORS

The model for the director which was to become standard in the major centres of theatrical activity was the exact opposite of that of the manager-director of the previous period. This has not only to do with a readiness to dismantle autocratic structures and to move towards new forms of communal activity. It is merely the most evident aspect of a complete shift in the directors' perception of their roles.

The experiences that formed directors who took up their posts in the early 1970s can be identified from a recent volume of reminiscences.[24] Most of them were then in their thirties and forties. They were distinguished by a radical scepticism towards the restoration of the Adenauer period in which they had grown up: full of mistrust for restrictive moral prejudices and the emptiness of conventions masked by official culture. They had been disturbed and shaken by revelations about their fathers' generation, which in spite of official silence had come to light in isolated political scandals and above all in the trials of Nazi war-criminals. Finally, they had been influenced by the experiences of student mass-protest, which had left an ambiguous impression in many cases: commitment and action seemed exciting and attractive, but the rapid swamping of the movement in ideological jargon and its subsequent fragmentation were repellent.

Their artistic inspiration derived less from contemporary literature and drama, let alone the repertoire of civic theatres, than from a rediscovery of the theatre of the 1920s, and principally from the forms of action that artists had developed after the Second World War: mobile events and happenings, and annual exhibitions of the international avant-garde.

These influences were responsible for a similar understanding of their function on the part of young directors of the period, in spite of other distinctions and oppositions. They were alert to the historical, social and political background of their work. This was reflected in productions underpinned by a greater degree of awareness, which could no longer be justified simply by recourse to the intentions of the author, but were also understood as a comment on the contemporary situation.

Second, there was a prevailing allergy to anything that might seem like convention and routine. No preconceived expectations were to be allowed to deflect the direct insight into people and behaviour that theatre should present; nothing should prejudice its implacable focus on and exposure of underlying motivation. In terms of scenic language this meant a search for hitherto unused forms of expression on the very verge of what could be said through theatre.

Third, allied to this was a specific appeal to the public. Each performance was an invitation to open up to new themes and unfamiliar forms, to the kind of directly relevant, if unpalatable, truths theatre dealt in.

In most cases it was not a question of having to combat the views of their predecessors, whose aims were reconciliation and harmony. The careers of Stein and Zadek are typical: the new directors did not get their early experience in the big houses. They achieved the break-through from the sidelines, from smaller theatres or university theatres.

Claus Peymann, for example, came out of student theatre, which was particularly lively in the 1960s; the annual international festival in the Bavarian town of Erlangen was an important forum for the exchange of ideas, differences of opinion, and hence programmatic proposals for the future. Others had attracted attention in provincial theatre: for example Hans Neuenfels in Heidelberg, with emotionally demanding, strongly psychological productions, and Hans Günther Heyme in Wiesbaden with an agitprop style which engendered much controversy. Following Zadek and Stein there were other significant debuts. The most important work from the end of the Hübner years was Klaus-Michael Grüber's minimalist *Tempest*; Grüber had previously worked with Strehler. In Bremen too the work of the Munich 'antitheatre' was presented by a troupe directed by Rainer Werner Fassbinder, in a style provocatively opposed to any claim to 'Art', consciously and exaggeratedly dilettante, heavily mannered.

It is characteristic that the new directors, in spite of differences in interest, working methods and signature, did not want to work in isolation. Conscious of differences, they nevertheless sought to work together and to construct a network of productive tensions arising from the juxtaposition of contrasting directorial styles in the same theatre. They highlighted contrasts through the programme, through particular perspectives on classical and modern plays, and through performance style, so as to create enduring tensions in the face of which the public could not remain indifferent. The results of this coincidence of opposites can be seen in the work of the two directors of the theatre in Frankfurt.

Here the scope of the work was determined from the beginning by the contrasting methods of Palitzsch and Hans Neuenfels, the second house-director. Palitzsch started from the principles of the Berliner Ensemble: he had begun there as assistant director under Brecht himself, and after Brecht's death, together with Manfred Wekwerth, had put his stamp on the second phase of work. He had left the GDR after the construction of the Berlin Wall, and had been able to demonstrate the considerable riches of authentic 'epic' theatre in the West, firstly as a guest director, then as artistic director in Stuttgart, where his work was followed with interest after years when no one had wanted to put on Brecht. He was not at all dogmatic or deferential: in Stuttgart Palitzsch often reacted quickly to actual political events and thus produced genuine political theatre. He had been able to demonstrate, above all with reference to Shakespeare and to contemporary English authors like Pinter and Bond, as well as to the plays of Peter Weiss, that Brecht's directing methods were not just relevant to his own work, but could be used to penetrate other dramatic forms and open them up to readings of their social significance.

This approach marked Palitzsch's work in Frankfurt also. It was based on Brecht's simplest and most important insight: the actor is always doubly present on stage, both in his own right *and* as the character he is depicting. To play a part therefore means to show it from a specific perspective, to endow it with a commentary from the person who is playing, to take up a position with regard to it. Palitzsch believed that actors were able not just to 'round' a character in a given context, but also to judge it and examine it using different and contradictory perspectives. It was no doubt this trust in the actor's ability to analyse a character, ultimately a trust in his rationality, which derived from Palitzsch's sense of his own individuality as an artist, and most profoundly motivated him to take the lead in promoting the participatory model and defending it against the massive resistance which soon surfaced.

All his Frankfurt productions were based on this faith in the rational powers of the performers. Characterization was built up from action with a cool, light and witty hand, but also with meticulous care and close involvement; Palitzsch employed Brecht's concept of the 'fable' here, in the sense of the interface of story and characters, of the material and emotional constraints that cause people to develop or block each other, to reveal their mutual attractions, repulsions, needs and motivations.

This working principle proved its worth in widely differing plays – it was particularly successful in Bond's *Lear*, which opened amid scandal, and in Wedekind's *Spring Awakening*, which was the most mature production of the whole period. In these productions the actors at the very least demonstrated more than the characters could know of themselves; they displayed what could additionally be gleaned about them from the development of the action, and thus offered, reticently and carefully, explanations for what the characters could only experience in their own limited self-consciousness as destiny.

Hans Neuenfels's productions were quite different. People in the grip of monomania became the force of destiny for themselves and for others. Palitzsch's characters had a built-in distancing mechanism in the actors' consciousness of role, which gave them freedom to express differing, contradictory qualities and modes of behaviour; under Neuenfels the actors sought to get as close to their characters as possible. They bored into them, as it were, and hauled their deepest and most secret fears, compulsions and ecstasies up to the surface. Neuenfels focused on characters in isolation, thrust them into extremes of intimacy, showing them reduced to their own resources, bound up in the net of their own psychic obsessions and thus held irrevocably apart. Limited to a few pathological traits, the characters lost all normal recognizable features and seemed like larger-than-life monsters, stumbling about unable to find a way out in a sealed, surrealistic nightmare world.

Neuenfels's style is reflected best in two very different groups of plays. In nineteenth-century plays like *A Doll's House* and *Hedda Gabler*, the characters' veneer of secure and comfortable bourgeois domesticity was stripped away to reveal hidden and twisted psychic depths. In this, Neuenfels was following Ibsen's intentions, albeit in a startlingly graphic manner. It was made clear that the bourgeois household is not merely built on lies and convention, but worse, that its relationships are rooted in psychological schisms and wildly irrational urges.

Neuenfels opened up classical works in similarly unexpected ways. In Euripides' *Medea*, which became the most discussed production of this period in Frankfurt, the sense of the archaic and the extreme, which is still difficult for us to grasp rationally, could be sensed in the exultant force of the characters. Euripides' characters appeared naked and covered in blood, a prey to manic erotic obsessions, enmeshed in feelings that offered no chance of escape, isolated in their mental worlds, meeting and touching only out of lust. The tragedy came alive in this way for a contemporary audience, although its historical and social – let alone religious – dimensions were less obvious. It was seen in this production as a consequence of internal upheaval, with the characters locked into bleak fantasies of eroticism and power.

The Frankfurt example shows that even where two directors were firmly committed to their own positions, they did not want to offer a one-sided view to the spectator. Any tendency for a particular perspective to become absolute was to be avoided by the practice of including totally opposing approaches within the same seasonal programme. The public was conceived of as having an active role in mediating between apparently irreconcilable opposites (Brechtian didacticism and psychological exhibitionism) and finding for itself the missing elements in both positions.

DEVELOPING A VISUAL LANGUAGE

At the Schaubühne, it was always the intention to promote two distinct directorial styles in parallel. At first this could only be achieved through distinctions between different plays on the pro-gramme: the juxtaposition of Peter Stein's opening première (Brecht's *The Mother*) and the following production initiated by Claus Peymann, Peter Handke's *Ritt über den Bodensee* (Ride over Lake Constance).[25] Whereas Brecht's play presented the possibility of changing reality, which it exposed as full of social contradictions, Handke's work questioned the status of reality itself. The Brecht play described the achievement of solidarity among the Russian proletariat and the emergence of a revolutionary collective; at the Schaubühne this was related to the situation of the company, who wanted to form themselves into a workers' collective. The Handke play took place in a setting given over to art (an intimate theatre), where figures from the world of art (bearing the names of famous actors) played out verbal rituals giving rise to purely symbolic orders in which the only 'realities' were entirely dependent on relative and subjective perceptions. Here was no such thing as a socially constituted reality, as in Brecht. Rather the reverse: social data revealed themselves as mere conventions and fictions, whose only claim to objectivity lay in the norms and rules of language, which require us to take words for things and attribute the status of 'reality' to them.

It was true, however, that a genuine balance between two different directorial personas was only achieved two years later, with Klaus Michael Grüber's first production at the Schaubühne. Since that date he has been employed there continuously along with Peter Stein. In order to describe the differences between Stein and Grüber, we need first to clarify what they held in common. They both subscribed to an aesthetic principle that was typical of the decade, and that was fully worked out first at the Schaubühne: the stage was considered as a pictorial space. Stein and Grüber, each starting from his own artistic temperament, took it to opposite extremes.

The origin of Peter Stein's *mise-en-scène* style has already been mentioned: it dates back to the co-operation on *Tasso* with set designer Wilfried Minks in Bremen in 1969. Before then Minks had stood out against the representational sets of the managers in company with younger theatre workers. They were firmly opposed to the monumentally symbolic or merely decorative sets which just provided external illustration of the action. The alternative was a thoroughgoing uncluttering of the stage. Minks's work for the Bremen productions of Zadek and Hübner illustrates this: empty, brightly lit sets, with an economy of visual elements, providing clear comments on the action (a blow-up photo in *Spring Awakening*, an exaggeratedly large Lichtenstein cartoon in Schiller's *The Robbers*). These sets focused attention on the actors, who could present their characters to the spectators like objects in an exhibition. Movement, rhythm, proxemics (spatial relationships), gestures and reactions could work as independent means of expression alongside the text, not merely illustrating or underlining the words, but also functioning as a physical language capable of narrating meaning.

Tasso was different. The director did not leave the space open to the spectators' gaze; he wanted to identify the characters with their surroundings by placing them in a self-contained artificial reality, where they could be seen from a distance. The set for *Tasso* moved beyond the previous alternatives – elaborate illustration versus expressionistic physical play in an empty space – by synthesizing physical language and stage space as complementary compositional elements. This production demonstrates essential features of the developments in set during the subsequent decade: set is no longer just a background to action, but furthers and expresses it; the stage becomes a metaphorical space. This is shown by one tiny detail, the bust of Goethe at the front of the stage. In itself it is just a reference to the author of the play and thus an indication of the date of its composition. But the bust takes on a new level of meaning, when the actor playing Tasso adopts flattering poses alone at his writing desk, which gradually call to mind all the clichés of well-known portraits of 'poets and thinkers': the pose becomes ecstatic, is taken to extremes, Tasso loses his balance and crashes to the floor. The bust comes to suggest that a famous man has created a monument for himself which needs its basic premises questioned. The play-acting shows up the monument as a stylization, an exaggeration of genuine sorrow into grandiose idealization.

Associations like this are repeatedly made possible on various levels by the fact that the stage forms an autonomous play-world composed of a montage of heterogeneous visual elements. It does not imitate a 'natural' environment, a historical ambiance or social milieu, but quotes these aspects by allusion through diverse detail. These details link up with the physical and verbal 'montage' of the actors to form new configurations of meaning. This stage language means that performance can be liberated from the chains of the literary text, and thus from the dictat of remaining 'true to the work'. Text becomes *one* expressive element amongst others of equal importance. It becomes a constituent of theatrical language, which can communicate meaning independently of the given text, going beyond it, being in dialogue with it, analysing and questioning it.

Furthermore, to make the stage into a metaphor enables the suspension of linear time. It removes the need to opt for a historically determined setting, to which the contemporary situation of the spectator would be opposed; the artificial world can merge time of action (in the court of Ferrara), time of composition (at the court in Weimar) and time of performance (1969). It also links the performers to the completion of a story that has a specific beginning and end.

In contrast, using set and stage space as a non-specific metaphor meant that the narrative flow could be dislocated and incidents could interpenetrate through a variety of temporal relationships. Frequently, all the characters would be on stage at once, their simultaneous gestures, actions and movements forming a commentary on each other. The total image yoked together actions far removed from each other in time and space, making them into expressive tableaux in the autonomous time/space-frame of the play. If narrative sequence was of little interest, so too was development of character. The essential determining features of each role were introduced from the beginning.

Since the language of the stage could free itself from the logic of narrative and psychological development, theatre could now tell another story on a higher plane – not just the one in the text, but along with that, one *about* the text. As the grotesque comedy of the Court poet's situation was being presented, the classical play itself was revealed as an expression of its dependent and limited status when reduced to mere decoration – a situation that is valid beyond the historical period of the original.

The example of the way the stage was used in *Tasso* thus shows the main gains of the visual aesthetic. The different elements theatre used to produce meaning were brought together. The hierarchy of important versus insignificant, central versus peripheral no longer applied. The set no longer illustrated the play or vice versa. A coherent theatrical language had become possible, and all components related to each other and were equally valid: text, scenic space and performers alternated as sources of meaning.

It is above all to the credit of the Schaubühne that this autonomous theatrical language could exhibit its potential, at least during the first ten years. Whereas in other places it often degenerated into mannerism and superficiality, here there was the leisure to engage in lengthy preparations and time-consuming rehearsal, so it could be applied to very different plays from varying points of view and produce original and convincing results.

The most salient features of his work on *Tasso* also characterized Stein's subsequent productions. They each afforded both a fully worked-out rendering of the play and a critical perception of it. *Peer Gynt* (1972) gave a broad insight into the nineteenth century by quoting from all its characteristic textual sources, from the grand concepts of idealistic philosophy through adventure stories to pure kitsch. They all became means to debunk the bold attempt to construct a concept of the 'great' individual (responsible only to himself, the sum of his own actions and achievements) as a (petty-bourgeois) illusion. Through Gynt the idea of the all-powerful 'personality' was shown to be a chimera, the wild dream of a bygone age; in Kleist's *The Prince of Homburg* the entire action was transposed to a dream atmosphere, and the protagonist was treated as a projection of the author's desires. His drama of the Prussian prince who refuses to obey orders in battle, is condemned to death but is finally pardoned and accepted back into his social circle, was interpreted as the poet's dream of a political order based on recognition of human idiosyncrasy and ability to integrate even the most sensitive outsider. Here too the ending shattered the illusion: as the officers carry out a lifeless puppet to the strains of the famous battle-cry 'In the dust with all enemies of the Brandenburgs', the Prince remains alone on the empty stage. An open-ended, naggingly ambiguous final image, but one strongly implying that Prussian military pragmatism had overtaken any hope of a reconciliation between politics and humanitarianism.[26]

To achieve a visual representation of such ideas, the stage – and not infrequently the whole auditorium as well – might be totally transformed. For *Homburg* a peep-hole set, plus a dream atmosphere invoked by colour and light, was sufficient. But for *Peer Gynt* the whole interior was included. The setting – a range of hills incorporating areas where scenes could be played simultaneously – ran through the length of the theatre. The spectators were seated on ramps along the walls, looking down on the shifting action in the centre. Later productions moved the spectators out of the theatre altogether and constructed environments that surrounded them in large sheds – for example, for *Exercises for Actors* (a prelude to Grüber's *The Bacchae*), and then for Peter Stein's two Shakespeare projects: *Shakespeare's Memory*, a theatrical introduction to the Elizabethan period, and, a year later, *As You Like It*.

Stein and Grüber worked from opposite ends of the spectrum. Stein's sets tended towards clarity, Grüber's towards the evocative and mysterious; Stein aimed to open up the formal and structural riches of a play, to analyse and criticize, whereas Grüber extracted individual motifs and sharpened them in the service of denunciation. Stein's productions offered comprehensive insights into the emotional and intellectual world of the play; Grüber moved more and more towards a disturbing vision put together from symbolic fragments, signs of a darkening world.

This frozen, final quality of Grüber's designs, in contrast to Stein's attempts to use stage space to instigate dynamic action, can be seen in his first production for the Schaubühne. Horváth's *Tales From The Vienna Woods* was set in an unreal landscape with fragmentary outlines – a ruined castle framed in glass, a stretch of road, a section of the façade of a house. This surrealistic montage expressed not a complete story, but only its bitter quintessence – the ruins and rubble of a story of ruined lives, failed hopes, fractured plans and disappointed desires for a better future.

This was Grüber's major theme, and he devised more and more severe visual equivalents for it. The tendency to fragmentation, reduction, minimalization intensified. The cold clinical space designed by painters Gilles Aillaud and Eduardo Arroyo for Euripides' *The Bacchae* still gave room for extensive associations between the archaic and the modern. In the production that followed, Hölderlin's *Empedocles*, the stage was dominated by a single image: an enormously enlarged poster reproduction of C. D. Friedrich's jagged landscape *The Failure of Hope, or Frozen Sea*, which hung opposite a grimy station waiting-room where homeless (contemporary?) figures moved in a dumb show. The second Hölderlin evening (*Winter Journey*; after texts from *Hyperion*) took the minimalization to the limit: the in-the-round action was almost swallowed up in the gigantic dimensions of the Nazi architecture of the setting, the Berlin Olympic stadium. The vast discrepancy in proportionate size evoked the gap in time between the writing of the text and its performance. Here again there was the sense of finality – an ancient piece of writing highlighted with quiet insistence at the moment of its perhaps inevitable disappearance. This produced a paradoxical effect: the pain engendered by the production arose from its emphatic fidelity to Hölderlin's vision, but its power derived from regret about a present in which such a vision could find no place.

SUMMARY AND RETROSPECT

This investigation of the history of West German theatre in the 1960s and 1970s, the most important post-war period, leads to the conclusion that the first real rupture in a tradition reaching back to the 1930s took place neither in 1945 (with the end of the war) nor in 1949 (with the founding of the Federal Republic), but in the early 1960s. From that time, numerous forms of political theatre opposed the representational theatre of the autocrat-managers, whose aesthetic, clothed in a classical or pseudo-modern veneer, dated from the Nazi era, and had allowed itself to be used as a shop-window for a spurious 'cultural miracle' as part of the *Wirtschaftswunder* (economic miracle) and the never-had-it-so-good years. As we have seen, to oppose this meant claiming access to new areas of concern, encapsulated it in historically relevant forms; above all, it meant reclaiming a tradition that had been contested and put under pressure, that of the 'theatre of contemporary realism' of the Weimar Republic.

The emergence of young directors at the end of the decade marked a second stage of development. To put it simply, after writers had discovered new kinds of political content, new forms of presentation followed, allowing theatre to free itself from the domination of literature and find its own means of expression. This can, it is true, be understood as abandoning the recently secured gains of political theatre. But the achievement of the young directors was rather to reverse its marginalization and give it universal validity. Confrontation with history and society became the kernel of all work in theatre. The previous dichotomy between contemporary plays, which were acknowledged as possessing a political dimension, and the classics, was dissolved; all plays were seen as political, and even the classics functioned as commentaries on contemporary events and conflicts. As we have seen from all the examples above, finding a new language for the stage entailed the politicization of all theatrical activity.

From here until the second half of the 1970s all further developments were extensions and variations on the same theme, a theatre awake to contemporary issues and confident of its aesthetic autonomy. It should be noted that innovation was not restricted to the new 'model theatres' described above. The change in personnel of 1971/2 had allowed young directors to take over in other theatres as well. Their potential could thus be demonstrated elsewhere, with results which extended the spectrum operating at the Schaubühne or in Frankfurt. It is true that this occurred mainly in the case of outstanding single productions, which were not underpinned by developments in structure, and therefore did not result in a house-style along the lines of the Schaubühne, or slightly less uniformly, the Frankfurt theatre. A similar degree of uniformity was achieved perhaps only at the Hamburg Schauspielhaus, under the direction of the former critic Ivan Nagel, and above all in Stuttgart: here, Claus Peymann developed a colourful style which simultaneously involved itself boldly in public affairs and was able to reach the spectators; moreover he took his company with him to Bochum in the early 1980s, the only successful such transfer of the decade. The limits to which the original intentions behind the work influenced company practices can be seen both in the many successes and in the two failures of Peter Zadek, who, taking the whole period into account, was certainly the most important director working in West German theatre. Zadek had many successful productions which took risks with conventions and expectations, and managed to present undogmatic and unconstrained insights into human motivation and action. He aroused new interest in a range of plays – Shakespeare, Chekhov, Ibsen, contemporary authors, review-style dramatizations of epic sources; there was virtually no repetition, no falling-back on routine; but as artistic director, first in Bochum and then in Hamburg in the 1980s, he failed to build up and retain a company. So those who continued to promote a view of theatrical practice as extending beyond one-off performances contented themselves with forming small groups that worked independently within (and against) the large theatre institutions. One example is that of the theatre laboratory run by Georg Tabori at the Bremen theatre in the second half of the 1970s.

The 1970s were not just notable for outstanding individual work; in general, it was more a period of taking stock and revising attitudes.[27] A popular slogan around the middle of the decade was *Tendenzwende* ('end of the trend', 'loss of momentum'). This was shorthand for a gradual faltering and eventual abandonment of the readiness to institute major changes and develop democratic structures in all areas of political and social life. That evidently had repercussions for work in the theatre. Here the turn-around meant a virtually total cessation of all the processes of change on which people with an eye on contemporary developments had placed high hopes. Total stagnation resulted. A final sign of the hardening of attitudes was what became known as the 'German autumn': the mobilizing of state power in tandem with terrorist attacks of 1977. It seemed as though people were faced by a political policy that abandoned political means, analysis, reflection and debate in the face of terrorism, and was only prepared to meet force with force. One of our previous examples shows how theatre reacted: Grüber's bleak juxtaposition of Hölderlin's vision of the achievement of human freedom with the gigantic architectural image of the apparatus of totalitarianism, was an open reference to the terrorist hunts of that year. Its title, *Winterreise* (Winter Journey), directly quoted the code-name for the secret police operations.

From one angle then, the balance of developments in West German theatre looks as though it is in deficit. In conclusion, one could suggest that what started with a breakthrough amid great hopes ended almost before it was begun, with a crisis. The volume of reminiscences of the protagonists in the new German theatre referred to earlier shows that they all see the current state as characterized by a profound paralysis, by a lack of concepts strong enough to build future plans on, by an absence of productions that could rise above the merely modish and inaugurate new directions. It is true that we are only considering the mainstream here, what stands out and can most easily be recollected and identified as historically significant. Alongside this there was much going on that outpaces all attempts to draw up a balance sheet; developments that are far from being concluded or have only just got under way. Let us briefly mention two of the most important here, with reference to the context we have established.

From its perception of the failure of a new start which was to have gone beyond theatre to include the whole of society, theatre drew different conclusions. The West German stage, more so than literature and film, developed a sharp 'evil eye' for a Republic which once more rested on the laurels of its economic success and formed its image accordingly. It is only a short step from here to a recognition that the official pronouncements of success are contradicted by the misery of the human condition, the compromises, the many situations for which no comfort is available; there are no utopias, only ugly emptiness. Theatre in the 1980s exposed this more uncompromisingly than anything else. Pina Bausch's dance-theatre, for example – neither ballet nor straight theatre, but a unique intermediary form – revealed, without dramatizing or sentimentalizing, the power games cynically cloaked in fine words that dictate all relationships, the false promises of fortune and love, and underneath them the abyss of indifference and of real despair, the opportunities lost for ever; all expressed in terms of what goes on in and between human bodies, as a theatre of gesture, of visual exchanges, of everyday physical rituals.

Internal examination of the Federal Republic is also to be found in the eloquent and witty plays of Botho Strauss, previously the dramaturge at the Schaubühne. Even after he had left that theatre, the link remained. Almost all the plays he wrote in the 1980s were given exemplary productions by Peter Stein or the young Luc Bondy at the Schaubühne.

Whilst Strauss's plays – contemporary fables about people who have made it in the world of art, ideas and business – were played elsewhere as light conversation-pieces or boulevard theatre, placing the emphasis on the author's powers as comic observer of the manifold confusions of living together and the mishaps and banalities of everyday life, in his 'home' theatre Strauss was presented rather as a radical diagnostician of contemporary life for the stage. The productions brought in all kinds of mythical, symbolic and literary allusions to suggest the varied pathology of contemporary life, its anxiety states, feelings of isolation, losses of and desires for faith. To many, this made the plays look like disguised essays on the 'in' themes of intellectual debate, based on the 'surface of big-city life in the West, the clichés about liberation and relationships, the psycho-jargon'.[28]

Botho Strauss's focus on the tribulations of life in the Federal Republic was put into perspective by plays by writers from the GDR (banned or censored in their own country) which had been put on in the West from the 1970s. Chief amongst these, Heiner Müller's performance texts give a different insight into the assumptions underlying the status quo. His themes were Nazi Germany, the war and its consequences, the two Germanies, with Western economic power as the winner and socialist utopia the loser in East and West. The results as presented in Strauss's work – as a nebulous zone of confused impressions, shifting opinions and untrustworthy feelings – look frail and questionable in comparison to the fatal contradictions and bloody conflicts Müller writes of. His uncompromising vision is reflected in staging too. After Wolf-Biermann's loss of GDR citizenship, many directors in East German theatre – including the most important – moved to West Germany, some as guests, others permanently. West German theatre not only gained from new personalities, but this move also signalled the arrival of a tradition which had really not been taken on board till then. Although the West had discovered Brecht in the 1960s as the author of the late parables, as the theorist of 'epic theatre' and the director of the great model productions of the Berliner Ensemble (and soon dropped him again as an 'ineffectual classic'), theatre practitioners in the GDR had tried to carry on the tradition by using the fundamentals of Brechtian dramaturgy (its materialism, its dialectic acuity, its anarchist and hedonist foundation) to stir up description and criticism of their social reality. The results became visible towards the end of the 1970s and during the following decade in West Germany. A broad spectrum of innovation gave rise to increasingly individualistic ways of harnessing the tradition, from the anarchic/plebeian directorial style of the duo, Manfred Karge and Matthias Langhoff, through the stark stylization and formal precision of Jürgen Gosch, to the dialectical, sharp and radically intelligent dramaturgy of B. K. Tragelehn. This kind of thing offered rough edges, showed the opposite side of the coin from endless variations on the theme of melancholia amidst empty material prosperity.

Perhaps it is precisely this tension which, in the context of contemporary events in Europe and the unification of the GDR and the FRG will prove productive for theatre in the old East *and* West. The question of what will happen in both former halves of the country opens up a whole new area of problems, which may legitimately become the sphere of theatre too. One thing only is certain: if theatre does become active in this field, then it will be in *opposition* to the instant solutions and hasty recipes that are currently making the running. The common denominator of directors from East and West is scepticism. It may work as a motivating force. At any rate, one may hope that theatre will not allow the past to be lost to sight, in a situation where people are mesmerized by the future. The last few years have seen the beginning of what is needed in order to achieve a proper perspective – a theatre that remembers.

NOTES

1 Henning Rischbieter, 'Theater', in: Wolfgang Benz, ed., *Die Bundesrepublik Deutschland*, vol. 3, *Kultur*, Frankfurt on Main, 1983: 81.
2 ibid., 82.
3 The dominant maxim of the programming in this theatre was 'pluralism', i.e. a broad spread of offerings of completely different plays, in order to satisfy the different expectations of the various groups of clientele. In practice this meant that classics, principally Shakespeare and Schiller, took the lion's share as against a few 'international successes'. 'Experiments', i.e. productions of plays less likely to fill the house, were in contrast marginalized by being put on in small, purpose-built performance spaces, usually called 'workshops'.
4 To be 'true to the work' was the watchword of all directorial practice of this era. The criteria had been laid down in the *Düsseldorf Manifesto* started by Gustaf Gründgens (1952), in which forty prominent cultural figures declared themselves 'against idiosyncratic interpretations of literature resulting from unjustified experiments which interpose themselves between work and receiver'. 'True to the work', understood in this way, therefore meant unconditional confirmation of the expectations of the public towards the plays in the repertoire, mainly the classics, and exclusion of any unconventional interpretation that might disrupt these expectations.
5 Thus Hans Mayer, Professor of Literature expelled by the Nazis, who held this post again in the GDR from 1948–63 and held a similar one after his return to the FRG, in *Zur deutschen Literatur der Zeit. Zusammenhänge-Schriftsteller-Bücher* (On Contemporary German Literature, Connections – Authors – Books), Hamburg, 1967: 300ff.
6 Theodor W. Adorno, *Jargon der Eigentlichkeit. Zur deutschen Ideologie* (The Jargon of Essentiality. On German Ideology). Frankfurt on Main, 1964.

7 Theatre critic Siegfried Melchinger in *Theater der Gegenwart* (Contemporary Theatre), Frankfurt on Main, 1956: 44.

8 In Peter Weiss, *Rapporte 2,* Frankfurt on Main, 1971: 91–104.

9 This is the key concept of political theatre as proposed by Weiss in 'Notizen'. From it appropriate forms of representation are derived in order to produce a genuine meeting between stage and auditorium; Weiss recommends the use of documentary material, in order to avoid predictable story-lines, general truths or abstract problems. Theatre should report on the state of the world and should declare its intention to do so. That, says Weiss, is why 'it abstains from all invention, it takes authentic material, respects the content and adapts the form, and gives it out from the stage'. Weiss is thus not primarily concerned to reproduce reality 'as it was and is': that would be simplistic realism applied to politics. 'Adapt the form' therefore means to prepare in the artistic realm of theatre a model of reality consistent with the limits of the author's political insight and the aesthetic capacities of the stage. The documents whose 'content is not tampered with' are artistic material serving the political aims of such an aesthetic. They are signs and evidence to enable the spectator to recognize the implications of what is being presented, and to form an opinion about it. Documentary theatre, as Weiss described it in 1968, functions above all as a democratic forum which uses theatrical means to clarify the current situation and the historical sequence that led to it.

10 ibid.: 91.

11 Rischbieter, 'Theater': 84.

12 Text and performance here interrelate to mutual benefit. The original works used as points of departure by young writers enjoyed a belated new lease of life in the programming of the period.

13 Peter Palitzsch, a disciple of Brecht, who will be discussed further below, put it on in Stuttgart in 1968, when the political situation was in the forefront of public awareness.

14 The dispute had, in fact, a sequel. The Munich production of *Vietnam-Diskurs* was taken over by the Schaubühne in Berlin, where it had also to be taken off following police intervention.

15 It is symptomatic that the new could at first only find expression in a very small theatre: 'Since the centres of theatre were firmly under the control of the autocratic manager-directors, any changes or challenges could only be developed from the grass-roots, from the depth of the provinces' (Rischbieter, 'Theater': 87). This is the case not merely for the work Hübner made possible in Bremen, but equally for his period of tenure in Ulm (1959–62). Palitzsch had directed here, and Peter Zadek had ensured a contentious climax with a lively and anarchistic rendering of Brendan Behan's *The Hostage*. Zadek's provocative and unfettered style was then employed in Bremen, chiefly for Wedekind (1965: *Spring Awakening*, on a bright, empty stage, symbolizing the sensuality and naïveté of early adolescence), Schiller (1966: *The Robbers*, distancing the rhetoric of the text and the pathos of the action by means of banal and comic quotation) and Shakespeare (1967: *Measure For Measure*, using an exaggerated body-language to push the attitudes of the characters to the limits).

16 cf. Botho Strauss in his account of the production, first in *Theater heute*, 5,

1969; subsequently in: Henning Rischbieter, ed., *Theater im Umbruch* (Theatre in Crisis), Munich, 1970; 118ff.

17 That can be seen also in the subsequent development of those involved in the production. The Bremen *Tasso* became a success, invited to numerous festivals, including international ones, and voted one of the best productions of the year by the jury of the theatre colloquium held in Berlin from 1963. However, the company found that being part of an artistic meditation on the dependent status of the artist did not solve the problem. In the very theatre where the unconventional Hübner was in post, successive conflicts with authority broke out. He was accused of censoring an interval-piece planned by the *Tasso* company, in which Stein and the actors intended to engage the audience in discussion. Further, another incident was interpreted by the company as a sign of the exercise of authoritarian power by the manager. Whilst *Tasso* was in rehearsal, a group of actors sought to suspend the normal hierarchy (director at the head, actors as mere instruments of his vision), and to work on an Aristophanes play with everyone having an equal say in directorial decision. The manager did allow this unconventional prepared piece to be premièred, but publicly distanced himself from it. The *Tasso* actors viewed both occurrences as further confirmation of the dependent status of the artists in their production, and accepted the logic of the situation: Stein and the actors handed in their notice.

18 Barbara Sichtermann and Jens Johler: 'Über den autoritären Geist des deutschen Theaters' (On the authoritarian tendency in German theatre), first published in *Theater heute*, 4, 1968. Reproduced in Rischbieter, ed., *Theater im Umbruch*: 130.

19 *Theater im Umbruch*: 139.

20 ibid.: 136f.

21 At the instigation of cultural departments that favoured reform, and on the recommendation of a committee of prominent theatre critics, a statute for the new form of theatre was drawn up, which accorded wide-ranging powers to the ensemble: it was to have the exclusive right to elect from its ranks the (eight) members of an 'artistic advisory group', which had to ratify the two directors directly appointed by the civic authorities; furthermore it could elect the third director, who was to represent the 'artistic base'. Directorate, advisory group and full meeting of the ensemble made up the internal communication network. Everyone should be equally well informed and participate in decision-making.

22 As in Frankfurt, the directorate was responsible to the whole company. The three artistic directors were elected by the company, and had to justify their decisions at a weekly meeting with six elected representatives. Detailed minutes of these meetings were published, so that all the (approx. 100) workers employed at the theatre could inform themselves about any relevant issues.

23 From the start, they took several forms. As distinct from Frankfurt, where actors were engaged from various places, so that they had to be moulded into an ensemble and acclimatized to the new working structures, the participatory system at the Schaubühne had the advantage of a group of actors who had been working closely together for several years. When

Stein moved to Berlin, the whole *Tasso* company – plus a few actors who joined during his brief stay in Zurich – moved with him. Similar views on the allocation of jobs and the aims of the work, a common determination to change working practices, evolved through long debate and experience, and a shared aesthetic, provided a sound basis for working together; whereas in Frankfurt a gradual process of getting to know each other was necessary. A further distinction was equally important. The civic theatres in Frankfurt had to work under the commercial pressures of big-city theatre. The main theatre (Grosses Haus) and the Chamber Theatre (Kammerspiele) had to put on an average of twenty productions each season. The Schaubühne was in the privileged situation in the early formative years of only having to mount about five. Thus in Berlin, without the pressure to meet the demands of an extensive programme, energy could be concentrated on a few projects which could be thoroughly prepared.

24 Wend Kässens and Jörg W. Gronius, eds, *Theatermacher. Gespräche mit Luc Bondy, Jürgen Flimm, Hans-Günther Heyme, Hans Neuenfels, Peter Palitzsch, Claus Peymann, Frank-Patrick Steckel, Georg Tabori, Peter Zadek*, Frankfurt on Main, 1987.

25 Owing to differences over interpretation and with actors, Peymann gave up the direction prematurely and the production was completed without him.

26 This reflects Kleist's experience: the poet's disproportionate hopes and visions were not fulfilled: the shock led him to commit suicide six months after completing the play, and the production ended with a reminder of this fact.

27 The clearest sign of the breakdown of the vision underlying the changes in management structure is the failure of the attempts to involve all participants in decision-making. This occurred as a gradual and unspectacular fade-out at the Schaubühne. The structures are still in place, but they have been overshadowed in everyday practice by the return of dominant personalities. Since Peter Stein's retirement, hopes for the future rest on the kind of impression individual directors like Luc Bondy or Jürgen Gosch make, rather than on collective activities. In Frankfurt the transfer back to the old system occurred through a symbolic act. As already mentioned, the participatory statute was only established here under strict conditions and with great difficulty. In many instances the public stayed away from productions, and some members of the company were not up to the extra time and effort required by joint administrative responsibility in addition to performance. Despite growing personal doubts and increasing criticism from outside, Palitzsch and many of his actors stuck to the participatory system until recently. The subsequent story of this model, however, shows unequivocally that the initial interest from theatre critics and civic cultural authorities very soon turned to profound mistrust, and finally to open hostility. Even during the second half of the 'Palitzsch era', criticism of the artistic inadequacies of several productions was linked to condemnation of the unsuitability of the participatory model. Any thought of modifying the system soon had no chance of success in the face of the growing opposition. At the beginning

of the 1980s the long-expected measures were taken. Palitzsch's successor was scarcely in post before the magistrate used a trivial incident (a demonstration by young people in the theatre) as an excuse to dissolve the participatory statute, and return to the managerial model of theatre.

28 Rischbieter, 'Theater': 99.

BIBLIOGRAPHY

Bahn, Volker, *Das subventionierte Theater in der Bundesrepublik Deutschland*, diss. Berlin, 1972.

Canaris, Volker, *Peter Zadek*, Munich, 1979.

Carstensen, Uwe B., *Klaus Michael Grüber*, Frankfurt on Main, 1988.

Daiber, Hans, *Deutsches Theater seit 1945*, Stuttgart, 1976.

Iden, Peter, *Die Schaubühne am Halleschen Ufer 1970-1979*, Munich, 1979.

Kässens, Wend and Gronius, Jörg W., eds, *Theatermacher. Gespräche mit Luc Bondy, Jürgen Flimm, Hans-Günther Heyme, Hans Neuenfels, Peter Palitzsch, Claus Peymann, Frank-Patrick Steckel, Georg Tabori, Peter Zadek*, Frankfurt on Main, 1987.

Kortner, Fritz, *Aller Tage Abend*, Munich, 1959.

Laube, Horst, ed., *War da was? Schauspiel Frankfurt 1972-1980*, Frankfurt on Main, 1980.

Mauer, Burkhard and Krauss, Barbara, eds, *Spielräume - Arbeitsergebnisse Theater Bremen 1962-73*, Bremen, 1973.

Melchinger, Siegfried, *Theater der Gegenwart*, Frankfurt on Main, 1956.

Nagel, Ivan, *Kortner. Zadek. Stein*, Munich, 1989.

Patterson, Michael, *Peter Stein*, Cambridge, 1981.

Piscator, Erwin, *Das politische Theater*, Berlin, 1929, rev. edn, Hamburg, 1963.

Rischbieter, Henning, 'Theater', in Wolfgang Benz, ed., *Die Bundesrepublik Deutschland*, vol. 3, *Kultur*, Frankfurt on Main, 1983: 73-109.

——, ed., *Theater im Umbruch*, Munich, 1970.

Rühle, Günther, *Theater in unserer Zeit*, Frankfurt on Main, 1976.

——, *Anarchie in der Regie?*, Frankfurt on Main, 1982.

Sichtermann, Barbara and Johler, Jens, 'Über den autoritären Geist des deutschen Theaters', in *Theater heute*, 4, 1968; reprinted in Henning Rischbieter, ed., *Theater im Umbruch*, Munich, 1970: 130-8.

——, ed., *Schaubühne am Halleschen Ufer/Am Lehniner Platz 1962-1987*, Frankfurt on Main/Berlin, 1987.

Vietta, Egon, *Katastrophe oder Wende des deutschen Theaters*, Düsseldorf, 1955.

——, ed., *Theater. Darmstädter Gespräch*, Darmstadt, 1955.

Weiss, Peter, 'Notizen zum dokumentarischen Theater', in *Rapporte 2*, Frankfurt on Main, 1971: 91-104.

Journal: Theater heute, monthly since 1960. From 1962 on, at the beginning of each season, an almanac has appeared entitled 'Chronik und Bilanz einer Spielzeit' (note especially *Theater heute*, Oct. 1970: *German Theatre 1945-1970*; and *Theater heute*, almanac for 1980: *German Theatre 1960-1980*).

5

SWITZERLAND

Ralph Yarrow

Swiss theatre in the years before and during the Second World War registered its importance on the European scene by staging Brecht at the Zurich Schauspielhaus. For a time in the 1950s and 1960s too, the plays of Max Frisch and Friedrich Dürrenmatt were among the most interesting European writing. These advantages seem to have been relinquished. Perhaps the most significant move in established theatre in the following decades was the Schauspielhaus's failure in its association with Peter Stein's politically and aesthetically innovative style (he left in the early 1970s). The story of civic theatre in German-speaking Switzerland largely follows the model of *Intendantentheater* in the Federal Republic of Germany, and economics seems to have played at least as strong a role as artistic criteria in the construction of programming: Stein could not fill the house in Zurich and left a large deficit; Zurich is a city run by bankers . . .

Like theatre in West Germany in the period under discussion, Swiss theatre is not merely one phenomenon. There is only space here to deal briefly with the German-speaking area, mentioning theatre in French-speaking Switzerland only in passing. Nevertheless, even that limited perspective needs to be broken down into several categories. Swiss theatre has its own folk tradition, still to some degree extant – though commercialized and sanitized – in the carnivals of Basel and Luzern; another branch of this tradition emerged in the strong (mainly anti-fascist) cabaret scene of the 1930s and 1940s. Cabaret also flourished as an avant-garde, intellectual form in Zurich in the Dada years. In common with much in Swiss society, cabaret since that time has tended to shy away from anything with political bite. Frisch's *Biedermann* satirizes the head-in-the-sand complacency of bourgeois society.

Cabaret also links with another important variant: theatre in the national/local language/dialect. 'Swiss-German' conceals many distinct dialect forms and is itself grammatically distinct from 'high' German. Major urban theatres mainly operate in standard German, since they make use of international work and performers; language, high prices and cultural exclusivity tend to restrict the clientèle to a relatively narrow social band.

Popular theatre, apart from cabaret or carnival, has seen something of a revival in the 1970s and 1980s. Here we touch perhaps the most salient distinction of all, however, that between subsidized and non- or minimally-subsidized theatre. If it is true in Britain that much of the energy for new performance styles and new writing is to be found in small-scale, mainly touring theatre, at least there is some financial support for it in the form – however minimal – of Arts Council subsidies. In Germany and Switzerland the imbalance between large publicly funded institutions and small-scale theatre of all kinds is perhaps even more marked, and it is consequently more difficult to be truly experimental; even to be so notoriously, like Stein, is to risk incomprehension or censure. I want then to look briefly at some examples of activity in various forms of theatre, in order to outline the major distinctions in aim and achievement.

MAJOR URBAN THEATRES: THE SCHWEIZERBÜHNENVERBAND

The Schweizerbühnenverband (SBV), or Union of Swiss Theatres, is made up of 17 major professional theatres (the Zurich Schauspielhaus, the Zurich Opera House, the Basel theatre, civic theatres in Bern, Luzern and St Gallen, the Grand Théâtre of Geneva, the Théâtre Municipale of Lausanne, and the Théâtre Populaire Romand (TPR). Most of these theatres have their own in-house companies; they receive subsidies and funding from the local canton and/or city, ranging from 750,000 Swiss francs (the TPR) to 60 million francs (Zurich Opera House) as of 1985.[1]

Policies have often favoured investment in the plant, or the hiring of 'star' performers and internationally known directors. To some extent this, plus the heavy reliance on subsidy and the need to cater for a fairly well-heeled sector of the community (seats are *not* cheap), has resulted in a certain complacency and lack of experimentation and/or of discernible directions in performance style or programming. The domination of the economic factor here, as in West

End and Broadway theatre, though perhaps less disastrous in terms of product, means that the repertoire may be expectation-led rather than proposing anything very new about the function of theatre in society. Brecht remarked to Frisch in Konstanz in 1948 that things had to be started all over again; the story is perhaps not so different subsequently. With reference to the figures quoted above, it is perhaps not insignificant that by far the largest amount of subsidy goes to the Opera House, which relies on attracting famous overseas artists and conductors and operates in a grand fixed building, whereas by far the smallest subsidy goes to the much more mobile model of the TPR, which operates a policy of making theatre available to the general public and of encouraging theatre in locations where it had formerly not been available – following to some extent the model laid down by Jean Vilar with his Théâtre National Populaire in France. It is also worth noting that when a recent change in civic government in Zurich threatened to cut some of the subsidy to the large houses, the Schauspielhaus responded by itself threatening to close not its traditional, but its experimental space, the Kellertheater. There have occasionally been flurries of interest, as for example in the hiring and firing of Stein, or in the recent production of a new Frisch play, *Palaver*, which dealt with the proposed abolition of the Swiss army; Dürrenmatt also did some direction in Basel for a time; but otherwise there seems to have been relatively little in the way of innovation, or of new writing.

SMALL THEATRES: THE SCHWEIZERISCHE KLEINTHEATER-VEREINIGUNG

The Schweizerische Kleintheater-Vereinigung (KTV), or Swiss Association of Small Theatres, is composed of around two hundred small-scale venues with between one and two hundred seats; for the most part they have a certain amount of professional input. KTV was founded in 1975: Claque, a small theatre company in Baden, was a major mover in this enterprise, as also in organizing in 1983 the Vereinigten Theaterschaffenden der Schweiz (VTS, or Association of Swiss Theatre Workers). Other members of the KTV include the Theater am Neumarkt and the Theater am Hechtplatz (Zurich), the IG Rote Fabrik (likewise Zurich), lots of small theatres, cultural centres/groups, café theatres and cellar theatres. In French-speaking Switzerland there also exists an organization called the Cartel des Petits Théâtres Romands, which is made up of eight producing theatres.

The aims of these associations are to promote small-scale theatre and to use it to bring new work and styles to the attention of the public. The participating members/organizations are at least partly professional and actors may work for them on a part- or full-time basis. They actively seek subsidies. They aim to foreground any or all of the following:

1 Swiss writing;
2 dialect plays;
3 collective planning and organizational structures, sometimes including collective direction; and
4 touring/outreach theatre, in order to create not a *Volkstheater* so much as a 'professional theatre for the people' – making professional theatre available in places and to sections of the population where it would otherwise not have been found.

The history of Claque is illustrative in many respects: it was started in the cellar of a former corn-hall (many towns experienced population shifts and changes of use in urban buildings, sometimes resulting in an influx of intellectuals, students or artists and the development of new venues in the period); it acquired a professional director early on – Jean Grädel had been associated with both the Schauspielhaus and the Neumarkt in Zurich, and moved to Baden in 1971 bringing with him some actors from Zurich in the wake of the disappointment caused by Peter Stein and Peter Löffler's removal from the Schauspielhaus, and by the failure to introduce a communal policy which would have involved actors in administration and so on at the Neumarkt; Claque adopted a communal participatory strategy from the start; and by the end of the 1980s, some degree of crisis is perceptible here and in some other small theatres.

They were able to fill a gap that in the early 1970s the large subsidized venues were unable or unwilling to tackle, namely the presentation of new and/or avant-garde work. However, the subsequent opening of more experimental in-house spaces by the larger theatres (such as the Kellertheater at the Zurich Schauspielhaus) to some extent took the wind out of the sails of the small theatre movement. The situation is still in flux; and furthermore the other aims of, for instance, dialect and touring theatre, are less likely to be catered for by the large houses. Clearly there is still a role for small-scale theatre, but that role – like everything in theatre – is constantly in need of revision. The Neumarkt's programme for 1990/1 may be seen as an attempt to balance the traditional and the new; on the other hand, it could be viewed as a relatively haphazard compilation and might suggest something of a lack of clear direction (*Macbeth*, *Waiting for Godot*, Frisch's *Biografie* make up half the offerings, the rest being given over to first performances either in Switzerland or in Germany of work previously performed elsewhere).

But it may be at this level (as for instance in the physical-and-mime-based small-scale theatre of Britain and France) that the energy for change is most active. New combinations and focuses arise and testify to the spirit of innovation. For example, the Rote Fabrik, which offered a space for political theatre for some time, has to some extent become an 'accepted', and thus less confrontationally potent, venue; but its function is being taken over by a new development at the Reithalle in the Gessnerallee in Zurich. The city authorities in Zurich also fund a September festival of performance art which seeks to bring together international performers working in many different styles in an informal atmosphere, and aims at a mixed audience, one including younger people who by and large have been unable to afford regular visits to the established venues. Amongst well-known contributions in recent years has been Peter Brook's *Mahabharata*, though for this performance the very cheapest seats to be had were at 45 Swiss francs. (In 1990 Brook's new French-language production of *The Tempest* premièred at the Gessnerallee from a more reasonable 25 francs.) The festival is currently subsidized to the tune of 55 per cent by local authorities, and this in itself is a comment on the situation of alternative forms of performance. In any case, international festivals, although certainly providing useful stimulus, do not always serve the best interests of indigenous theatre.

Some critics feel that the most interesting developments in the last few years have been in the area of dance and movement theatre; there have also been some developments in feminist theatre, and at least one all-female company is in operation. On the other hand, Erika Hänssler (see below) suggests that the emphasis on dance may itself be one of the phases and crazes that periodically strike theatre practitioners. Similarly, she is sceptical about the 1990 rush to perform the work of Gottfried Keller, the Swiss national writer, simply because it happened to be his centenary.[2] This kind of historical reminiscence merely puts theatre in the position of jumping on a commercial bandwagon, rather than constructing and performing something to which writers and performers are genuinely committed.

A further reason for some of the stagnation in established theatre is that the large theatres in German-speaking Switzerland operate with fixed companies, which therefore tend to grow as each new director brings with him actors from his previous venue. Actors may therefore be required only to perform one or two small roles each year; this naturally leads to larger and larger budgets and less and less vitality. To counteract this directors tend to bring in star performers from outside, at even greater expense. An alternative model in the French-speaking part of Switzerland is that followed generally in France, where only the director is attached to the theatre, and then hires actors for each production. But the problem of maintaining venues or plant is not restricted to the larger established theatres. The energy of the Kleintheater movement has also in large measure been expended on the maintenance of venues in small locations, rather than on production of innovative forms of theatre (though of course a valuable function may be served by keeping performance-and-arts-centres open in small towns, and so on).

OTHER FORMS OF THEATRE

Carnival and cabaret have already been mentioned; they offer some contact on a large or small scale with aspects of theatrical activity. There are a couple of other companies which seem to fall under no convenient label, and are interesting precisely because of this. Mummenschanz, a Swiss company originating at Jacques Lecoq's Paris school, have an international reputation for mime/mask work. Like most of Lecoq's pupils, they have developed their own idio-syncratic style out of precise physical discipline; their work is able to transcend the boundaries of language-confined theatre, or the other registers which may exclude sections of the populace, by being based mainly in mask, movement and gesture, and by drawing on the techniques and traditions of clowning, mime, circus, spectacle and direct audience contact. But, largely for the same reasons, Mummen-schanz does not have any very strong links with Swiss tradition or culture *per se*. They are thus not really significant in any development of that tradition, since their work does not really engage with it either to support or challenge it.

The other enterprise is possibly unique anywhere, and even more remarkable in Switzerland. Zbigniew Stok and Erika Hänssler's Kammertheater am Hirschengraben in Zurich exemplified even more than other small professional theatres, a complete dedication to all aspects of the process of theatre. Stok, who died in 1990, walked across Europe in the war, and he and his Swiss partner, Hänssler, compiled their own performance texts, made masks and props, rehearsed, performed, and even sold the tickets themselves. Their work centred on figures in crisis or states of psychic estrangement (Artaud on Van Gogh, Kafka and the metaphor of imprisonment, Rilke's articulation of puppet and mask). The Stoktheater's repertoire reads like a catalogue of confrontational writing in modernist art – confrontation with the limits of experience and the limits of expression: Strindberg, Arrabal, Beckett, Van Gogh, Artaud, Kafka, Picasso, Brenton . . .

Through fragments of text, commentary, mask and mime, Stok and Hänssler gave shape to the theatre of the subconscious, the repressed, the visionary, the marginalized. Working entirely at their own prompting and pace, without subsidy, living amongst the materials of their craft, they created from texts and physical forms, from bodies and from the resources they possessed, a textual and intertextual collage. They operated no *abonnement* scheme because they refused to mount a play until they felt it to be ready, and were prepared to take it off if they were not satisfied with it.

Other groups (many of those from Lecoq's school) build up a performance score from improvisation, from fitting together text and gesture from collaborative input. Such groups have been guests in Stok's theatre: among them Bread and Puppet, and companies from Vienna, Warsaw and Berlin; the theatre has hosted café-theatre, music/circus, film. In the Stoktheater, performance was a means to challenge the restrictive norms by which creative forces are caged up; the aberrant is celebrated because it reveals what, as Rilke put it, we cover up and keep out of sight most of the time. Theatre here is a kind of madness, and it is only in acknowledging that madness that its energies can be released. A theatre then which is essentially Artaudian in focus, which aimed to reflect the hidden and the taboo. That such a theatre was *tolerated* may perhaps be the worst thing that could happen to it, since its function is primarily to incite incomprehension, panic or amazement. On the other hand, its existence and continuation may argue for a kind of psychic health in the community. The issue is one which can be related to much 'alternative' performance work, of course. Cynically, it is always possible to argue that the society can pat itself on the back for its own liberal behaviour by maintaining the token presence of something it knows most people will never visit. In contrast to Mummenschanz, however, Stok established a presence on the Zurich theatre scene; he and Hänssler represent a powerful statement about the nature of performance as a total act, about text as a continuum from source material to physicalization, about the experience of theatre as an encounter with the marginalized and the subliminal reaches of human life. Indulgently tolerated or studiously ignored, their work still stands out as a marker of the total investment of commitment and physical capacity in the value of a living art-form. Theatre practitioners could do worse than learn from their example.

Hänssler is also both a remarkable performer, often taking virtually the whole weight of the performance, and a living statement of the intellectual and artistic resources of women: one production proposed the female body as the site of a 'transvaluation of all values', materializing texts from Nietzsche through the actress as masked figure, dancer, musician, puppeteer, as she who plays and incorporates the spirit of 'lila', the continual migration of form as opposed to the stone tablets of patriarchal law.[3]

This boldness and originality of vision has underpinned all of Stok and Hänssler's work; Hänssler justifiably figures in a forthcoming volume of profiles of leading women in business, politics and culture, by Sonja Buchholzer, entitled *Aufbruch* (Break-out); the celebration of the twentieth anniversary of Stok's activity in Zurich (1970–90) is among the most significant, if less well publicized, events in European theatre.

Otherwise the story of Swiss theatre since the 1950s is relatively depressing. As such it is perhaps symptomatic of events elsewhere in Europe. Where theatre is dominated by economic considerations, whatever the input of directorial concern or performance talent, the resultant product (the word 'product' is itself significant, suggesting a package for easy consumption) tends to the mediocre, the safe norm – both in terms of repertoire and of performance. There is an inherent contradiction here, which all performance art is constantly coming up against; its existence, as a fluid and unpredictable mode, poses a challenge by its structure to the desire of society to establish safe limits and conventions. Not surprisingly, Switzerland is an excellent example of this.[4]

NOTES

1 A useful source of information about the small-scale theatre movement in Switzerland is Peter Arnold's *Auf den Spuren des 'anderen' Theaters* (On the Trail of 'Alternative' Theatre), Limmat Verlag, Zurich, 1987.

2 From conversations with the author in July 1990.

3 *Ohren für Unerhörtes, oder Jenseints von Gottvater, Sohn & Co* (Ears for the Unheard-of, or Beyond Godfather, Son & Co.), theatre project by and with Erica Hänssler and Zbigniew Stok, with texts by Friedrich Nietzsche, Kammertheater Stok, Zurich, 1987.

4 Thanks are due to the following, who gave their time and experience in discussion with the author: Erika Hänssler and Zbigniew Stok (Stok Kammertheater); Dr Jakobi (Neue Zürcher Zeitung); Peter Müller (Tages Anzeiger); Dr Emanuel Steck; Res Bossart (Präsidialabteilung der Stadt Zürich).

6

AUSTRIA

Susanne Chambalu

INTERNATIONAL CONNECTIONS

Austrian theatre has always had strong connections with the dramatic and theatrical traditions of its German-speaking neighbours, Germany and Switzerland. At the same time Austrian writers, actors and directors have often made their mark in these countries. There is a continual exchange of artists, which occasionally leads to controversy over what is regarded as German infiltration of such cultural institutions as the Burgtheater. Another less obvious influence is the fact that Austria shares borders with countries that used to be behind the so-called Iron Curtain. Plays by Vaclav Havel or Pahvel Kouhout, often banned in the authors' country, had their world premières in Vienna.

Musicals are a fairly new and imported aspect of Austrian theatre. The long run of *Cats* which started in 1983, led to the translation and production of other musicals: *A Chorus Line, Les Misérables, The Phantom of the Opera*. Sell-outs are proof of their popularity with audiences, who often come from as far away as Germany and Switzerland. At the same time these productions are accused of being alien to Vienna's cultural climate.

The Salzburg Festival is an international festival of opera, theatre and dance, with foreign productions as well as productions created for the festival only. Other international festivals include the Bregenz Festival (opera and theatre), the Vienna Festival (a festival that covers every aspect of the performing arts together with exhibitions and a symposium, held together by a common theme every year) and the biennial dance festival (where dance and dance theatre companies from all over the world are invited to present their work). The

Steirischer Herbst in Graz is an avant-garde festival, bringing together new and commissioned works from the worlds of theatre, art, music and literature under such titles as 'Guilt and Innocence in Art', 'Chaos and Order', 'Up and Away: a Nomadology of the Nineties'.

BURGTHEATER

Aside from performing arts festivals, of which there are quite a number, Austrian theatre centres very much on Vienna. The Bundestheater – the administrative body for the Burgtheater and the Akademietheater as well as the Staatsoper and the Volksoper – represents a tradition rooted in the Austro-Hungarian Empire, with the Burgtheater celebrating its centenary in 1988. The German theatre director Claus Peymann was appointed director of the Burgtheater and Akademietheater by the Minister of Art and Education. The appointment of a German to what is considered the most prestigious and influential post in the performing arts in Austria sparked off a heated discussion about the nature and responsibility of the Burgtheater as the major exponent of an Austrian national theatre. Criticism centred not only on the fact that a foreigner had been appointed to the post of guardian of the nation's dramatic tradition, but also on the fact of his open political sympathies for the left. Among those opposing him were a large number of the acting ensemble at the theatre who criticized his confrontational working and employment methods.

Claus Peymann had been artistic director in Stuttgart and Bochum. He had put the Bochum Schauspielhaus on the map for German theatre critics, who used to travel to his productions from all over Germany. They enthused about his productions of German classics like *Die Hermannsschlacht* (The Battle of Teutoburg Forest) by Kleist (long considered unstageable) as well as premières of contemporary playwrights. One of these was the Austrian Thomas Bernhard, whose plays caused controversy in his native country. Once Peymann became Burgtheater director in Vienna, Bernhard's plays became one of the important features of the repertoire of both the Burgtheater and the Akademietheater. Productions from Bochum or Salzburg, where they had been premièred, transferred to Vienna. His last play to be staged at the Burgtheater in November 1988, *Heldenplatz*, caused a controversy that extended far beyond the theatre.

The play is set in 1988. In a flat overlooking the Heldenplatz (the square where in 1938 Austrians had cheered Hitler, as he announced Austria's *Anschluß* to Germany) the relatives of a philosopher meet after his suicide. He had been forced to emigrate in 1938 but had returned to his professorship at Vienna University in the 1950s. In 1988 he commits suicide, because Austria is now 'noch viel schlimmer als vor 50 Jahren' ('much worse than 50 years ago'). In this as in many of his other writings, Bernhard insists that Austrians have never come to terms with their involvement with fascism, anti-semitism and the Third Reich. Instead, they live with thinly covered-up lies, unable to change. No one escapes his verbal attacks directed against politicians, academics, the Catholic church, industrialists and the average citizen.

On the insistence of the author and the director, the text of *Heldenplatz* was not published until after the first night. Nevertheless some passages of the text became known. There were moves to cancel the production on the grounds that the Austrian taxpayers (the theatre is state-funded) could not be expected to pay for a production that only intended to insult them. On the opening night a demonstration was staged outside the theatre. In many ways the controversy surrounding the production illustrated another line from the play, Österreich selbst ist nichts als eine Bühne ('Austria itself is merely a stage'). Thomas Bernhard died in February 1989. In his will he explicitly forbade any new productions of any of his plays or publication of any of his writings in Austria after his death.

The repertoire of the Burgtheater and the Akademietheater, as well as their equivalents in the capitals of Austria's *Bundesländer*, includes German classics by Goethe and Schiller as well as those by Austrian playwrights such as Grillparzer, Raimund and Nestroy. Shakespeare and Molière also form part of the traditional repertoire. There are a number of renowned contemporary playwrights, such as Peter Turrini and Peter Handke, whose plays have been staged and sometimes even commissioned. Peter Turrini's plays look at social issues, his latest *Der Minderleister* dealing with unemployment. Peter Handke, who started his career as a playwright in 1966 with his play *Publikumsbeschimpfung* (Insulting the Audience), has been translated into several languages. His latest play *Das Spiel vom Fragen* (Game About Questioning), staged by the Burgtheater in 1990, is a philosophical discourse: eight actors, impersonating different types, wander in a no man's land without aim, as they question, meditate and investigate the question of questioning.

It is an important fact of Austrian theatre politics, that Elfriede Jelinek's plays are not to be found in the main subsidized sector of the theatre in Austria, but are produced by big theatres in Germany. The fact that only fringe theatres produce some of her plays shows an attempt at marginalizing an uncomfortable writer.

FREIE GRUPPEN

Although most of Vienna's main theatres have a long and often eventful history, their historic buildings limit their ability to try out new ideas: very often they have a traditional audience with certain expectations regarding 'their' theatre and 'their' actors. The numerous so-called 'Freie Gruppen' (independent companies) have no such qualms. Indeed, they are often without a theatre building of their own and instead use more unusual spaces.

'Serapionstheater', founded in 1980, uses texts as a starting-point for their imagination, ranging from Balzac to André Heller (a contemporary Austrian songwriter, singer, actor and producer). With the aid of music, masks, costumes, mannerisms and choreography they tell stories without text, leaving the audience to use its own imagination and associations. They tour abroad quite extensively. They started in a small theatre, but their productions are now staged in the newly renovated Odeon Building.

Daedalus is the name of an ensemble that mounts its productions not just as performances, but together with a range of installations, lectures, films and exhibitions. Their subjects are the perspectives and often unusual connections between artistic phenomena, like the spiritual connection between Antonin Artaud and Vincent Van Gogh. Their latest project (1989) was *Das Leben der infamen Menschen* (The Lives of Infamous People). As a homage to the French philosopher Michel Foucault, who had dedicated his œuvre to society's outcasts, their production attempts to draw a picture of the consequences of the economic crises around 1700 for thousands of people in Europe, as well as society's measures to contain the army of beggars, smugglers, prostitutes and children roaming the streets.

TheaterAngelusNovus, which dissolved in 1988, based its work on Brecht's *Lehrstücktheorie*. Their emphasis was on the material they worked with and they chose such texts as Homer's *Iliad* or Brecht's unpublished 'Fatzer' material. They looked for actors free from the conventions of the traditional theatre, and a theatre that would be a laboratory for social experiment. They found that in the society they were living and working in, there was no room to develop their utopia of what theatre ought to be. But their attempt to encompass both theory and practice resulted in a co-operative venture by members of the group, students and a member of staff at the Department of Theatre Studies at the University of Vienna. A project under the name of 'Fatzerversuche' attempted to bring together the different attitudes in approaching a text in the context of Theatre Studies and in the work of the actor.

BIBLIOGRAPHY

Dace, Wallace, *National Theatres in the Larger German and Austrian Cities*, New York, 1981.

Hadamowsky, Franz, *Bücherkunde deutschsprachiger Theaterliteratur 1945– 1979*, Part II, Böhlau, 1972.

Haider-Pregler, Hilde, *Theater und Schauspielkunst in Österreich* and English translation *The Theatre in Austria*, Vienna, Federal Press Service, o.J., 1970.

Steinberg, Michael P., *The Meaning of the Salzburg Festival: Austria as Theatre and Ideology, 1890–1938*, Ithaca, Cornell University Press, 1990.

Theater in Österreich: das österreichische Theaterjahrbuch, Wien/Darmstadt, Zsolnay.

Wertjanz, Ursula K., 'Theaterpolitische Ziele in Österreich: eine Inhaltsanalyse zum aktuellen Stand der kultur- und theaterpolitischen Diskussion', unpublished dissertation, University of Vienna, 1988.

7

ITALY

Christopher Cairns

THE CONTEXT TO 1960

The situation of the Italian theatre since the Second World War is, to a very significant extent, a result of political and social ferment in a country struggling to find its feet internationally and attempting to come to terms with economic and cultural realities in a *European* context after the traumas of war, occupation and liberation. This is because the parties of the left-wing opposition have always seen cultural activities as an important means of communication with the working classes, and because the left in Italy is stronger and arguably more significant than anywhere else in Western Europe. Hence the (sometimes hasty) identification of all 'official' initiatives, *teatri stabili* (permanent, established theatres) with an element of state subsidy as tools of the establishment, of authority, of government – therefore of a reactionary right wing associated (for all the thirty years of this period) with the ruling Christian Democrat Party. Theatre by its nature is a collective cultural enterprise, and so it is no surprise that the history of the Italian theatre since 1960 is often described in terms of authority and freedom, hegemony and influence, communication and revolt, and so on – all terms of political and social relevance. It is a story of repression and state interference, communication and censorship, the heyday of the director and the drafting of manifestos, of influence from, and competition with, the cinema, of interaction with the other arts, but of influence from abroad above all, in the ferment of debate that characterized the opening-up of the country's frontiers and communication with Europe and the world after the walls of fascism had been breached. The post-war years have seen dramatic changes in the Italian theatre, above all and in a rising crescendo, in the years 1960–9, with the discrediting of *teatri stabili*

110

formed in the immediate post-war enthusiasm for democratic state-subsidized institutions, disillusionment with the 'official' nature of production by directors (the gurus of this system), the so-called *regia critica* ('critical' theatre direction), and that watershed of political debate, the uprisings in France and Italy of 1968, causing rethinking of a fundamental kind about the relationship of theatre to society and its use as a means of (primarily political) communication.

Naturally, the roots of the situation in the 1960s go back to the immediate post-war years: 1947 saw the foundation by Giorgio Strehler and Paolo Grassi of the Piccolo Teatro in Milan, a theatre that was intended to serve the needs of the people for the first time. Audiences were to be drawn from all walks of life, including workers and young people. The aims of the Piccolo Teatro in those years were to foster the participation of the whole society in theatre with convenient season-ticket arrangements, to avoid the simple formula of a repertory of classics leavened by some new writing, to break down the closed elitism of traditional theatre and mirror contemporary issues of universal interest. And the first initiative of 1947 was the classic and long-running *Harlequin, Servant of Two Masters* by Goldoni ('classic' because on the 'hinge' of Goldoni's 'new' theatre of freedom from the constraints of the *commedia dell'arte*), followed by memorable productions of Shakespeare, Ibsen, Chekhov and others. Thus began the work of post-war reconstruction based on contemporary ideals (at that time, of the Resistance) by a director, Strehler, of vision and experience, that was soon to become a model for developments elsewhere.

The previous year (1946) saw the career of Eduardo de Filippo reach a significant climax with *Filumena Marturano* and consolidate a dialect-based theatre rooted in the exact representation of middle-class (and Neapolitan) family life. Sharing some common ground with Luigi Pirandello's theatre of the early 1930s (though this is discussed below), and indeed collaboration with him, down to the diverse experiments of the 1960s – the historical drama *Tomaso d'Amalfi*, the meditation on the play-within-a-play of *L'arte della commedia* (The Art of Comedy) and others – Eduardo's career, as we shall shortly see, mirrors some of the twists and turns of the story of the Italian theatre.

Similarly, Ettore Giannini was searching for new forms of theatre in Naples in these years with realistic sets, dance and music in *Carosello napoletano* of 1950; Visconti's production of Miller's *Death of a Salesman* (1951) looked for new depths of interpretation, above all of character, and concentrated on interpretation, 'critical' direction and relevance in his production of Goldoni's *Locandiera* (Mirandolina); Gianfranco de Bosio brought new insights to his version of Ruzante's *Moscheta* (Posh Talk) in 1951, while Visconti experimented with Williams's *A Streetcar Named Desire* and Luigi Squarzina tried *Hamlet* (1952) with the renowned Vittorio Gassman as Hamlet. So throughout the 1940s and 1950s there were some genuine attempts to break the mould of the past: Gassman's Hamlet moved away from traditionally Italian 'declamatory' styles of acting to focus on the character's psychology; directors such as Strehler, de Bosio and Squarzina were clearly seeking, in these early years, a more tangible place for theatre in the complex of social and political ideals of post-war Italy, convinced that they had a duty to communicate contemporary issues through the director's (new) interpretation of texts.

Theatrical life in Italy in the 1950s was still dominated by Strehler at the Piccolo Teatro in Milan, with the significant landmark of Brecht's *Threepenny Opera* in 1955, and the gradual formation of *teatri stabili* in major Italian cities. The arrival of Brecht in Italy represented a major triumph for Strehler, who went on to study his theories and to direct other works by him – notably historic and imaginative performances of *Galileo* and *St Joan of the Stockyards*, widely recognized (also by Brecht himself, and later, his widow) as classic productions. Brechtian theories also emerged in innovative productions of *Coriolanus* and a Chekhov adaptation, *Platonov e altri*, in these years. Eventually these successes – crowned also by unprecedented audiences – were recognized by state subvention, and there followed recognition of the Piccolo Teatro as an independent organism, free from the restrictions of state control (1959). Thus the Piccolo Teatro was to become the model for the formation of other *teatri stabili*, six of which were in being before 1960, as Franco Quadri has documented. Yet, as we have seen, the acquisition of official status, the battles forced on such institutions by the bureaucratic results of state subvention, possibly also the nature of the power-structure within them (where the model was Strehler's absolute control of the theatrical process and artefact), carried, in a sense, the seeds of their own destruction. Suzanne Cowan writes:

Given the historical period, the political climate in which they were operating, and particularly the organisational principle upon which they all, to one extent or another, were established, they could not have developed otherwise – short of voluntarily divesting themselves of their public finances, and, like St Francis, seeking support among the poor and disinherited.[1]

THE CRISIS OF THE THEATRE

It is to the crisis of the Italian theatre that we now come, and the variety of responses to it in the 1960s. Consciousness of this crisis is seen in manifesto and programme; openness to foreign (and expatriate) influence characterizes the period; a march forward in step with the progress of social and political change in a much closer relationship and interdependence than formerly, and a fragmentation and dispersion of initiatives which has tended (in more recent years) to return the Italian theatre to the realm of an intellectual elite: groups perform to groups, united in the pursuit of aims that they share, but perhaps somewhat remote from the everyday aspirations of ordinary people.

One symptom of the crisis in the theatre was the appearance of television in Italy in 1953 and the vigorous growth of the cinema in the 1950s: both providing Italians with available alternative mass-media entertainment, and removing the theatre's popular base. Statistics show that theatre audiences, standing at 6 million in 1950, had been halved by 1959, while dialect theatre had its audience figures drastically cut from 5 million to 1 million in the same decade. Ironically, the cinema itself showed one way forward in the films made precisely in 1960: Fellini's *La dolce vita* and Antonioni's *L'avventura*. The former projected a pessimistic but very theatrical vision of modern Rome, while Antonioni's film was an epoch-making attempt to see the inconsequentiality of life as it really is, using the camera and its angle in a new and exciting way that presages developments in theatre staging. Antonioni himself directed Isherwood's *I Am A Camera* in the theatre in 1958 as if to underline the point about cinematic vision.

Second, the introduction into Italy of the works of Samuel Beckett and Eugene Ionesco – in a word, the Absurd, or the assault on language as expression in all the written arts – happened in this period. Fundamental to the new spirit in the Italian theatre was the pessimism, the inconclusiveness and the breakdown of all communication central to Beckett's method. *Waiting for Godot* had an important production by Mondolfo in 1954 in which a rapid succession of scenes included clowning and a new degree of improvisation with Moretti (formerly Strehler's Harlequin) and Claudio Ermelli as protagonists. Forward-looking, too, was the activity of the group led by Aldo Trionfo in Genoa who showed their interest in contemporary European developments by staging works by Ionesco, Adamov, and Prévert, and Beckett's *Endgame*, while a point of arrival was marked in 1962–3 with important performances of *The Devil and the Good Lord* by Sartre, directed by Squarzina in Genoa, and Strehler's production of *Galileo*, as we have seen. The Sartre was characterized by a full range of theatrical effects suggested to the director by the text, and a full-blown examination of the play's philosophical tensions. Strehler's *Galileo*, by contrast, successfully combined the rigours of Brecht's method with a lyrical and poetic theatrical vision which was Strehler's great strength. Nevertheless, most critics at the time concluded that these were beacons shining in considerable darkness.

From about 1963 the directions taken by Italian theatre diverge sharply into apparently opposing areas: continuity and change characterize the scene. Continuity in the primarily comic forms of people's theatre, building on past traditions, of the actor-dominated comedy of Totò, Eduardo de Filippo and Dario Fo; and change in the more intellectual and iconoclastic forms of Gruppo 63, and the various conference, enquiries and manifestos which generated continuing debate *about* the theatre in the mid-1960s – and were often in part reactions to movements that had begun outside Italy. By contrast, the theatre of Totò, Eduardo and Fo (before 1969) were built on the solid foundations of popular dialect theatre, the *commedia dell'arte* and the *mattatore* (actor–manager) tradition of the primacy of the actor. It has to be said that since the deaths of Pirandello, Ugo Betti and Dego Fabbri, the most enduring 'new writing' has been by Eduardo and Fo, whose works have been almost the only Italian theatre to be widely performed outside Italy (although, as we shall see, Eugenio Barba is a special case, and three others will be briefly considered below).

One of the first initiatives towards renewal through experimentation came from the Gruppo 63 headed by Giuseppe Bartolucci in Palermo. He proposed a renewal of theatre in the wake of the impact in Europe of the works of Genet, Adamov and Beckett; the attack on the primacy of language in the theatre was to lead to important results, among them the concept of *scrittura scenica* (writing for performance; see below), which links the work of the group above all to the director Carmelo Bene, although they were also to be linked to the various 'foreign' influences discussed below. The group also promoted a form of 'interdisciplinary' theatre called *poesie di teatro*, through the works of poets like Giuliani, Balesini and Porta, who had already tried their hands at electronic and visual poetry. Francesco Leonetti had published his *Il malpensante* and *Teatro in versi* in 1961, and Giuliani's *Povera Juliet* and *Urotropio* are not dissimilar. And so the influence was not only from poetry: the group also received strong stimulus from painting and music, and even from contemporary disciplines not normally considered cognate like contemporary philosophy, structuralism and psychoanalysis. It cannot be said that such experiments produced great theatre, or that a school was founded to endure beyond initial iconoclastic enthusiasms, but the principle of the assault on traditional canons was probably more important than the detail. The question was posed: 'what is theatre?' The edifice of theatre as an organ of the state came under attack, until – perhaps inevitably – members of the group dispersed to former homes and disciplines.

Others, however, made use of the Gruppo 63 experiment. Perriera continued with adaptations of Shakespeare and Ionesco within the framework of 'metatheatre'. Giuliano Scabbia, more importantly, brought a new vision to his *Zip* (performed Venice, 1965) by utilizing traditions from the Italian past as diverse as futurist theatre and the *commedia dell'arte*. Again, others have built on successive waves of influence from abroad to indicate new directions.

Carmelo Bene, already mentioned, deserves a place here. Initially operating in the closed atmosphere of an experimental workshop and attracting attention only superficially at first, Bene began to work in the early 1960s towards a negation of the power of the director, an assault on the dramatic text through *scrittura scenica* in which the intervention of the director as mediator, interpreter or critic is dismissed. Thus Bene promoted a process by which the language of theatre grows from the action itself; all the traditional relationships between text, delivery, set and effects are broken down. Yet again, it is difficult to point to enduring results which have stood the test of time, but Carmelo Bene promoted new freedoms from tradition for the theatre that have had a lasting influence on succeeding generations. Of historic importance were his productions of *Lo strano caso del dottor Jekyll e del Sig. Hyde* (The Strange Case of Dr Jekyll and Mr Hyde), *Pinocchio* and *Hamlet*; his principal contribution was the evolution of *scrittura scenica*; and yet his anguish through characters who seem at odds with society, the hopelessness of man, the impossibility of harmony, all remind one irresistibly of his contemporary, Beckett, and emerge most strongly in his adaptations of Shakespeare throughout the 1970s (*Hamlet*, 1975; *Romeo and Juliet*, 1976; *Richard III*, 1977; *Othello*, 1979).

From the mid-1960s, consciousness of crisis became revolt. Complaints were heard on every side that there was no rapport between intellectuals and the theatre, that audiences were fading and companies dissolving, that literature and the theatre were becoming mutually exclusive and that language was the crux. Pasolini was emphatic on this last point:

> Even the Piccolo Theatre is always academic: its speech does not correspond to the real speech of the audience: they are two different spoken languages. It is not an academic convention based on the real speech of the audience, but a hypothetical speech which does not exist.[2]

This was one of the responses to a poll conducted by the leading drama journal *Sipario* in 1965 to ascertain the causes of the malaise in the Italian theatre. Writers and artists were asked to comment and concluded that Italian theatre was out of step with the times. Although some writers (notably Pasolini himself) sought to remedy the situation by writing plays themselves, there seemed no obvious solution and debates and accusations continued unabated. In the midst of all this – in March 1965, to be precise – the Living Theater erupted onto the scene with their revolutionary concept of theatre as a total event, involving the audience actively in a shared experience, transmitting a message in language far from what Italians expected from theatre, and systematically destroying structure and theatrical convention alike in an 'immersion' process of considerable violence. The performance of *The Brig* and *Mysteries* acted like some long-awaited catharsis for Italian audiences who saw techniques imported from dance, music, painting and sculpture (as we have seen for Gruppo 63), but going on to project anarchic principles and to smash a range of social taboos, including violence and sexuality, rarely if ever seen on the Italian stage at that time.

Although Living Theater rapidly acquired the status of a cult and made disciples wherever they went, the recipe was too hot for a traditionally conservative and Catholic society to absorb at a stroke. Just as Squarzina's production of *Il diavolo e il buon Dio* (The Devil and the Good Lord) had been accused of insult to religion and its tour prevented from reaching Rome, the papal city, and Luigi Lunari's

Tarantella on One Leg had been broken up by police in 1962 in Naples, so now Living Theater's performance in Trieste was interrupted; the actors were arrested and charged with obscene acts; the *teatro stabile* was accused of complicity, and the government threatened withdrawal of subsidy. Again, after the presentation of their *Frankenstein* in Venice, members of the Living Theater were arrested, accompanied to the frontier and deported. Thus it was that the theatre in Italy assumed an increasingly more radical stance. Once again, *Sipario* published a species of manifesto signed by many interested parties which tried to promote an Italian avant-garde, but it was the conference at Ivrea in 1967 that yielded perhaps the most constructive discussions. Mention was made of 'collective' and 'laboratory' theatre in a direct relationship with society, of new plays and new structures, and the consumer circuit (the closed circle linking production and consumer) was vehemently attacked. A thousand 'little' theatres, springing up wherever there was space, was the current dream, and the aims of the theatre were to be overtly and unashamedly revolutionary.

Meanwhile, a glance across the map of Europe reveals much that was to be important in the world of Italian theatre (and the significance in Italy of 'cross-cultural perspectives') on the eve of 1968. On 1 October 1964, Eugenio Barba, until recently a wandering student on a scholarship, founded the Odin Teatret in Oslo; Stockholm had seen the staging of Brecht, Ingmar Bergman and the first (American) 'happening'. A German who had spent much time in Stockholm had just written *Marat/Sade* (1964). Taviani writes:

> One by one, the themes of the Absurd were being replaced in the theatre by those of madness, of excess, of the violence of institutions. Those distinctions which, in the 1950s, placed in opposition the political theatre and the theatre of the existential anguish of the individual were falling away ... the ideological clarity of Brecht's theatre and the paradoxical clarity of the logical pessimism of Beckett and Ionesco were gradually disappearing.[3]

Peter Handke, capturing the rebellious spirit of the young, had written *Publikumsbeschimpfung* (Insulting the Audience) in 1966. *McBird* (a play about the Kennedy assassination and the Johnson government) created a scandal in the United States, and Peter Brook put together a play about Vietnam. When the Odin Teatret was founded in 1964, very few had heard of Grotowski, few had seen

Living Theater, Peter Brook's injection of Artaud into *Marat/Sade* was yet to have its effect, and Dario Fo was known in Italy mostly as the author of surreal and satirical farces and revue.

The popular movements in France and Italy which characterized the years 1968–9 soon changed all that. Sparked off originally by French students and workers and spreading in an unprecedented revolutionary fervour to Italy, the uprisings, street demonstrations, strikes and manifestations against the prevailing social and political order, were to have widespread repercussions in the Italian theatre, since artists, creators and all kinds of intellectuals were soon swept up in the general enthusiasm for, and commitment to, change. It seemed as if the directions indicated by (until then) isolated pockets of theatrical innovation, with their quota of radicalism, violence and social commitment, were now to become established principles in the life of the theatre. And it is noteworthy that only Barba is Italian, and that his innovations had begun outside Italy. Strehler was obliged to resign as director of the Piccolo Teatro, the *teatri stabili* came under renewed attack, and theatre 'collectives', self-supporting and independent of the webs of Italian bureaucracy, began to appear, the most famous of which was undoubtedly the foundation of Nuova Scena in 1968 by Dario Fo, as we shall shortly see.

And yet this brings us to one of the most striking cross-cultural perspectives of these years. Taviani notes that:

> A few months before [Eugenio Barba] had organised the tour in Denmark and throughout Scandinavia of [Dario Fo's] *La Signora è da buttare*, an anti-American satire. Fo had become one of the great actor-authors in Scandinavia. He had held a seminar at Holstbro in which he had given a series of practical demonstrations based on the ancient texts of Italian popular culture. These demonstrations were to become the basis for *Mistero Buffo* which, in Italy, was to become the new symbol of a new theatre capable of cutting all links with the economy, the organisation and audiences of Italian middle-class theatre, and directing itself openly to middle-class audiences and the militant left.[4]

Barba's activities were indeed becoming international. Having begun in Denmark with a handful of actor-rejects from official drama schools a species of drama-laboratory, untaught and untrained, the group began a process of experimentation within closed doors on the basis of Barba's commitment to the principle of self-discovery through training as actors. Their first show, *Ornitofilene* in 1965, in which an embargo on the hunting of birds becomes an allegory for the Nazi depredations of the war years, was characterized by striking innovations of all kinds: performance space was fluid; actors mingled with audience; counterpoint was set up between different acting styles and different forms of delivery; multiple tensions were created (for instance, between violence in war and violence in peace); and actors transformed themselves into different characters under the gaze of the audience.

Odin Teatret performed its second show, *Kasparina* in 1967, also at the Venice Biennale, and chose to dramatize the contemporary debate about education, the transmission of culture, the arguments about 'teaching' and indoctrination which had wide social and ideological ramifications, through a story of a young man 'rescued' from a wild and untutored state by the education process in Nurenberg in 1828, and assassinated shortly afterwards. Meanwhile, Odin was growing in experience, publishing books and magazines and organizing seminars – possibly contributing more than any other group to the international dimension of European theatre at this time. They studied the theory and practice of *commedia dell'arte*, Russian theatre, Indian theatre, Piscator's political theatre, Noh theatre and the work of Decroux, Grotowski and Craig, inviting representatives to participate in their seminars from all the most important branches of world theatre, including the director Luca Ronconi from Italy, and, as we have seen, Dario Fo.

In Italy itself, it was Ronconi's *Orlando furioso* staged in 1968 which most caught the public imagination: a dramatization of Ariosto's Renaissance epic poem which encouraged audiences to think of the actors as mobile, sets as fluid, and even of themselves as constantly in movement. Mobile stages and seats either enclosed spectators or obliged them to move in order to follow the course of the action – a theatrical concept that was strikingly new and attempted to identify the 'spirit' of the drama, abandoning stereotyped spatial conventions. Theatre had become a popular festival rather than representation and, typically, Odin invited *Orlando furioso* to Denmark as part of an extended European tour.

EUGENIO BARBA: ODIN

Thus can be seen the extent to which, in this sketch-map of the Italian theatre since 1960, all roads lead back to Eugenio Barba and the Odin

Teatret. It is worth pausing, therefore, to consider this phenomenon – of European dimensions – in more detail. Perhaps no one more than the 'Europeanized' Barba has contributed more to the ways we think about theatre today, and the ways we have accepted (or rejected) the lessons and events in Europe since 1960.

The Odin Teatret perhaps represents four fundamental principles (though this must, of necessity, be an all-too-brief summary of a highly complex phenomenon): isolation (therefore, detachment) from the main centres or 'schools' of theatrical activity; 'training' for the actor (understood in the physical sense: the word has gone into Italian on the wave of interest in the group in recent years); and the important principle of self-teaching, deriving from the complete lack of formative influences from outside currents of thinking, schools and academies. (This does not mean, of course, that Odin has not absorbed contemporary influences, but it has achieved an undisputed influence and prominence from a unique base: a total commitment of life, resources and fortunes that has frequently been compared with that of a monastery.) Fourth, Odin has arguably done more than any towards the systematic dismantling of the 'fourth wall' dividing actors from audiences in traditional performance situations.

First of all, detachment from theatre's traditional power-base: despite its fame, Odin has maintained a distance from the (corrupting) influence of institutions, state subvention and established theatre. Even when touring or accepting invitations to international festivals, the Odin Teatret only do so under conditions that guarantee their freedom of action and autonomy of performance. This regard for their independence (to some obsessive, or even fanatical) extends also to soundings locally to ascertain what reaction there might be to their revolutionary style. Given the background, examples of which we have seen, it is not hard to see the strength of this dedication.

Second, the (physical) training for the actor, as Taviani has noted, seems sometimes marked by the same degree of monastic fervour bordering on obsession. Far from the normal preparation of the professional actor (post-acting school) of rehearsals (for specific performance, Odin's actors work as far as they can from the concept of the actor as a tool in the hands of the director to be used in the process of fashioning a commercial product. Training for Odin is not a search for a theatrical language or just the urge towards renewal of an old profession: it is self-taught, a process of self-realization through practical experience of all possible theatrical languages, experiments by each individual actor with (for instance) dance, mime, gymnastics, acrobatics, styles of delivery of speech, in different languages, and so on. One would not wish to enclose Eugenio Barba within any restrictive analogy, but the same kind and range of experimentation characterizes the long history of the *commedia dell'arte*.

Third, the principle of self-sufficiency has been total; the group has always worked towards the discovery of itself, taught mainly by its own practical performance experience. Barba himself wrote in 1979:

> In order to evaluate the work of the theatre as a social and cultural phenomenon, one looks automatically to the audience. But the relationships between audience and actors only become important at a second point in time. Before that, the relations between the actors are supremely important. The first 'social' phase of theatre happens within the groups: it is the way different individuals control their work relationships and socialise their needs. The nature of this initial socialisation decides the place of the theatrical group within the society and its influence on it.[5]

From this kind of theoretical and practical basis the Odin Teatret has gone from strength to strength. This philosophy has revolutionized thinking about the theatre, doing away with the 'distortions' of 'performance', realizing drama as a lived reality within the group before it is 'projected', performed or played. What is conventionally termed 'theatre' as an event in time and circumscribed space is only a part of the Odin experience. Between 1976 and 1979 this discussion became a world-wide issue. Making contact on tour with groups in Yugoslavia, Italy, Peru and Spain, Barba has shown that Odin struck a chord in many diverse societies outside official theatre networks and circuits, an influence that is no longer even European. Significantly, this now includes Britain (Cardiff in 1980 and 1990).

The period from 1969 to 1972 saw the performance of *Ferai* and *Min fars hus* (The Father's House) and contributed with further examples to its influence in Europe and the world. In France, Belgium and widely in Italy, *Min fars hus* was no longer a performance in the accepted sense (conventional time- and space-limits), but became much more like a total seminar in which Odin's actors related to local groups (for days at a time) in a total mingling, exchange and fusion: a 'workshop' in which roles are unclear, but in which the 'play' becomes the culminating stage. This process (partly dictated by practical considerations since only a few spectators were admitted) allowed genuine rapport between groups throughout Europe who wanted to

share this totality of experience. Since those years, with the foundation of the International School of Theatre Anthropology (ISTA) in
1979, the world tour we have referred to, publications, films, Barba's
manifesto for a *Third Theatre* (1976)[6] and further important productions (*Come and the Day Will Be Ours* (1976) and *Brechts aske*
(Brecht's Ashes, 1980–2)), the message of Odin Teatret has continued
to stimulate and stir the theatre world.

DECENTRALIZATION

Returning to Italy after the momentous events of 1968, we find one
response to the malaise of the *teatri stabili*: decentralization.
Initiatives of this kind were to bring theatre to outlying areas, to
respond to the need for new audiences, to create a closer bond
between theatre and everyday life by putting it on in the very midst of
society. This phenomenon has been variously described (by one
committed writer as a 'colonialist picnic') but did have the advantage
of tapping into new audiences, away from the *centri storici* of large
cities with low-priced tickets. The most famous example of this was
the celebrated *Harlequin, Servant of Two Masters* which Strehler put
on in a circus tent on the outskirts of Milan. The production was a
huge success, as were plays by Brecht, Büchner and Ionesco, among
others, which performed outside Turin. Sometimes, too, as is more
common today, workshops followed in the wake of such local
performances, and these had solid benefits for the 'social integration'
of the theatre, particularly for children and young people. In some
places, centres for cultural interchange have survived to provide a
place for theatre-in-society consistent with the thinking of the times;
in others, such moves were of short duration. The aim was, of course,
to set up genuinely reciprocal cultural activities through theatre rather
than to present merely the packaged products of the *stabili* in tents.

Apart from the sometimes promising results of decentralization of
the activities of the official theatre of the *stabili*, there were a number
of more 'unofficial' initiatives in the wake of '1968' springing from
the example of Odin, from the visit of Living Theater and from the
Bread and Puppet Theater. One critic has called the period the boom
of '*teatrini* off' (again, the internationalism of the jargon is
significant). Dario Fo reigned supreme on the alternative circuit,
while Eduardo de Filippo, his older contemporary, was now winding
down, as we shall shortly see; but there was an explosion of
experimental theatre in many parts of Italy.

Carlo Cecchi's Granteatro performed a mixed repertory of classics from Europe (including Brecht) and more experimental shows with more than a dash of the old Neapolitan popular comedy. Notable by Mario Ricci was a laboratory production of *Moby Dick*, while the Ouroboros group in Florence 'saw theatre primarily as a form of play intended to express unconscious instinct and liberate collective fantasy through the use of highly surrealist techniques sometimes reminiscent of Futurist theatre';[7] and the Milanese Teatro del Sole, with its masks and puppets, echoed Fo's *Grand Pantomime with Flags and Small and Medium-Sized Puppets* (see below) and the Bread and Puppet Theater. Broadly, there was movement towards visual, exterior forms of theatre which echoed the most ancient of Italian traditions as well as building on messages received from the international circuit.

NEW WRITING

In the area of new writing for the theatre in this period, it is perhaps ironic that the ferment (particularly since 1968) has not produced works that have carried far beyond the Italian frontier, except in the cases of Eduardo de Filippo and Dario Fo. Ironic because it has been these two writer-actors who have continued the centuries-old traditions of the Italian comedy: Eduardo built on the solidly Neapolitan traditions of Petito, Scarpetta and Viviani, whereas Fo uses traditions as diverse as popular theatre and literature, variety and the *commedia dell'arte* in the service of a theatre now firmly committed to ideological functions. Both, in their different ways, have brought striking innovations in dramatic language to the Italian theatre – another irony, since this is precisely the area which has come under the lash of critics of the *teatro stabile* system like Pasolini. It will be clear by now that Barba stands outside this category. Nevertheless, there has been new writing in the theatre that has received recognition within Italy, and we should now look briefly at Patroni Griffi, Giovanni Testori and Franco Brusati.

Patroni Griffi has consistently echoed the themes of modern Italy in our period, paying close attention to the dilemmas of post-war Italians. *D'amore si muore* (One Dies of Love) had considerable success in 1958 with its very topical setting in the world of the cinema and characters using it to climb the ladder of success. *Anima nera* (The Dark Soul, 1960), deepens the sense of alienation felt by a favourite Griffi character (a young man uncomplicated by any sort of moral pre-conditioning). He marries Marcella who then leaves him after finding out about his doubtful past. The struggle to win her back invests the character with a renewed sense of personal moral integrity. Griffi went on to construct an autobiographical play about the strain of being a Neapolitan adrift in Rome. This was his *In memoria di una signora amica* (In Memory of a Lady Friend, 1963) set in the bureaucracy of contemporary Rome. The play projects the hand-to-mouth survival techniques of this displaced Neapolitan in a language which, though not dialect, makes wide use of the inflections of Naples. Probably his most successful play was, however, a dramatization of the new 'permissiveness' of the 1960s and recounts the search for moral integrity of a couple in a society with few rules and restrictions: *Metti una sera a cena* (One Evening at Dinner, 1967). Since then, Griffi's drama has taken different directions, preoccupied with the plight of the homosexual in today's society, and using progressively more modern techniques. Perhaps the most significant of these plays is *Prima del silenzio* (Before Silence, 1979), which examines the impossibility of communication between the usual amoral young man and an ageing poet, isolated in a warehouse of books.

Giovanni Testori, a poet and narrative writer as well as a playwright, seems rather more enmeshed in the modern ferment of Italian theatre. Still rather in the grip of neorealism in the early 1960s, his plays are set in Milan and attempt to discover the tragic essence of society through his dramatization of mainly working-class characters. *Maria Brasca* (1960) tells the story of the heroine's obsessive pursuit of a worthless suitor; *Arialda*, on the other hand, is a play about the tragedy of ordinary people and a victim of destiny, the homosexual Eros, denied the opportunity of love. The fact that the play attracted censorship problems perhaps says more about the date (1960) than the play itself. Possibly Testori's plays achieve more authentic tragic values in his *La Monaca di Monza* (The Nun of Monza) and *Erodiade*, both of 1967, which document the author's revolt against society's strictures. As its title indicates, *Erodiade* is set in the time of Herod; it is marked by some unusually explosive language which, in the eyes of some critics writing in these crucial years before 1968, led to definition of his work as 'protest drama'.

In the 1970s Testori devoted his attention to tragedy in the classic sense, creating versions of *Hamlet* (1973), *Macbeth* (1974) and *Oedipus* (1977) which have been seen by some as the highest achievement of this playwright. They continue his search for tragic authenticity, perhaps questioning the existence of tragedy since the passing of the tragic visions of Genet and Beckett. The pessimism of the author emerges powerfully in these adaptations, productions of great linguistic richness, in which the audience feels the sense of loss of absolute values along with a despairing consciousness of the isolation of the individual. In the end, this seems to denote the death of tragedy. As Testori himself has admitted, the success of these productions of the 1970s is closely linked with his relationship with the theatre (the Salone Pier Lombardi), and with the mastery of the actor, Franco Parenti, in all the principal roles.

Since this important phase of his work, Testori has moved away from tragedy to religious themes (following his own re-conversion after the death of his mother) and we have *Interrogatorio a Maria* (Questions for Mary, 1979) and *Factum est* (1981) in this vein, as well as *Post-Hamlet* (1983) and *I promessi sposi alla prova* (The Betrothed on Trial, 1984). 'Oratorios' as some have defined them, these late plays belong to a different tradition, intended for believers, and possibly outside the mainstream of Italian theatre in this generation.

Franco Brusati came to the theatre as a creative artist already successful as a film director. His first play, *Il benessere* (Wealth, 1959), was a portrait of a corrupt society which laid greater stress on wealth than on moral values. Yet critics felt that the portrait was rather superficial, and were unhappy about the ending (the death, in the course of an erotic game, of the protagonist). *La fastidiosa* (The Fastidious Woman) of 1963 owed its considerable success to the creation of a classic Italian wife-and-mother figure in the protagonist, Lidia. Her integrity and moral sense are pitted against an unfaithful husband and deceitful son in a finely crafted and elegantly written play. As so often, the success of the piece was partly due to a fine performance by the actress Eva Magni; the play was revived in 1966.

In that year, Brusati moved from the traditional domestic sphere to an ambitious allegory of our time with *Pietà di Novembre* which uses the story of Lee Harvey Oswald (alleged assassin of Kennedy) as a parallel to his (Italian) protagonist, whose escape from his own inadequacy into violence the author sees as a sign of the times. *Le rose del lago* (Roses by the Lake, 1974) was far less ambitious and returns to the process of documenting changes in Italian life in this period by placing five characters in a general strike where their façades and appearances are stripped away to reveal base humanity. This dramatic process vaguely echoes *Huis clos*, although Brusati's play scarcely lifts the argument to a universal plane. In the end, the 'unmasking' has neither the power of Pirandello nor the weight of Sartre. And much the same could be said for Brusati's most recent play, *Una donna sul letto* (A Woman on the Bed), written in 1984.

Eduardo de Filippo

We have already noted the extent to which the most enduring and internationally acclaimed theatre in Italy in our period has its roots in popular origins and an emphasis on comedy. For both Eduardo de Filippo and Dario Fo, springing from contrasting backgrounds, represent centuries-old traditions from the *commedia dell'arte* to Neapolitan dialect theatre (Eduardo), from *commedia* practice to the rebirth of medieval literature through popular comedy (Fo). The problem for the present sketch-map is that Eduardo was 60 when the period covered by this book opens, so we must look briefly back before documenting the shifts in his theatre since 1960. His younger contemporary, Fo – enjoying the friendship of Eduardo and influence from the Neapolitan actor-playwright that he has often admitted – attracted attention fairly precisely as this period opens. They share the common and very Italian traditions of the *commedia dell'arte*, though for Eduardo this was inherited from the long Neapolitan traditions of Petito, Scarpetta and Viviani in the centrality of Pulcinella, whereas for Fo, *commedia* was stumbled on, almost by accident, as we shall shortly see, in a relationship that was only formalized in 1985.

The influences on Eduardo were, above all, Neapolitan and initially dialect-orientated. Stemming from the satire and pathos of Petito's comic theatre in the nineteenth century, via Eduardo Scarpetta, his successor in the period either side of the First World War, Eduardo emerged in the late 1920s, with his brother Peppino and sister Titina, as an authentic force in the comic theatre. Actor, playwright, director and *capocomico*, he inherited the twin influences of Petito's nineteenth-century *pulcinellate* and Scarpetta's skilfully crafted 'urban' comedies. He was to go on to inherit more from Pirandello in the 1920s and 1930s and indeed collaborated with him. And yet the thread that runs all through his drama is the irreparable conflict between man and society, envisaged in a process that veers from the comic to the pathetic and the tragic and (in its social ramifications) brings Eduardo firmly into our period. Just as the theatre of Dario Fo mirrors its times both before and after 1968, so his older contemporary,

Eduardo, acknowledged internationally as an actor-playwright of world stature, felt the need to attract an audience wider than the regional restrictions of Neapolitan dialect allowed and began, after the Second World War, to mirror the social preoccupations of *Italians*. Neapolitan comedy became a metaphor for the plight of all Italians, and (to the nostalgic regret of some critics) aimed its shafts at the middle class.

But before this, Eduardo's reputation rests on a long history of memorable productions in the theatre, from the language of everyday speech and the fantastic variety-orientated one-act farce of *Sik-sik* (1929) to the post-war reflection of sombre realities (poverty, the black market, and so on) of *Napoli milionaria* (1945) in the first fervour of Italian neo-realism of De Sica, Visconti, Rossellini and others, and the opening-out of the lens of film and theatre to the harsh aftermath of the war. Eduardo's realism anticipates the advances of the neorealist film in this portrait of a Neapolitan family forced to undergo the hardships of unemployment, the compromises of the black market, and deportation by the Germans of the husband, Gennaro, who returns to find his family up to their necks in illegal trafficking. His moral stance is contrasted with the 'reality' of the situation forced on his family by circumstances.

The other landmark in de Filippo's work in this post-war period must be *Filumena Marturano* (1946) which broadcast his reputation as a dramatist, being performed throughout Europe as well as in Russia. In this play we have one of the most significant heroines in post-war Italian theatre. Filumena is depicted in her struggle against hardship, and the contrasts the play projects are summarized thus by Mignone:

> On one side we have the rancour of the woman humiliated, the fury of the threatened mother, the rebellion of the working woman vilified; on the other, male egoism, the hate of the lover who is badly treated, the insidiousness of revenge, and the sarcasm of the victory. In the end, there is prayer, weeping and forgiveness.[8]

The energy is created by a cruel 'husband' cohabiting with Filumena for many years, seducer of another, who is tricked into marriage by Filumena's pretence of serious illness. The couple's antagonism is finely dramatized with psychological perception and a forward-looking vision of women's rights (accounting perhaps, in part, for the play's continuing popularity). The piece deserves more space than we have here, but in their 'contemporary' struggle towards self-discovery,

Eduardo's characters look back to Pirandello and forward to Betti, and the play uses a 'modern' range of expressive stage-techniques.

On these foundations rests Eduardo's reputation (in a long and productive life), so we should now consider his late works since 1960. In recent years he has moved further away from his Neapolitan and dialect roots and attempted to project the dilemma of a whole society; *Il sindaco del rione Sanità* (The Mayor of Sanità District, 1960) which meditates on the problem of human justice and its shortcomings, echoing (back, not forward, this time) similar themes in Betti's drama. Don Antonio Barracano is a kind of people's hero who supplies the sort of justice the state cannot provide, inviting consideration of conscience, piety, questions of brotherhood and solidarity, and compassion for the poor and exploited. There is a tacit appeal to the organs of the state to be more understanding in their treatment of ordinary people, and the protagonist, Don Antonio, is clearly a redemption symbol, and so tends to eclipse the psychologies of minor characters.

Tomaso d'Amalfi (1963) attempts a fusion of music and history in a setting (1647–8) which seems almost of Manzonian derivation. This is a radical new departure for Eduardo, with a musical chorus and a 'message' about the ethics of power (to the people). We have a colourful backdrop of Naples – reflected by chorus and dance – against which the drama of the protagonist is played out. Masaniello is a man of complex psychology who leads his people in their struggle for political freedom against the aristrocracy, and yet who appears weak and believably human. Clearly an allegory for his own time, Eduardo's 'musical' captures the spirit of struggle in a mingling of chorus, music, poetry and dance with pictorial effects, placed in a precise historical setting, with possibly the gains (and disadvantages) of *Les Misérables* avant la lettre.

With *L'arte della commedia* (1965), we are on rather solider ground, as de Filippo has used an old device (the programmatic manifesto play about the nature of theatre itself, as in Goldoni's *Il teatro comico*) for specific modern and topical reasons. With it, he joined the fairly widespread chorus of disapproval of the *teatri stabili* as fossilized bureaucratic institutions in the grip of state subvention (control), which, as we have seen, was a prominent feature of the 1960s in the Italian theatre world. But the way in which this criticism is achieved has echoes far and wide in European theatre and is also an examination of the nature of theatrical reality, the fiction of the actor who 'becomes' another person through acting, and the 'schizophrenic' possibility of confusing the two. In an interview with a bureaucratic representative of the state, (a sort of latter-day chairman of an arts council), a *capocomico* accuses him of non-comprehension and an uncaring attitude towards the theatre (the critique of the *stabili*) and succeeds in removing his appointment-list bearing the names of the next people to be ushered in. Then the *capocomico* threatens the bureaucrat that his actors will impersonate these 'characters' and that the bureaucrat will not know the difference! The 'characters' enter one by one, and indeed the question of whether they are impersonations or 'real' is never quite resolved in a plot that this summary cannot detail. But the echoes are clear: back to Stanisławsky, sideways to *Kean*, perhaps, but surely back to Pirandello (the *Six Characters in Search of an Author* and *Henry IV*), possibly even forward to Fo's maniac in his *Accidental Death of an Anarchist* (1970); and ultimately, back to Freud, in the twentieth-century perennial fascination with the nature of personality and 'acting' in all its forms.

The year 1965 also saw Eduardo's *Il cilindro* (The Top Hat), and the return to domestic (low) life in Naples. The top hat becomes a symbol of formality and authority against which, on the side of the poor and dispossessed, the play operates, with deception in a fake suicide as the principal weapon. Presented at the 1967 festival in Venice, *Il contratto* (The Contract) returns to Eduardo's themes from previous works. The striving for wealth looms large; the character Geronta appears to possess miraculous powers; and once again Eduardo has dramatized in his protagonist the other, more humanitarian, face of state repression and bureaucracy. De Filippo himself described his play's targets:

> The aim of all those who come near Geronta is to grab as much as possible with no concern for his neighbour; the main aim of the state is to dispossess and oppress the citizen, and the Church has betrayed the teaching of Christ by allowing itself to become involved in material interests which are often the antithesis of Christianity.[9]

Although he is never far from the central preoccupations of the world of Italian theatre in these years (post-war disillusionment, the plight of the dispossessed and oppressed, the repressive image of the state), Eduardo adapts popular traditions to the uses of the times, rarely with overt didacticism, but with a deep moral sense. Originally the leading exponent of a dialect theatre – consequently of somewhat limited range and appeal – he has in recent years broadened its appeal with a language which is dialect-influenced Italian. He has widened the range of his theatre's social sphere, and lifted its meaning and significance to a national Italian level, bringing it, at times, on to the world stage. His theatre, even in its more complex or intellectual subjects, always retains the stamp, freshness and immediacy of a popular genre.

Dario Fo

Unlike that of Eduardo, Dario Fo's career as actor-playwright, already successful in review (notably *Il dito nell'occhio*, The Finger in the Eye, in 1953) was projected beyond the Italian frontier precisely in 1960 with a performance of *Gli archangeli non giacono a flipper* (Archangels Don't Play Pinball) at Zagreb in Yugoslavia. From here he has moved ahead and it is now widely accepted that he is the most performed living playwright in the world. Again, by contrast with Eduardo, Fo came to the theatre after studying architecture (he still designs his own sets) and evolved his own individual brand of farce, combining the grotesque, music, mime, variety and satire, and (like Eduardo) using puppets from Sicily and the improvisation and masks from the *commedia dell'arte*. Alongside Eduardo's Pulcinella, Fo has placed his Harlequin in its modern satirical and subversive twentieth-century formulation and since the momentous political events of the late 1960s, he has used these talents specifically in the service of the militant left. Now, with Franca Rame, he includes women's rights in Europe in the struggle for the assertion of a more equitable place in society for modern woman.

Owing to the recent publication of his company's statistics, it is now possible to measure the impact of the theatre of Dario Fo and Franca Rame between 1960 and 1989.[10] We find that the hard-hitting farce *Accidental Death of an Anarchist* has absolute pride of place, having been performed in translation or adaptation in 41 countries world-wide, and bringing its devastating and hilarious revelation of police corruption and cover-up to countries where the message might have had potent force, such as Argentina, Chile, South Africa and Ceauşescu's Romania. In part this is doubtless due to the play's flexibility in performance, as less dependent on Dario Fo's unique acting talents. By contrast, *Mistero Buffo* is so dependent, but this has not prevented it from being performed in 27 countries, and for many television services, including the whole of Catholic Europe.

Finally, the emergence of Franca Rame as a militant force with her brand of political commitment and feminist polemic is (in statistical terms) no less striking for the 1980s, as her first monologues, *Tutta casa, letto e chiesa* (known in Britain as *Female Parts*) has been performed on its own in 35 countries, and (with other monologues) in about 30. This is only matched by *Can't Pay, Won't Pay*, now seen in 35 countries. Suffice it to say that in the theatre season 1989–90, there were 53 separate productions of 18 different shows in about 20 different countries, including China, Israel, Paraguay and Japan, from which it seems clear that Fo and Rame are bringing new meaning to 'cross-cultural perspectives'.

The 1960s began for Dario Fo with *Archangels Don't Play Pinball* which mocks the oppressive hierarchy and obstructionist bureaucracy of post-war Italy through the hilarious adventures of a petty criminal who dreams he has suffered from a loss of identity (he has no papers) and other misfortunes, buffeted this way and that by the inexorable machinery of state. 'The play was performed with the same rhythm as a film, where scenes and events followed a cinematic kind of sequence',[11] wrote Fo. But this was good-natured satire, on a Pirandellian theme, hardly militant protest. *Isabella, tre caravelle e un cacciaballe* (Isabella, Three Sailing Ships and a Con-Man), however, first performed in Milan in 1963, used historical research to project a message through a (fictional) Columbus in his dealings with the power-base (the Spanish Court) to show, in a Brechtian mixture of comedy and commentary through songs, the plight of the individual at the mercy of the ruling class. This period had seen the formation (1958) of the Compagnia Fo–Rame (in the Italian tradition of the *mattatore*) which was now producing shows for a bourgeois audience. In 1962, as well, the now famous incident of the TV variety programme *Canzonissima* occurred; after a few episodes, Fo and Rame walked out as their merciless satirical portraits of Italian politicians and institutions became too hot for the times and were altered by the censors.

Continuing to cement their reputation – by now firmly established throughout Europe – Fo and Rame created satirical plays throughout the 1960s until the episode of *La signora è da buttare* (Throw the Lady Out, 1967), an anti-American satire, brought them firmly to the forefront of the 1967–8 movements in Italy. The show was a characteristic mixture of satire, topical comment (Vietnam, Lee Harvey Oswald, the Kennedy assassination) and circus acts (a flea circus, clowns), and was indeed set within a struggle between two rival circuses. One result was that Fo was officially accused of disrespect towards a foreign head of state (President Johnson), and he was for long denied a visa to enter the United States. At this time, spurred on by the growing unrest, Fo and Rame began to reject their role as entertainers of the bourgeoisie on the commercial theatre circuit and disbanded the Compagnia Fo–Rame to form Nuova Scena. This new company was to perform as a service to the proletariat in workers' clubs, factories and other public spaces, an instrument – now quite specifically – of political change in collaboration with ARCI (the cultural wing of the Italian Communist Party), and it was intended that the company should be run on Brechtian/Communist principles of evenly shared responsibilities. There followed the *Grand Pantomime with Flags and Small and Medium-Sized Puppets* (1968), Fo's most overtly ideological show to date, in which puppets and other devices, manipulated by strings and sticks in full view of the audience, projected the struggle of the proletariat and the bourgeoisie; as well as masks, as much rooted in Roman Comedy as in the *commedia dell'arte*, and a monster puppet always on stage representing fascism (and giving birth to all the subsequent incarnations of its philosophy of repression: a king and queen, the middle class, a general, a bishop and the Italian confederation of industry).

1969 and 1970 saw the gestation and performance of Fo's two most celebrated works, *Mistero Buffo* and *Accidental Death of an Anarchist*, which, as we have seen, are now considered classics and are performed world-wide. But the same period saw also *L'operaio conosce 300 parole, il padrone 3000, per questo lui è il padrone* (The Worker Knows 300 Words, The Boss Knows 3000 . . .) and *Legami pure che tanto io spacco tutto lo stesso* (Chain Me Up and I'll Still Smash Everything), less well known, but which served to define Fo's ideological viewpoint and to underline his stand against the rigidities and bureaucracy of the Italian Communist Party. As a result, Fo was attacked by Communists writing in *Unità*, members of the Party began to boycott his shows, and the Party threatened to obstruct his access to playing spaces in halls and similar venues. This led to Fo's secession from Nuova Scena and the formation of the collective La Comune in 1970, a major alternative theatre circuit in Italy.

Mistero Buffo is Fo's most famous one-man-show and has been played by many actors in many languages. It is a *tour de force* of Fo's own acting style, however, and uses a unique blend of illustrated lecture/introduction to the sketches and comes across entirely (in the original) in an 'abstruse language of the *giullari* ', a form of northern Italian dialect which echoes the linguistic virtuosity of the medieval strolling player who had to adapt his discourse to different audiences. The play takes the sources of its satirical polemic from medieval literature (suitably adapted to Fo's purpose), church history and the Bible, 'demythologizing' sacred and profane alike to show how the peasant/worker has been exploited and misrepresented down the long course of history. In 1986 Ron Jenkins wrote:

> If there is a single work that embodies the essence of Fo's epic clown it is *Mistero Buffo* . . . Fo's masterpiece. It provides a key to understanding the extraordinary performance techniques required to animate the texts of his large-cast plays. . . . Fo infuses every story with the rhythmic drive of a jazz improvisation, the immediacy of a newspaper headline, and the social scope of a historical novel.[12]

After Dario Fo had performed it in London, the critic from *The Times* described it as 'a revelation comparable to London's first sight of the Berliner Ensemble'.[13]

Accidental Death of an Anarchist, on the other hand, got as close as Fo has ever done to contemporary reality, dramatizing the police cover-up following the fall from a police station window of an anarchist accused of implication in a bombing in Milan in 1969. The immediacy of the events (the play was performed during the trial following the assertion by *Lotta Continua* that a police inspector had pushed the anarchist from the window, and the newspaper was being sued by the inspector) was unique in modern theatre. The subsequent murder of the inspector in real life only served to thicken the soup of circumstantial evidence, claim and counter-claim. The play uses the device of a certified lunatic who, having infiltrated the police station, strips away the layers of pretence, lies and fabricated evidence by impersonating an anarchist, a judge and a bishop, and ironically subjects the culpable to a travesty form of cross-examination in which defence becomes more and more hilariously impossible; the policemen sink deeper and deeper into the swamp of their own making. Franco Quadri writes:

> This is an example of great theatre, in which the wild inventiveness of the writing blends harmoniously with the aims of counter-information and succeeds in having a concrete effect on consolidating public opinion in a way one rarely sees happen.[14]

As we have seen from its impact, *Anarchist* thrives after twenty years; popular trust of the forces of law and order has not increased down the years; nor has the comic device of the maniac (here *comic*, but with many other previous associations) lost its appeal as one of the classic roles for the modern actor. Its secret, perhaps, is that the clown-as-madman unites many themes – twentieth-century fascination with impersonation, the actor/role dualism, Freud, Pirandello, Stanisłavsky, disguise, identity, and so on – in a way that is as compellingly universal as Fo's *guillare*/raconteur in *Mistero Buffo*. Descended from medieval *jongleur*, Harlequin, Chaplin, Fo's own *Poer nano*, he strikes a universal chord. If *Mistero Buffo* is diminished in other hands than Fo's ('hands' used advisedly: Fo is the champion of mime after Lecoq, from whom he learned so much), and *Anarchist*'s message has been somewhat muted in some adaptations, nevertheless, these two plays are now central to the modern canon of committed European theatre.

After two such masterpieces, one might expect a downward trajectory, but Fo's vigour has scarcely diminished since 1970; he has written plays in support of Palestinian liberation (*Fedayin*, 1972), the South American ideological scene (*Gerra di populo in Cile*, The People's War in Chile, 1973), generating the usual opposition, censorship or police intervention and the (intended) debate. Dario Fo was arrested and briefly imprisoned in Sardinia; Franca Rame was abducted and beaten up in Milan; they have suffered harassment of all descriptions. *Can't Pay, Won't Pay* (1974) faced the issue of civil disobedience (hard-pressed workers steal from supermarkets) of which Joel Schecter wrote: 'Rabelais's grotesquery has given way to antic transformations more suitable for an age of inflation, shoplifting and miracle salad dressing'.[15] Both this and *Clacson, trombette e pernacchi* (Trumpets and Raspberries, 1981) ran successfully in London's West End, the latter using a classic personality-doubling technique to pillory an industrial baron (Fiat's Agnelli) and related social and political issues.

Since 1970 the *Mistero Buffo* one-man-show formula has been built on with the *Storia della tigre* (Tale of a Tiger, 1978) and *Fabulazzo osceno* (The Obscene Fable, 1982) and the work of Fo and Rame has taken in the place of woman in society with the highly topical *Coppia apertu* (Open Couple, 1983), which exposes the double standard in male pretensions and asserts the equality of the sexes. Franca Rame's *Female Parts* ('hers' in the sense that she performs alone) has also had an impact as great as that of Fo's classics, as we have seen, with productions continuing throughout the world. It has caught the imagination of society since 1977 and mirrors very contemporary preoccupations with feminism and the modern emancipation of women. From the first performance of these monologues to this day, the detachment, hard-edged polemical thrust and ideological commitment of the pieces have built a permanent place for them in the repertoire of the actress, above all in Western Europe, but increasingly also in countries where the centuries-old yoke of male domination continues unabated. Significantly, Britain has seen 21 separate performances of *Female Parts* (plus two more-or-less clandestine ones that I am aware of!).

Since 1985 Fo and Rame have continued their activities in various fields, now including television. She is an undisputed leader of feminist theatre in Europe; he is offered a university chair in Rome; *Harlequin* (1985) crowned a workshop/partnership with the university of Rome and actually builds on remarkable similarities between Fo's performance style (audience feedback, dialogue with spectators, universal 'language' and so on) and the improvisation and masks of the *commedia dell'arte* tradition. Increasingly, Fo directs: opera in Holland, Molière in Paris. He performs 'retrospective' collections of his pieces, and has even returned to film. The post-performance debates are perhaps fewer, the harassment less pronounced in more tolerant times, and he has had to face the irony that the sheer theatricality of his shows continues to win converts, even among those who lack his political courage. The most recent show, *Il Papa e la strega* (The Pope and the Witch, 1989) investigates the growing international drug problem, linking it to predictably capitalist interests and making use of a gently satirical portrayal of Pope John Paul II (so there are opportunities to satirize Vatican attitudes to abortion, birth control and so on) with a wealth of topical allusions and devices as 'theatrical' as any in the past. Indispensable professional partners in performance as well as in the writing and revision process, sharing a dedication to the theatre of commitment through comedy: the solidarity of Dario Fo and Franca Rame looks set to continue.

As we go to press, a new *Anarchist* in English has toured thirty-three British theatres, sold out at the National, and won 'Best Comedy Actor' for Alan Cumming who played the maniac, testifying to an enduring vitality. *The Pope and the Witch* transfers to the West End from Leeds. Eduardo received an honorary degree from Birmingham University shortly before his death; and Eugenio Barba returned again to the Cardiff Centre for Performance Research in September 1990 with Odin's *Talabot*. From our standpoint in Britain, it is these three names (Eduardo, Fo and Barba) who have done most in the recent past and present to give Italian theatre a European and world dimension, or cross-cultural perspective.

NOTES

1 Suzanne Cowan, 'Theatre, politics and social change in Italy since the Second World War', in *Theatre Quarterly*, 7/27, 1977: 29.
2 Quoted ibid.: 30, from F. Quadri, *Il rito perduto*, Turin, 1973: 35. See also Pasolini, 'Manifesto per un nuovo teatro', in *Nuovi Argomenti*, 9, 1968: 3–19.
3 Ferdinando Taviani, '1964–1980: da un osservatorio particolare [E. Barba]', in F. Cruciani and C. Falletti, eds, *Civiltà teatrale nel XX secolo*, Bologna, 1986: 351–84 (here my translation, but this important essay is also in E. Barba, *The Floating Islands*, Holstebro, 1979).
4 Cruciani and Falletti, *Civiltà*: 359; and see now Eugenio Barba and Nicola Savarese, *Dictionary of Theatre Anthropology*, London, 1991.
5 Quoted in A. Attisani, ed., *Enciclopedia del Teatro del '900*, Milan, 1980: 261.
6 In E. Barba, *Beyond the Floating Islands*, Holstebro, 1986: 193–212.
7 Cowan, 'Theatre, politics and social change': 34.
8 Mario B. Mignone, *Il Teatro di Eduardo de Filippo*, Rome, 1974: 123.
9 Quoted ibid.: 272.
10 Information derived from Piero Sciotto, ed., *Il teatro di Dario Fo e Franca Rame: rappresentazioni all'estero dal 1960 al 1989*, Milan, 1990.
11 Quoted by Tony Mitchell, ed., *File on Dario Fo*, London, 1989: 19.
12 ibid.: 37.
13 Irving Wardle in *The Times*, 5 Jan. 1984.
14 Quoted in *File on Dario Fo*: 45.
15 Quoted ibid.: 58.

BIBLIOGRAPHY

General

Of far-reaching importance throughout and beyond the confines of this book, is the widely respected *Enciclopedia dello spettacolo*, whose *Aggiornamento* volume for 1955–65, Rome, 1966, just comes within the scope of this volume. We now have in addition Antonio Attisani, ed., *Enciclopedia del Teatro del '900*, 1980, excellent for all major figures, trends and movements up to 1980, all of which receive concise but full summary treatment. Central to this chapter was Ferdinando Taviani, '1964–1980: da un osservatorio particolare' (the standpoint is Barba's Odin Teatret), in F. Cruciani and C. Falletti, eds, *Civiltà teatrale nel XX secolo*, Bologna, 1986: 351–84. This whole volume is of interest and contains one of the most up-to-date bibliographies to about 1985.

In English (apart from Dario Fo) there is little, though a good general survey is S. Cowen, 'Theatre, politics and social change in Italy since the Second World War', in *Theatre Quarterly*, 7/27, 1977: 25–38, which takes the story up to the late 1970s, while (for Milan) there is a study of the early 1980s: T. A. Joscelyne, '*Gesto o testo?* The crisis of the Milanese avant-garde in the early 1980s', *Theatre Research International*, 9/3, 1984: 50–8.

See also Barba's own *The Floating Islands*, Holstebro, 1979.

Specialized

For the journal which he edits (*Sipario*) and his books, the primacy in this area is held by F. Quadri whose four titles comprehensively cover 1960–80: *L'Avanguardia teatrale in Italia* (covering 1960–76), Turin, 2 vols, 1977; *La politica dei registi* (covering 1967–79), 2 vols, Milan, 1980; *Il teatro degli anni '70: Tradizione e ricerca*, Turin, 1982; and *Invenzione di un teatro diverso*, Turin, 1984.

For the story into the 1980s, see, for example, Oliviero Ponte di Pino, *Il nuovo teatro italiano*, Milan, 1988.

For the roots of much that was to emerge (only in its postscript about our period), see Claudio Meldolesi, *Fondamenti del teatro italiano*, Florence, 1984.

For 'New Writing' in general (with useful summaries of the plays themselves), Giovanni Antonelli, *Storia del teatro italiano del novecento*, Rome, 1986.

For Eugenio Barba and the Odin Teatret, see Ferdinando Taviani, ed., *Il libro dell'Odin: il teatro laboratorio di Eugenio Barba*, second edn, Milan, 1981; on Eduardo de Filippo, see F. Di Franco, *Il teatro di Eduardo*, Rome/Bari, 1975; on Dario Fo, perhaps alone in his generation in having secured a reputation and following in the English-speaking world, see Tony Mitchell, *Dario Fo, People's Court Jester*, London, second edn, 1986, and David Hurst, *Dario Fo and Franca Rame*, London, 1989.

8

SPAIN

Gwynne Edwards

No discussion of Spanish theatre since 1960 can begin without reference to events a quarter of a century before, for the triumph of Franco at the end of the bitterly contested Civil War (1936–9) marked the beginning of a political and artistic repression that would last until his death in 1975. The cold-blooded murder of Federico García Lorca by Franco sympathizers in the summer of 1936 can be seen, indeed, as highly prophetic of the years of intolerance that lay ahead for all writers and theatre exponents other than those who toed the official line. On the one hand, the political, economic and social conditions of the Franco years, with their grinding poverty and social injustice, were those most calculated to inspire drama, in particular a drama of protest and opposition. On the other hand, a ruthless official censorship, lack of resources and a virtual absence of opportunity were the realities with which prospective dramatists were obliged to contend. Given these circumstances, the fact that so much drama of such high quality was written and performed in Spain, not least between 1960 and 1975, is quite remarkable.

COMMERCIAL THEATRE

The commercial theatre, as in most of Europe, followed its traditional path, providing entertainment for relatively well-heeled audiences. Lorca's complaint in 1934 that 'a man, by the mere fact of having a few millions', was able to become 'a censor of plays and arbiter of the theatre', pointed to a situation that was much the same in 1960 – the ownership of most of the theatres of Madrid and Barcelona, the two main centres of theatre, by impresarios who, in the interests of profit, took no risks and so discouraged theatrical experiment.[1] A glance at the Madrid theatre scene on 15 November 1960, for example, reveals the prevalence of comedies and well-established plays, some Spanish, some foreign. Tejedor's *Operación divorcio* (Operation Divorce) ran at the Teatro Goya and another of his plays, *Las mujeres y yo* (Women and Me), publicized as 'lots of fun', at the Teatro Fuencarral. Foreign plays included Colette's *Cheri* at the Teatro Reina Victoria. Ten years later the situation had barely changed, for the programme on 15 November 1970 included at the Teatro Marquina Leonard Gershe's *Las mariposas son libres* (Butterflies Are Free), described as 'a steamy piece of eroticism revealing the serious problem of today's youth', and, amongst well-known foreign plays, Coward's *Private Lives*. Needless to say, there was no serious new work of any kind.

After Franco's death the situation changed only in the sense that much of the entertainment provided by the commercial theatres acquired a pronounced sexual emphasis. In an article in 1978, for example, Javier Maquea drew attention to the prevalence of nude shows and reviews in Madrid and noted the failure of the impresarios both to retain their old, middle-class bourgeois audience and, confronted by the challenge of television, cinema, and other leisure activities, to appeal to a new, younger, more liberated body of theatregoers.[2] The 1978 season in Madrid included, for instance, such titillations as *Enséñame tu piscina* (Show Me Your Swimming-Pool), *Pijama de seda* (Silk Pyjamas), *Mi marido no funciona* (My Husband Doesn't Function), *¿Con quién me acuesto esta noche?* (Who Shall I Sleep With Tonight?), *Sexorama, Locuras eróticas* (Erotic Follies) and *¡Oh, Calcutta!* If in the new Spain it was believed that the commercial theatre could survive on a diet of soft porn, the evidence reveals a progressive decline in audiences that has continued until today and is leading to the closure of more and more theatre buildings. A recent article in the daily newspaper, *El País*, notes the actual or imminent closure in Madrid of the Fuencarral, Larra, Martín, Alfil, Beatriz and Monumental, many of them important and elegant theatres in years gone by.[3] In many respects and much to the delight of their opponents, the commercial theatre and the impresario would appear in 1988 to have had their finest hour.

NEW WRITING

As far as new writing was concerned, 1960 proved to be a crucial year, though its relevance cannot be fully appreciated without reference to the previous decade and the emergence of the two most significant

dramatists of the last forty years: Antonio Buero Vallejo (1916–)
and Alfonso Sastre (1926–).[4] Buero Vallejo's *Historia de una
escalera* (The Story of a Stairway) and Sastre's *Escuadra hacia la
muerte* (The Condemned Squad), presented in Madrid in 1949 and
1953 respectively, marked in effect the beginning of a genuine serious
post-Civil War drama whose influence on the writers of the 1960s and
1970s was to be profound. *Historia de una escalera*, set in a tenement
building in post-Civil War Madrid, portrays the lives of four Madrid
families over a period of thirty years and sets their dreams and
aspirations against the depressing reality of the poverty and lack of
opportunity that constitutes their lives. *Escuadra hacia la muerte* is the
story of five delinquent soldiers and a corporal, punished for their
crimes by being sent on a suicide mission at the beginning of the Third
World War. In an effort to obtain their freedom, the soldiers murder
the dictatorial corporal only to be defeated by the consequences of their
action and the general circumstances in which they find themselves.
Both plays announce a preoccupation with the problems of contemporary Spain in relation to the individual that would become a
dominant feature of all serious Spanish drama for the next thirty years.
In terms of style and technique too they point the way ahead. *Historia
de una escalera* reveals the continuity of the Spanish naturalistic
tradition from the short plays of Lope de Rueda and Cervantes in the
sixteenth century to the more modern so-called *género chico* with its
emphasis on popular types and low-life society. At the same time the
play's naturalism is balanced by a marked symbolism, as in the case of
the stairway that the characters repeatedly climb and descend, which
reveals the influence of Ibsen in particular on Buero's early work.
Escuadra hacia la muerte is also broadly naturalistic but has too a
strong element of symbolism and expressionism. Towards the end of
the 1950s the work of both dramatists would also become strongly
influenced by the theories of Brecht. It is within the broad context of
these influences that much, if not all, serious Spanish drama of the last
three decades has to be considered.

The success of Buero's *Historia de una escalera* in 1949 – 187
consecutive performances at the Teatro Español in Madrid – and the
suppression of *Escuadra hacia la muerte* in 1952 after only three
performances at the Teatro María Guerrero, reveal both a particular
contrast between the two dramatists and a more general problem
posed by the dictatorship itself. In general, Buero's plays were
powerful but often oblique comments on Franco's Spain, while
Sastre's approach was essentially confrontational. In consequence, it

was Buero who achieved by far the greater success, even in the commercial theatre, and Sastre who was constantly gagged. But it cannot be disputed that he proved to be the more inspirational figure for the younger writers of the early 1960s.

The publication in 1960 of Sastre's manifesto of the Grupo de Teatro Realista (Realist Theatre Group) proved, indeed, a key moment for the group of writers who emerged at that time and came to be known collectively as the 'Generación Realista' (Realist Generation).[5] The manifesto advocated, above all, a theatre of 'social realism', which meant for Sastre himself a theatre which is concerned with the issues of freedom, responsibility, guilt and salvation; which embodies those issues in dramatic characters who, as is often the case in the work of Arthur Miller, are not isolated individuals but part of the society in which they live; which is in its general thrust ethical rather than artistic, the latter serving the former; and which, above all, sets out to overturn the status quo.

The term 'Generación Realista' was given by the theatre critic, José Monleón, in an article of 1962 to a group of writers, influenced by Buero Vallejo and Sastre, whose work belongs to the late 1950s and early 1960s and who, in particular, made a great impact between 1960 and 1965.[6] They include Ricardo Rodríguez Buded (1928–), Lauro Olmo (1922–), José Martín Recuerda (1925–), Carlos Muñiz (1927–) and José María Rodríguez Méndez (1925–). Until this time, Monleón observed, only Buero and Sastre were, as dramatists, concerned with the contemporary social reality of Spain. Now a number of writers shared that concern and were linked by certain common features of their work: (1) the assumption of a moral position in relation to current social and political problems; (2) a belief that theatre has the power to move and influence emotionally and intellectually; and (3) the desire to create theatre that is 'popular' in the sense that it deals with ordinary men and women of the working or lower middle class, including the unemployed and the emigrant worker. In terms of style and technique there were, of course, important differences between the writers in question, but in broad terms the nature of their subject matter demanded naturalism, or naturalism injected with a degree of expressionism or even the grotesque. As far as influences were concerned, it is worth noting that in general the impact of twentieth-century European theatre was denied. Rodríguez Méndez, for example, has expressed a positive dislike of Brechtian theatre, and has been echoed in that view by Lauro Olmo and Martín Recuerda. Similarly, Artaud, Arrabal and

Peter Weiss have been described as having little relevance. Of European dramatists it was an older generation – Chekhov, Hauptmann, Ibsen, Strindberg – that was approved of. In addition, American dramatists of the 1950s, in particular Arthur Miller, were considered to deal with the social themes close to the hearts of the Generación Realista and to do so in a style which they found appropriate. But above all it was the strong, broadly naturalistic Spanish tradition from the sixteenth century to the present day which they all proclaimed as their real source of inspiration: *La Celestina*, the theatre of Lope de Vega, the picaresque novel, the nineteenth-century realist novelist Pérez Galdós, and, amongst twentieth-century dramatists, Carlos Arniches, Ramón del Valle-Inclán and Lorca.[7] Two points need to be made here. First, if the assumption of naturalism in the 1960s seems somewhat old-fashioned, the truth is that the writers in question used it in their own way. Second, the fact that they dismissed as irrelevant to their needs the theatre of major European figures does not mean, necessarily, that their influence was not felt. Brecht, as has been pointed out, had a significant effect on the work of Buero Vallejo and Sastre from the early 1960s and would prove influential in relation to the other dramatists as they in turn moved away from the naturalistic plays of the early 1960s to the subsequent treatment of historical subjects.

Carlos Muñiz's *El tintero* (The Ink-Well, 1962) and Lauro Olmo's *La camisa* (The Shirt, 1962) can be taken as examples of the themes and style of the generation. The action of *La camisa* is set in a poor, run-down area of Madrid and focuses on the struggle for survival of some of its inhabitants, in particular Juan, who is unemployed, and his wife, Lola. In a desperate attempt to improve their fortunes, she emigrates to Germany in search of work – a common enough practice in the Spain of the 1950s – while Juan, refusing to be driven out and so acknowledge failure, remains to face a hopeless future. The world of *El tintero* is that of the office where Crock, a humble clerk, struggles to earn a meagre living. Refusing to sacrifice his individuality and become, like his fellow-workers, a mere automaton, blindly accepting authority, he is ruthlessly mocked, humiliated and finally driven to suicide.

In style *La camisa*, with its run-down buildings, working-class characters and colloquial language, is a good example of the naturalism of many of the plays of the early 1960s.[8] But it is a naturalism that, far from being merely photographic or decorative, penetrates beneath the surface appearance of things to reveal the painful reality of despair and hopelessness that dominates people's lives. The influence of Buero Vallejo's *Historia de una escalera* and the long tradition of Spanish naturalism that lies behind it is very clear. *El tintero*, on the other hand, reveals a strong element of the grotesque, which in Spain may be traced to Francisco de Quevedo, Goya and, above all, as far as theatre is concerned, the technique of 'systematic distortion' practised by Ramón del Valle-Inclán in his plays of the 1920s;[9] and if European influence is admitted, the impact of Kafka, Expressionism and the Absurd is also evident in the black humour and the machine-like, dehumanized characters who inhabit the world of this play. Naturalism and the grotesque, frequently interwoven, are thus important features of the plays of social protest of the early 1960s, and many of them share too the notion of the 'closed space' – an enclosed physical setting, be it a room, an office, a tenement, a run-down neighbourhood – which suggests the absence of hope and opportunity of those who live there.[10] In general, however, these are plays that present the social and moral problems of contemporary Spain without openly attacking the dictatorship.

It goes without saying that the dramatists of the Generación Realista achieved little public success. Productions of their plays, as in the case of *La camisa* and *El tintero*, had to contend with a hostile censorship and a largely disinterested theatre-going public. Consequently, productions were often small-scale and non-professional, and runs were short. It was little wonder that, in the course of the 1960s, these writers should come to regard themselves as having been effectively silenced.[11]

BRECHT AND THE TREATMENT OF HISTORY

Another important trend in the drama of the 1960s, and extending into the 1970s, concerns the treatment of Spanish history. In the years just before and after the Civil War dramatists like José María Pemán had written historical plays that were intended to extol traditional virtues, falsifying history for political ends: *Cisneros* (1934), *Metternich* (1942). The only real exceptions to this were plays like Lorca's *Mariana Pineda* (1925), which dealt with the subject of liberal opposition to Ferdinand VII in the nineteenth century, and Rafael Alberti's powerful *Noche de Guerra en el Museo del Prado* (Night Attack on the Prado Museum, 1956), in which the atrocities of the Napoleonic invasion of Spain, so vividly depicted by Goya, were linked to the first aerial attack on Madrid by Franco's nationalist forces. In the 1960s, however, dramatists began to explore the potential of the historical play in a much more sustained way, believing, perhaps, not only that the past was a mirror for the present, but also that it afforded opportunities for making statements about the present which, being oblique, might circumvent censorship. In a consideration of this important trend Brecht was, of course, a key figure.

For Buero Vallejo, whose familiarity with Brechtian theory stemmed from the late 1950s, theatre demanded audience involvement and the awakening of strong emotions. The effect of alienation, with its attendant sense of critical awareness on the part of the spectator, is therefore balanced in Buero's historical plays by a degree of audience participation which varies from one play to another. *Las Meninas*, premièred in 1960, deals with events surrounding the painting of Velázquez's famous picture, in particular with the accusation, brought against him by his enemies, of immorality and disloyalty to the King, and Velázquez's denunciation of the corruption of the Court and the ills of Spain. On the one hand, there are clever Brechtian elements: the framing of the action by two narrators; direct address to the audience; the creation of a stage within a stage; and the breaking of illusion through moments of deliberate theatricality. On the other hand, there are many moments of powerful emotion involving love, grief, jealousy and anger, which ensure audience involvement, in particular with Velázquez, and allow it not merely to judge the events but also to be moved deeply by them.[12]

Indeed, in *El sueño de la razón* (The Sleep of Reason), premièred ten years later, the balance has shifted quite significantly towards audience involvement at the expense of distancing. As its title indicates, the play is concerned with the life and times of Goya, his state of mind in the years of the so-called 'Black Paintings', and his vision of Spain as a country inhabited and ruled by monsters and demons. While Brechtian elements are still in evidence, the most striking technical feature of the play is Buero's use of the 'immersion effect'.[13] The audience is made, by means of a series of brilliant dramatic strokes, to share both Goya's deafness and his vision of the world in which he lives: characters shape their words but make no sound or rage inaudibly, and normal human sounds become in Goya's head the cackling of hens or the braying of donkeys. The audience sees the Spain of Ferdinand VII through Goya's eyes as grotesque, and it is made too to feel his fear and disgust. The separation of stage and auditorium, allowing for critical judgement, is thus constantly bridged, the stage transformed into a mirror in which we see our own grotesque reflection. In its richer mix of influences – not merely Brecht but also the grotesque and the Absurd – the play is characteristic of the serious drama of the period. On the other hand, Buero's success in the theatre was never shared by his contemporaries. *Las Meninas*, for example, opened on 9 December 1960, at the Teatro Español in Madrid and ran for 260 performances, an even longer run than *Historia de una escalera* eleven years earlier.

The post-Brechtian thrust of the mid-1960s is exemplified too by Alfonso Sastre's *La sangre y la ceniza: Diálogos de Miguel Servet* (Blood and Ash: Dialogues of Michael Servet), written between 1962 and 1965 but not performed in Franco's lifetime.[14] It puts into practice Sastre's notion of *tragedia compleja* ('complex tragedy') in which the traditional Aristotelian catharsis should be simultaneously the recognition or assumption of a moral position, and the process of distancing should also become an identification.[15] Consisting of a prologue, three acts of eight, five and four scenes respectively, and an epilogue, the play deals with the life of the sixteenth-century Spanish doctor and philosopher, Miguel Servet, whose writings incurred the wrath of the Inquisition, who fled from Spain, and who was finally burned at the stake by the followers of Calvin. On the one hand, Sastre distances his audience. In this respect scenes are self-contained and are introduced by a kind of chapter-heading, reminiscent of the fiction of Cervantes or the picaresque. This sense of Brechtian distancing is also accompanied by devices of alienation drawn from the traditions of the grotesque and the theatre of cruelty: the anti-heroic presentation of the protagonist, who is small, pale, thin, limping and often cowardly; the use of puppets at given moments; and the wearing of masks and hoods by the committee which condemns Servet to death. On the other hand, the sense of audience involvement is often very strong: actors are placed in the auditorium; Servet delivers a sermon from the stalls; the police enter through the aisles; loudspeakers transmit cries and screams; and Servet's anti-heroic character gives way to a moving defiance. And, finally, the relevance of past to present is established by the introduction of Nazi salutes and frequent references to torture and intellectuals in hiding. For Sastre, then, that awakening of social conscience which inspires revolutionary action can be achieved only by a form of drama that combines a critical awareness with emotional involvement and therefore goes beyond the theatre of Brecht.

Finally, under this heading, José Martín Recuerda's *Las arrecogías del beaterio de Santa María Egipcíaca* (The Women Prisoners of the

Convent of Santa María Egipcíaca), written in 1970, banned under Franco, and finally performed in 1977, also merits consideration. Like Lorca more than forty years earlier, Martín Recuerda takes as his subject the persecution, imprisonment and execution of the nine-teenth-century liberal heroine, Mariana Pineda, but his use of the stage in this re-creation of Spanish history could not be more different. The play's subtitle, *Fiesta española* (Spanish Festival), points to the spectacle and atmosphere that the dramatist seeks to create, but in this respect his most striking innovation is the transformation of the entire theatre into the location of the *fiesta*. As the audience arrives, the presence of actors in the auditorium, singing and distributing flowers, creates an immediate sense of involvement. The bridge between the auditorium and the stage is established literally by the fact that the theatre aisles extend onto the stage itself. When the action of the play begins, flamenco song and dance creates a strong sense of identification between the actors and the public, and this is intensified from time to time when actors perform their songs and dances in the aisles, while others perform them simultaneously on the stage. The sense of horror and disgust awakened by the persecution of a nineteenth-century liberal becomes in effect some-thing that is felt and shared by Spaniards living in the shadow of another dictatorship.[16] In short, if Brechtian influence had been strong in Buero's *Las Meninas* in 1960, it is weak here. The treatment of history in the drama of the 1960s and 1970s reveals thus both a constant modification and weakening of Brechtian theory. This is hardly surprising, given the emotional nature of Spaniards and the strong feelings awakened by the Franco oppression.

OTHER EUROPEAN INFLUENCES

The silencing of so many dramatists in the 1960s and early 1970s meant that younger writers had little or no immediate source of inspiration. Their natural reaction, therefore, was to turn to European models, and the work of this new generation of writers, the so-called Nuevo Teatro Español (New Spanish Theatre), is distinguished by elements drawn from 'epic' theatre, the Absurd, the theatre of cruelty, metatheatre and the 'happening', as well as from earlier Spanish dramatists, principally Valle-Inclán, who wrote in a similar vein.[17] The Absurd, dispensing with logical and coherent plot development, argument and characterization, clearly proved attractive to writers for whom the society in which they lived and attempted to work had no apparent logic. The continuing influence of Brecht is evident too, though again dramatic treatments of historical subjects can be seen to mix Brechtian and other elements in a generally free-ranging style. Needless to say, the problems in relation to performance remained: on the one hand, a watchful censorship up to the time of Franco's death; on the other, a lack of opportunity for work that was essentially non-commercial.

Post Mortem, by Luis Matilla (1939–   ), was written in 1970 and reveals the clear impact of the Absurd. A young man and a young woman, who have lost father and mother respectively, discover that for the undertaker death has become both a way of life and a source of profit. They attempt to bury the bodies in free ground only to discover that the entire country is slowly being purchased by the undertakers. The theme of the play is, of course, the slow asphyxiation of the rebellion of the young in contemporary Spain, and the triumph of a prevailing order which itself makes no sense. The influence of the Absurd is to be seen in the basic situation, the dehumanized figure of the undertaker and the mad logic for which he stands.

Jerónimo López Mozo (1942–   ) exemplifies both the anger of the younger Spanish dramatists and, in *Guernica* and *Anarchía 36*, written in 1969 and 1971 respectively, a much more direct treatment of Spanish history than most dramatists dared contemplate. *Guernica*, drawing on multi-media techniques such as sound-effects and photographs flashed on screens, is an attempt to re-create in the audience the emotions of the inhabitants of Guernica during the bombing of 1937. *Anarchía 36*, less ambitious technically, utilizes factual sources and real speeches, presents the conflict within the Republican forces more objectively, and in the end is a more effective and moving play. As a dramatist, López Mozo is a good example of the eagerness of the writers of his generation to experiment, and of the way in which by the 1970s the treatment of history in the theatre owed less to Brechtian theory.

INDEPENDENT THEATRE GROUPS

Independent theatre groups began to appear in Spain in the mid- to late 1960s, were largely political in character, and comprised left-wing university radicals and professional actors disillusioned with the poor quality of the commercial theatre. While the latter, as well as the serious dramatists previously discussed, were mainly Madrid- and

Barcelona-based, the independent groups were essentially regional: Els Joglars, Els Comediants, La Claca (Catalonia); Tábano, Los Goliardos (Madrid); La Cuadra and Esperpento (Seville); Akelarre (Bilbao); La Carátula (Alicante); and so on. Moreover, the law of censorship, which was invoked to prevent them indulging in political theatre by banning street performances and allowing a maximum of two performances in any one location, had the effect of transforming them into itinerant groups and of causing independent theatre to flourish throughout Spain.[18]

In its general character independent theatre was essentially popular, its intention to reach audiences who did not normally go to the theatre at all. Its themes reflected the condition of contemporary Spain, while performance style was influenced both by the kind of audience it sought to reach and the censorship it had to circumvent. In one way or another all the independent groups reflect these factors, as the work of Tábano and Els Joglars suggests.

Tábano was founded in 1968 by Juan Margallo and disillusioned professional actors, and since its purpose was to bite and enrage the establishment, took its name from the gadfly. *Castañuela 70* (Castanet 70), presented in 1970, was indeed the most successful popular left-wing show of the last years of the Franco regime. Taking as its targets the familiar sacred cows of traditionalist Spain – family life, religion and so on – and the country's increasing consumerism under Franco, the show was cast in the form of the traditional itinerant vaudeville, divided into a number of scenes and backed by a well-known group of musicians, Las Madres del Cordero. 'Reinar después de morir' ('To Reign after Death') is, for example, a scene intended to satirize the Spanish acceptance of the miseries of this world as a prelude to the pleasures of the next, and takes the format of the popular television show in which members of the public are chosen to appear as dead king or queen of the week. This week's winner, the deceased Doña Juana, is wheeled on by her delighted husband, Don Cosme; is invited to dance with the programme's presenter; and for her prize is placed in a jewel-studded coffin. Another scene, 'La caída del imperio romano' ('The Fall of the Roman Empire'), is an oblique satire on Franco's policy of allowing the United States to install military bases on Spanish soil. The Roman Empire is seen to be in decline through the influence of the USA. The Americans enter Rome in the person of Cianón, an expert in military strategy who worships the dollar and whose companion is Hippia, a flower-power pacifist whose real objectives are money, drugs and sex.

After its two permitted performances, *Castañuela 70* was taken up, quite unusually, by the Teatro de la Comedia, a commercial theatre in the centre of Madrid, where it ran for over a month and was seen by 52,000 people before it was banned. Further problems with the censorship led Tábano to a tour of South America in 1973. It presented another hugely successful show, *Cambio de tercio* (Change of Regiment), in 1975 after Franco's death, and continued its vigorous work until 1984.

Els Joglars, founded by Albert Boadella in 1962, is one of Spain's most celebrated independent groups. Its early work, which was not especially political, owed much to the mime tradition and was not text-based, and when, after 1968, a political emphasis appeared in such pieces as *Diari* (Newspaper), *Cruel ubris* (Great Cruelty) and *Mary d'ous* (Mary of the Eggs), the same techniques were central to the performance. A good example is the torture scene in *Cruel ubris* which is given the form of a circus act. The two secret policemen who torture the prisoner have a female assistant in shimmering costume. A drum-roll precedes the delivery of blows, after which the girl steps forward, inviting applause. When the prisoner has been punched and kicked, the smiling assistant lights matches placed beneath his nails. By means of such techniques the company largely avoided trouble with the censors, for the use of mime, circus and vaudeville elements led them to believe there was no overt political intention. Indeed, it was after Franco's death that real problems surfaced. In 1977 *La torna* (The Weight) attacked the military in no uncertain fashion, the show was stopped and several of the group arrested. Only after the eventual intervention of the Spanish King were they finally pardoned.

The mid-1970s in general, however, saw independent theatre in a state of crisis, especially in Madrid. Between 1977 and 1978 the number of companies in the capital dwindled from seventeen to six as a result of their failure to obtain government support, despite the fact that between them they had produced 74 productions, given 15,000 performances, and been seen by 4 million people. Thus, a vigorous movement which for a decade had developed a practical, alternative and decentralized theatre, was in serious danger of extinction, ironically through the failure of a socialist government to support it. There were other reasons too, of course. As Guillermo Heras, one of Tábano's driving forces, noted in 1978, the end of the dictatorship had deprived the independent groups of their *raison d'être*.[19] Many were no longer prepared to tolerate the discomforts of constant touring and began to settle for a more comfortable form of theatre activity. In such circumstances it was inevitable both that the number of independent companies would decline and that the nature of the work of those that remained should be somewhat different.

AFTER FRANCO

While the death of Franco weakened independent theatre, it also had its effect on many of the serious writers previously discussed. On the one hand, those whose work had been suppressed finally saw it performed. On the other, the removal of the tyranny that gave them inspiration created different problems, and there was not, after 1975, a sudden flowering, either of the older or the newer writers. Indeed, a writer like Buero Vallejo found it difficult to scale, after 1975, the artistic heights he had previously achieved. The earlier discussion, indicating the extent to which the serious dramatists of the Franco years were 'political', suggests in turn that in the new democracy they required time to adjust. But in the last years of the decade, steps were at least being taken that pointed in new directions.

The most important included the introduction, on 1 April 1977, of a law permitting freedom of expression, and, on 27 January 1978, another which abolished the censorship of plays. Another important advance concerned the creation of the Ministerio de Cultura and, as part of it, the Dirección General de Teatro y Espectáculos (General Administration of Theatre and Spectacle). From this came the establishment in 1978 of the Centro Dramático Nacional (National Drama Centre), operating at the Teatro María Guerrero and the Sala Olimpia in Madrid, the former dedicated to the performance of established plays, the latter to new work. Since 1975 the number of theatre companies and organizations has grown rapidly: in Madrid, for example, the work of the Sala Cadarso; in Barcelona the Instituto de Teatro, the Sala Villaroel and the Regina. Again, youth theatre, seriously neglected under Franco, has begun to develop in various ways through the efforts of actors and teachers.[20] Worth mentioning in this respect is the Teatrejove, a company of young professional and semi-professional actors. Administered by the Fundación Shakespeare in Valencia, the company now has links with the National Youth Theatre of Great Britain and in 1987 presented their version of *Romeo and Juliet*, in Spanish, in London. It provides an example of the greater opportunities and the broader horizons that at last are becoming evident in Spanish theatre.

As far as the classics are concerned, Spain has not had, until the creation of the Centro Dramático Nacional in 1978, any kind of company or theatre remotely comparable to the National Theatre or the RSC. The performance of the great plays of the past – of Lope de Vega, Tirso de Molina and Calderón – as well as of more recent times – Ramón del Valle-Inclán, Lorca – depended largely therefore on individual directors and commercial theatres willing to present particular plays. The Madrid theatre seasons referred to previously – 1960 and 1970 – contained, for example, commercial productions of Spanish and foreign 'classics', from Lope de Vega's *La estrella de Sevilla* (The Star of Seville) to Zorrilla's *Don Juan Tenorio* and Chekhov's *The Cherry Orchard*. The early 1960s began to witness the first productions of Lorca's plays since his death: *Yerma* in 1961, *La casa de Bernarda Alba* in 1964; and in 1972 the famous and brilliant 'trampoline' production of *Yerma* by Victor García with Nuria Espert as the eponymous heroine. But such occasions were sporadic and it was not until after Franco's death that a more consistent policy emerged in relation to the performance of the classics. The Teatro María Guerrero, currently headed by Lluis Pascual, has produced in the last ten years the works of Spanish dramatists old and new – Cervantes, Galdós, Valle-Inclán, Lorca, Alberti – in a thoroughly modern and exciting style, culminating in the 1986–7 Lorca half-centenary celebrations and a memorable world première of *El público* (The Public), notable for its visual imagery, brilliant lighting and exciting choreography. The work of the Teatro Español, directed by Miguel Narros, is also significant.[21] During the Franco dictatorship this famous theatre, traditionally associated with the production of the Spanish classics, had been placed under the jurisdiction of the Ministry of Information and Tourism, and had lost both its freedom and much of its former glory. Destroyed by fire – curiously enough in the very year of Franco's death – it opened again in 1980, restored to the financial control of the municipality, and began a period of vigorous work which has included Calderón's *La vida es sueño* (Life is a Dream), Lope de Vega's *El castigo sin venganza* (Punishment Without Revenge), Lorca's *La casa de Bernarda Alba*, and Shakespeare's *A Midsummer Night's Dream* and *Julius Caesar*. In addition, in 1985, the Compañía Nacional de Teatro Clásico (National Company for Classical Theatre), directed by Alfonso Marsillach, was formed for the specific purpose of staging the Spanish classics, of which the production of *La Celestina* in the spring of 1988 was a notable example. Significantly, the company is based at the Teatro de la Comedia, one of Madrid's best-known commercial theatres of the past, providing an indication of the way in which in general subsidized theatres and organizations are finally ousting private enterprise.[22]

In terms of finance and organization, the commercial theatres of Madrid and Barcelona were controlled until fairly recently first by businessmen, and second by 'star' actors. In effect, the former rented the theatre to a company in which the influence of a big-name actor or actress usually proved decisive in relation to the company's repertoire, the latter depending less on quality than on the extent to which a part might allow the 'star' to display his or her talents. Companies were thus extremely hierarchical, actor- rather than director-orientated, leading Lorca to complain in 1934 of their inordinate influence over writers.[23] The situation has been slow to change, and so, of course, has the profit motive in determining not only the choice of plays but the frequency of performance. Until 1972 plays were performed twice nightly – at seven o'clock and half-past ten or eleven – for seven nights a week. Needless to say, such exploitation of actors hardly allowed them time to ponder on or polish their work.

In the Franco years new work of the kind already described was largely the province of small, unsubsidized groups – in part independent, in part university-based – producing and performing on a shoestring. Such was the production of Lauro Olmo's *La camisa* in Madrid in 1962 when it was presented in an important theatre, the Teatro Goya, by an independent group containing no big names. The other important writers of the period – Carlos Muñiz, Rodríguez Méndez, Martín Recuerda – were similarly denied the resources and publicity afforded by the commercial theatre, and suffered for the most part the consequences of having their work channelled into small-scale productions that did it less than justice. Thus the most vital and innovative theatre of the 1960s and early 1970s remained, in effect, marginalized.

The independent groups themselves provided, in terms of structure and finance, an alternative to the commercial theatre that could not be more marked. Most of the groups began as co-operatives in which directors, actors and designers enjoyed equality of status, and this applied to performance too, with writers acting and actors writing. In the Franco years the groups received no state support, surviving, like those on the London 'fringe', on takings at the box-office but simultaneously keeping prices down in order to build a popular audience. Needless to say, production costs were kept to a minimum,

Tábano's *Castañuela 70* costing a mere 10,000 pesetas (a little more than £60 in 1970).[24]

In the new democracy, with the commercial theatre in decline and state subsidy more in evidence, accusations have, of course, been made – of money wasted by the state on centres such as the Centro Dramático Nacional at the expense of smaller groups.[25] Yet it is true that in Spain today there are many smaller centres, like the Centro Cultural Galileo in Madrid, and smaller companies, like the Teatro de la Ribera in Saragossa, which are subsidized and do excellent work. And if the independent groups have declined in number and some survive unsubsidized, there are others, like La Cuadra de Sevilla, which are government-sponsored and able to take their work abroad.

CONCLUSIONS

This examination of Spanish drama since 1960 suggests quite clearly that the period falls into two distinct halves, the first up to, the second following, Franco's death, and that each is different from the other in terms of the social, political and economic forces that shaped the theatre in terms of its themes, its style and its relationship with its audience. The conclusion that emerges very clearly is that the changes that took place were almost entirely responses to the political climate.

During the dictatorship the issues with which almost all serious dramatists confronted their audiences were those directly connected with it: the lack of opportunity, the poverty and despair of the lower classes so vividly exemplified by Juan in Lauro Olmo's *La camisa* (1962), as well as the break-up of the family through his wife's departure in an effort to find work; or, as far as the lower middle classes are concerned, the need to submit unquestioningly to authority in order to prosper at work, as exposed in Carlos Muñiz's *El tintero* in the same year. In the early 1960s, as these and other plays suggest, contemporary subjects were presented in contemporary images. By the mid-1960s, although the issues were the same, the form in which they were presented was more historical: the persecution of a sixteenth-century intellectual in Sastre's *La sangre y la ceniza* (1965); the clash of liberal ideals and authoritarianism in the form of Goya and Ferdinand VII in Buero Vallejo's *El sueño de la razón* (1970); and the ruthless destruction of liberalism by tyranny in Martín Recuerda's *Las arrecogías del beaterio de Santa María Egipcíaca* (1970). In part the choice of historical subjects as a way of commenting upon the present was an attempt to circumvent censorship and to counteract the relative disinterest with which 'contemporary' plays were received, but the fact that two of the plays mentioned above were not performed until after Franco's death shows too how difficult it was for many of the dramatists of the 1960s to make their statements in any form on a public stage. As for independent groups, the work of Tábano and Els Joglars reveals essentially similar concerns presented in much more popular and immediately appealing forms. Curiously enough, although the restrictions controlling performances were extremely harsh, the success of independent groups in commenting on the contemporary scene was quite remarkable.

The dramatic change in the political climate after 1975 meant, clearly, that the dramatists whose work was so dependent on the circumstances of the dictatorship found themselves adrift, the very object of their opposition transformed into the freedoms for which they had fought for so long. Indeed, in the new democracy Spain has become the land of pornography, drug-abuse and muggings, a country where the old values, needing to be overturned to some extent, are in danger of being thrown away completely. Theoretically, this should be the material of the new drama, but new and significant dramatists have not appeared. The older dramatists, like Buero Vallejo, now 72, attempt to learn new but less effective tricks, or like Sastre, now 62, live in the Basque country, supporting the Basque cause.

The predominant style of the social drama of the early 1960s was, as we have seen, naturalistic: scenes of social deprivation and emotional despair re-created on the stage, placed before an audience for its contemplation.[26] The process was one in which suspension of disbelief was all-important, in which, as in *La camisa*, the audience's identification with the problems of the despairing Juan and his wife was complete. In this respect the re-creation on the stage of a physical world – of shabby, run-down houses or tenements – familiar to the audience had a sense of immediacy and impact from which its observers could not easily escape. One of the features common to these plays, the 'closed space' – be it room, house, tenement, neighbourhood or office – would have created in the audience of the play precisely that sense of 'no escape' experienced by the characters and would, hopefully, have stirred its social conscience. In particular, bourgeois theatre-goers had been accustomed in the past to seeing on the stage images of its own comfortable world. The experience of seeing 'how the other half lives' would, the dramatists hoped, prove both uncomfortable and disturbing. In practice, the bourgeoisie averted its eyes or avoided the plays, and the dramatists preached to the converted.

The immediacy and involvement of naturalism yielded by the mid-1960s to a stage–auditorium relationship involving greater critical judgement and a drama owing much to Brechtian ideas, though individual dramatists varied in the degree to which they practised them. The historical play, seen by dramatists as a means of drawing parallels with and commenting on contemporary issues, also required, of course, if this was to be achieved, a degree of collusion between dramatist and audience, a kind of intellectual rapport which naturalistic drama does not have or need. *Las Meninas* (1960) is an early example of this new relationship. The use of two narrators, the re-creation on the stage of settings and characters from the past, including those who figure in Velázquez's famous painting, create the sense of distance that allows the audience to observe and assess the action set before it. Part of it involves Velázquez's powerful attack on the moral deficiencies of those in power and their exploitation of a poor, suffering nation. The attack is specific, related to the seventeenth century, but delivered to an audience which experiences such ills in its own time. Moreover, the dramatist's presentation of Velázquez as a man of integrity and dignity is designed to make the audience warm to him and share his point of view. The sense that his words are equally applicable to contemporary Spain becomes a truth that, through that affinity with him, each member of the audience is invited to accept in the privacy of his own mind. Pure intellectual truth becomes personal conviction through a subtle manipulation of the stage–auditorium relationship.

In general, though, it was the need of dramatists to involve their audiences as strongly as naturalistic drama did that largely shape the treatment of history on the Spanish stage. In Sastre's *La sangre y la ceniza*, and more so in Martín Recuerda's *Las arrecogías*, it is less a question of the stage as stage than of the entire theatre – both stage and auditorium – merged in a total suspension of disbelief. Even before the action of *Las arrecogías* begins, the auditorium has become, through the presence of actors in it, an extension of the stage. Thereafter, the frequent spilling-over of the stage-action into the auditorium, combined with the use of familiar and emotive songs, creates between the actors and the audience a total sense of rapport, and thus of outrage at the on-stage events. The commitment of Spanish dramatists in the politically difficult Franco years was never one that allowed them or their audiences to make mere intellectual judgements.

In the case of independent theatre, collusion between the actors and the audience was frequently a vital factor. The shows themselves, often cast in the form of vaudeville and circus acts, were parodies of those people – Franco, the military – who ruled Spain, but because of censorship were forced to make their points indirectly. Words and actions therefore acquired double meaning, and a coded language developed between the actors and the audience.[27] As we have seen, a scene in Tábano's *Castañuela 70* is set in Rome, though the real object of attack is Franco's Spain; and in *Cambio de tercio* (1975) a musical melodrama set in the dictatorship of Primo de Rivera in the 1920s provided ample opportunity to comment on the parallel situation in the early 1970s. The censorship could do little to suppress such shows, though the audience understood their meaning perfectly.

In conclusion, the content and form of serious drama in Spain since 1960 have been shaped by political events – first by dictatorship, then by democracy – to a degree that makes it unique in Western Europe. But if this is a drama conditioned by national events, the point must be made that its appeal and quality go far beyond the boundaries of Spain, for if the dramatists responded to their own particular circumstances they did so in a voice and style that is universal.

NOTES

1 In an interview for the newspaper *El Sol* and quoted in *Federico García Lorca, Obras Completas* (Complete Works), ed. Arturo del Hoyo, 2nd edn, Madrid, Aguilar, 1955: 1630. The translation is my own.

2 In 'El empresario se confiesa', *Pipirijaina*, 7, 1978: 5–11.

3 See Eduardo Haro-Tecglen, 'Desaparecen las salas', *El País*, 2 May 1988: 30.

4 For detailed studies of these dramatists see Gwynne Edwards, *Dramatists in Perspective: Spanish Theatre in the Twentieth Century*, Cardiff, University of Wales Press, 1985; 172–247; R. L. Nicholas, *The Tragic Stages of Antonio Buero Vallejo*, Madrid, Estudios de Hispanófila, 1972; R. Doménech, *El teatro de Buero Vallejo*, Madrid, Editorial Gredos, 1973; F. Anderson, *Alfonso Sastre*, New York, Twayne Publishers, 1971.

5 The Grupo de Teatro Realista was founded by Sastre and José María de Quinto in 1960 and, as well as publishing its manifesto, presented three plays between January and March 1961. The 'Generación Realista' is, of course, a more general term used to describe the dramatists of the early 1960s whose aims were similar.

6 José Monleón, 'Nuestra Generación Realista', *Primer Acto*, 32, 1962: 1–3.

There are useful sections on the writers of the period in Francisco Ruiz Ramón, *Historia del teatro español Siglo XX*, Madrid, Cátedra, 1980, and María Pilar Pérez-Stansfield, *Direcciones de teatro español de posguerra*, Madrid, Ediciones Porrúa Turanzas, 1983. See too César Oliva, *Disidentes de la generación realista*, Murcia, Universidad de Murcia, 1979.

7 The dramatists of the Generación Realista used the word 'naturalistic' loosely to describe a tradition in Spanish literature in which the events and characters portrayed are of the people. The Lorca of *The House of Bernarda Alba*, for example, might be described as naturalistic in this particular sense, though the play is often highly stylized.

8 Others are Rodríguez Buded's *La madriguera* (The Den) and *Un hombre duerme* (A Man Sleeps) (both 1960); Martín Recuerda's *Las salvajes en Puente San Gil* (The Wild Women of Puente San Gil, 1963); and Rodríguez Méndez's *Los inocentes de Moncloa* (The Innocents of Moncloa, 1960).

9 Disillusioned by contemporary events, Valle-Inclán evolved a style in his plays of the 1920s that he considered suited to the expression of the grotesque reality of Spain: a style based on the kind of distortion achieved by viewing reality in a concave mirror. Only by such distortion, he believed, could the true reality of Spain be reflected.

10 The point is well made by Francisco Ruíz Ramón in his introduction to his edition of two plays of José Martín Recuerda, *Las salvajes en Puente San Gil; Las arrecogías del beaterio de Santa María Egipcíaca*, Madrid, Cátedra, 1985: 30-5.

11 The point is well made by Francisco Ruíz Ramón in *Historia del teatro español Siglo XX*: 441-6.

12 See Gwynne Edwards, *Dramatists in Perspective*: 196-7.

13 Buero's use of the 'immersion effect' in this and other plays has been examined at length by Victor Dixon, 'The "immersion-effect" in the plays of Antonio Buero Vallejo', in James Redmond, ed., *Drama and Mimesis*, Cambridge, Cambridge University Press, 1980: 113-37.

14 The play was finally presented in 1977.

15 For Sastre's ideas on the 'tragedia compleja', see chapter 9 of his book *La revolución y la crítica de la cultura*, Barcelona, Ediciones Grijalbo, 1971.

16 There is a useful study of the play by Francisco Ruíz Ramón in his introduction to his edition of two plays of José Martín Recuerda.

17 For informative accounts of the work of these writers, see Francisco Ruíz Ramón, *Historia del teatro español Siglo XX*: 527-71; María Pilar Pérez-Stansfield, *Direcciones del teatro español de posguerra*: 279-307; and George E. Wellwarth, *Spanish Underground Drama*, University Park and London, Pennsylvania State University Press, 1972.

18 Independent theatre is discussed at length by Francisco Ruíz Ramón, *Historia del teatro español Siglo XX*: 455-84. See too a recent study by Eugène vàn Erven, 'Spanish political theatre under Franco, Suárez and González', *New Theatre Quarterly*, IV, 1987: 32-52.

19 In '¿Resurrección o autopsia?', *Pipirijaina*, 10, 1978-9: 7-11.

20 Essays and discussions concerning recent developments are to be found in Luciano García Lorenzo, *Documentos sobre el teatro español contemporáneo*, Madrid; Sociedad General Española de Librería, 1981; and *Teatro*

español actual, a series of talks published by the Fundación Juan March, Madrid, Cátedra, 1977.

21 I am grateful to the administration of the Teatro Español for providing me with an account of the theatre's history: *El Teatro Español: de corral a coliseo*.

22 For a discussion of the place of the classics in contemporary Spain, see 'Debate sobre la representación actual de los clásicos', *Primer Acto*, 217, 1987: special supplement.

23 See n. 1.

24 See Eugène vàn Erven, 'Spanish political theatre under Franco': 40.

25 In particular, see Guillermo Heras, '¿Resurrección o autopsia?', and Alberto Miralles, '¡Es la guerra, más madera!', *Pipirijaina*, 7, 1978: 12–24.

26 Most studies of modern Spanish theatre have concentrated on theme and character and have neglected aspects of staging and the relationship of stage and auditorium. The latter is discussed, with particular reference to Valle-Inclán, Lorca, Alberti, Buero Vallejo and Sastre, in G. Edwards, *Dramatists in Perspective*.

27 See Eugène vàn Erven, 'Spanish political theatre under Franco': 34.

BIBLIOGRAPHY

General

Edwards, Gwynne, *Dramatists in Perspective: Spanish Theatre in the Twentieth Century*, Cardiff: University of Wales Press, 1985.

Halsey, Martha T. and Zatlin, Phyllis, eds, *The Contemporary Spanish Theatre*, New York, University Press of America, 1988.

Holt, Marion P., *The Contemporary Spanish Theatre (1949-1972)*, Boston, Twayne, 1975.

Oliva, Cesar, *Disidentes de la generación realista*, Murcia, Universidad de Murcia, 1979.

Pérez-Stansfield, María Pilar, *Direcciones de teatro español de posguerra*, Madrid, Ediciones Porrúa Turanzas, 1983.

Ruíz Ramón, Francisco, *Historia del teatro español Siglo XX*, Madrid, Cátedra, 1980.

Wellwarth, George E., *Spanish Underground Drama*, University Park and London, Pennsylvania State University Press, 1972.

Articles

Casa, Frank P., 'The theatre after Franco: the first reaction', *Hispanófila*, 66, 1979: 109–22.

Dixon, Victor, 'The "immersion-effect" in the plays of Antonio Buero Vallejo', in James Redmond, ed., *Drama and Mimesis*, Cambridge, Cambridge University Press, 1980: 113–37.

Halsey, Martha T., 'Dictatorship to democracy in the recent theater of Buero Vallejo (*La Fundación* to *Diálogo secreto*)', *Estreno*, 13, 1987: 9–15.

—— 'The violent dramas of Martín Recuerda', *Hispanófila*, 70, 1980: 71–93.

Giulano, William, 'Lauro Olmo and *La camisa*', *Revista de Estudios Hispánicos*, 5, 1971: 39–54.

Nicholas, Robert, 'The history plays. Buero Vallejo's experiment in dramatic expression', *Revista de Estudios Hispánicos*, 3, 1969: 281–93.

Norrish, Peter, 'Farce and ritual: Arrabal's contribution to modern tragic farce', *Modern Drama*, 26, 1983: 320–30.

O'Connor, Patricia W., 'Post-Franco theater: from limitation to liberty to license', *Hispanic Journal*, 1984: 55–73.

Pasquariello, Anthony M., 'Alfonso Sastre: dramatist in search of a stage', *Theater Annual*, 19, 1962: 19–26.

Pronko, Leonard C., 'The "revolutionary theatre" of Alfonso Sastre', *The Tulane Drama Review*, 5, 1960: 11–20.

Sheehan, Robert L., 'Censorship and Buero Vallejo's social consciousness', in *Aquila: Chestnut Hill Studies in Modern Languages and Literatures*, vol. 1, The Hague, Nijhoff, 1969: 121–37.

Zatlin, Phyllis, 'Theatre in Madrid: the difficult transition to democracy', *Theatre Journal*, 32, 1980: 459–74.

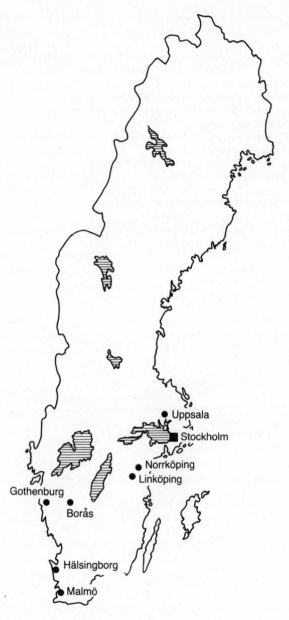

Figure 9.1 Cities with state-supported theatres in 1960 (adapted from Niklas Brunius, Göran O. Eriksson and Rolf Rembe, *Swedish Theatre*, Stockholm, 1967)

9

SWEDEN

Margareta Wirmark

A NEW CULTURAL POLICY

Compare Figures 9.1 and 9.2, two maps from 1960 and 1989, respectively. Thirty years ago there were only a few theatres in Sweden, almost all of them in the southern part. North of Uppsala no theatre company was to be found. Stockholm and Gothenburg, the two biggest cities, were also the dominant theatre centres. By the 1990s the situation has radically changed. Many local theatre institutions have been founded and they are no longer concentrated in the densely populated areas; they are situated all over the country. Today most of Sweden's twenty-four counties have a theatre of their own.

Discussion of cultural rights dates back to the early 1930s; thirty years later the discussion started anew. Since then a remarkable effort has been made to develop the possibility for every citizen to have access to culture independent of residence and parental background. In 1974 the Swedish Parliament passed an Act which came to influence not only the theatre but all aspects of the arts. This Act built on the ideas presented two years earlier in a White Paper, *Kulturrådets betänkande* (A New Cultural Policy). 'Cultural politics shall contribute to improvement of the social environment and promote greater equality.' This is the main goal of the new cultural policy. The starting-point for all this is a comprehensive view of the role culture plays – or should play – for each individual in society. Freedom of speech can also be interpreted as the individual's access to the languages of art. Each child has a right to learn how to play an instrument and to listen to music. Each individual has a right to use the language of theatre: to try to express himself or herself through drama and to see professionals perform. Culture is not only a way of

161

enriching the individual's life, it is also a means to critical examination of society.

Also in 1974 *Statens kulturråd* (the National Council for Cultural Affairs) was established. This Council is responsible for carrying out the policy based on the goals from 1974. Every Swedish institution – the National Board of Education, the National Board of Health and Welfare, and so on – shares in this responsibility. The National Council for Cultural Affairs also distributes state subsidies to theatre and other art-forms.

THE SWEDISH THEATRE NETWORK

Two of the theatre institutions still in existence date back to the eighteenth century when King Gustavus III established Dramaten and Operan, the two national theatres of Sweden. Dramaten (the Royal Dramatic Theatre) is situated in Stockholm and performs on six different stages. This theatre is for spoken drama. Operan (the Royal Opera) is also situated in Stockholm and has one stage. The Opera House gives both opera and ballet performances. These theatres are owned and subsidized by the state.

During the last thirty years a lot of new theatre institutions have been created. Regional and local theatres are now to be found in nineteen of the twenty-four counties. Every regional theatre has its own ensemble, usually located in the biggest town in the county. Most of the ensembles are small. These theatres have a responsibility to serve the whole region and to play to everybody who lives there. The companies do a lot of touring; often they bring a tent or a small stage along with them. Each theatre has to serve a population of about 200,000 inhabitants spread over quite a large geographical area. Half the population of Sweden lives in municipalities of fewer than 15,000 inhabitants.

Most regional theatres use the spoken word as their medium, but there are also a few that specialize in musical theatre.

The regional theatres strive to root themselves in their region and each company tries to develop its own specific identity. It is important to keep the dialogue open between the company and the audience. The ensemble usually stays together for many years. The employees of the theatre are protected by the same laws as other occupational groups; once an actor has been employed by the theatre he can stay as long as he or she wants, unless otherwise agreed from the outset.

The regional theatres are subsidized from three different sources.

Figure 9.2 State-supported regional and local theatres (triangles) and operas (circles) 1988/9 (adapted from *Swedish State Cultural Policy*, Stockholm, 1990: 182)

The state pays 55 per cent of the wage-costs of each employee and provides about one-third of the total cost. When the regional theatre is new the state subsidy tends to be bigger. The subsidy provided by the municipal council usually amounts to more than one-half the cost. The third source of subsidy is the county council which usually provides about one-tenth of the cost.

This network of regional theatres is not the first effort made to provide most Swedes with theatre. By the 1930s Riksteatern (the Swedish National Theatre Centre) was established. This organization is still in existence and has its base in the southern part of Greater Stockholm, in Hallunda. From here its productions are sent out on tour all around Sweden. This organization performs all types of theatre. Some of Riksteatern's main tasks are to serve those regions that have no theatre of their own and to act as a complement to regional theatres already in existence. There is a branch within the organization, Unga Riks (Children's Theatre) which performs to school and pre-school (2–6 years) children. Another group, Tyst teater (the Silent Theatre), performs to deaf people in sign language. Yet another group, Pionjärteatern (the Pioneer Theatre) performs in prisons. At present there is a discussion going on about the future of Riksteatern: probably the organization will continue to exist but decline in importance.

There are also a lot of independent theatre groups in Sweden, co-operatives that work on their own. About sixty such groups exist at the moment and they date back to the late 1960s and early 1970s. They came into existence as a protest against a theatre considered to be too hierarchical and too inclined to please a bourgeois public. At that time most of the groups shared a politically radical outlook. Today many of the theatre groups formed in the 1970s have ceased to exist, or their ideological basis has waned. Some groups have changed their way of existence. Many actors have left the groups and moved to the new institutions. Few groups have stuck to the old habit of touring all over the country. Usually they have found a base in a town, and about half of the groups have their own stage. Today the majority of the independent theatre groups have clustered around Stockholm where the possibility of getting a job is greatest. Many of the independent groups have specialized in a certain field of theatre; some perform to grown-ups, others play to children. Many groups play to pre-school children.

None of the independent theatre groups is heavily subsidized. Some of the groups get small subsidies from the state or from the municipal council, or from both. Many of the groups get no subsidy at all and have to earn their living by selling their performances to schools and others.

There are very few private theatres in Sweden – only around ten – most of them concentrated in Stockholm. These theatres play American musicals, English comedy or German light opera. The private theatres get no public support, and the ticket price is much higher (usually three times that in the publicly supported theatres).

All art-forms get public support in Sweden, but theatre is the one most heavily subsidized. Of the total state subsidy 30 per cent goes to theatre. For the budget year 1987/8 this subsidy amounted to almost 600 million Swedish kronor (or £60 million). Almost one-half of this sum went to the two state-owned theatres, the Opera (£16 million) and Dramaten (£9 million). Riksteatern received one-quarter (£13 million) and the rest was divided between the regional theatres (£16 million) and the independent theatre groups (£2.3 million).

The subsidies from the county councils and the municipal councils to the regional theatres are also very substantial. These subsidies amount to around £40 million a year. That means that every seat in a Swedish institutional theatre is subsidized to a great extent. To buy a ticket here is usually quite cheap in the Swedish context (around £10). Children's theatre is often free of charge for the individual; school performances are usually paid for by the county council.

In almost all parts of Sweden you can see theatre now and then. But the difference between those who live in Stockholm and those who live in the rest of the country is still very large. Those living in the neighbourhood of Stockholm are best furnished; every individual in this group is offered more theatre opportunities than a Londoner (see Figure 9.3).

The total number of productions for all Swedish institutional theatres during one year (1987/8) was about 350. Dramaten offered 24 productions a year, the Opera 46 and Riksteatern 44. The independent groups offered another 200 productions. During the year 1987/8 the Opera gave 301 performances, Dramaten 1,076 and Riksteatern 2,088 performances. The number of people visiting these three institutions during the year amounted to 232,000 for the Opera, 297,000 for Dramaten and 397,000 for Riksteatern. Around 6,000 performances were given by the independent theatre groups to an audience of about 800,000 people.

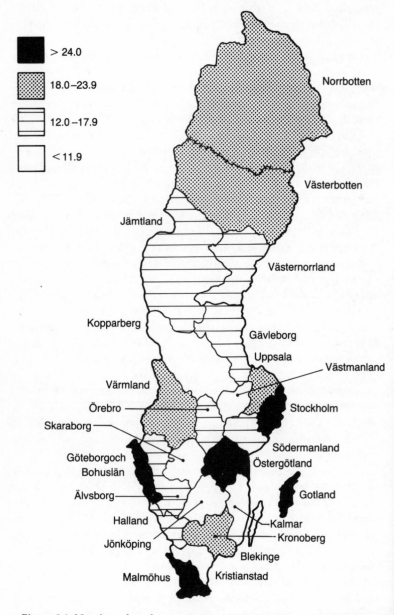

Figure 9.3 Number of performances per 10,000 inhabitants in 1985/6 by county (adapted from *Swedish State Cultural Policy*, Stockholm, 1990: 209)

THE THEATRE AUDIENCE

Sweden has 8 million inhabitants. Every year about 3 million visit the theatre. If everyone in Sweden went to the theatre equally frequently, it would mean that they would each go once every two years. This is of course not what happens; most people never go to the theatre. In the early 1990s every fourth Swede goes to the theatre once or twice a year. Every sixth Swede goes more often. A small minority, 2–3 per cent, visit the theatre every month. The majority takes no interest in theatre.

The well-educated are in the majority among theatre-goers even today. Out of this group 50 per cent go to theatre at least once a year (compared with 14 per cent among those whose school education is very short). The typical theatre habitué of Sweden is a well-educated woman who lives in the neighbourhood of Stockholm. Pre-school- and school-children – and this is worth noting – go to the theatre more often than the average population. This is due to the fact that school theatre has become more or less compulsory in our country. Children do not have to choose; they are provided with theatre by the school.

The annual theatre audience has doubled during the last thirty years. At the beginning of the 1960s the total number of visitors during a year was 1.5 million. The growth of the theatre audience was greatest during the early part of the 1970s. After that the increase stopped altogether, to be followed by a decrease. This decrease includes the total number of performances given in Sweden as well as the size of the total annual audience. During the same period that the number of theatres has increased, the total number of performances has diminished.

One of the aims of the new cultural policy is to make theatre accessible to everybody. If you judge by the theatre map of 1989 in Figure 9.2 you may think that this goal has more or less been reached already. From the statistics of theatre audiences and the reports about people's theatre habits, you get quite a different impression, however. It is perhaps true that most people today have access to theatre in geographical terms, but this does not mean that they use this opportunity. The vast majority ignore theatre.

What prerequisites should be fulfilled to provide a country with a vital theatre important to many people? An international discussion on the situation in Sweden has taken place recently and the report has been published by the European Council. Four experts from England,

France, Turkey and Norway find the work of the regional theatres quite promising but lay stress on the fact that the total audience has not grown during the last decade. They also recommend quality criteria to be used regularly when state subsidies are distributed to these theatres.

CHILDREN'S THEATRE

The most positive development in Swedish theatre during the last thirty years is that of children's theatre. The relative quantity of productions for children has grown and – more importantly – the quality has increased. Many of the new regional theatres devote much time to developing children's theatre. When Norrbottensteatern (the Norrbotten County Theatre) began working in 1967 in the very north of Sweden it was decided that 35 per cent of the theatre resources should go to productions for children and young people. Today many of the regional theatres play every second performance to children.

The development began in the late 1960s. The new signals came from the independent groups, especially from those young actors who had been trained in the student theatres of Stockholm and Lund. What they dreamt of was a revolt against a tradition where children's theatre was seen as an extra – something that took place once a year, usually around Christmas. At that time a fairy-tale was staged – the same production year after year – and that was that. The student actors wanted to discuss the problems of today with their audience. They believed in socialism as a way of changing society and were much preoccupied with man's responsibility in a starving world. They wanted to make children aware that it is possible to change the world. For these actors contact with the public was essential. They chose to perform in a milieu familiar to the child, in its everyday context – in gym halls, classrooms and leisure centres. Of course, this was no easy task, since teachers and parents did not always accept the group and its message.

For the groups that were successful, a time of bold experiment began. At the end of the 1960s children's theatre became an important platform for experimentation; this audience was a lively one and it did not react negatively to what was new. The actors renounced tradi-tional theatre-forms too dependent on props and lighting. This was partly a consequence of the milieu where they had chosen to work. Little or no scenery was used, and many groups preferred to play in ordinary daylight. The only essential thing was the close contact between the three or four actors and the small audience of about a hundred schoolchildren.

The script was usually new, written by a member of the group. Some groups preferred improvising together with the audience. Usually the play was written in co-operation with the children. Sometimes the actors stopped the play before the ending, and the children themselves had to work out an ending in discussion; after that the actors played the story the way the children wanted it to conclude. This method of working out a script together with an audience and then testing the play on the same audience is very common even today among those who work with children.

Suzanne Osten is one director who has developed this method over the decades. She began working in student theatre in Lund and in 1967 she founded Fickteatern (the Pocket Theatre) together with some others. Fickteatern went on tour most of the time and worked in gym halls and class-rooms. From 1974 onwards Suzanne Osten has been artistic director of Unga Klara (Young Klara), an independent theatre group within Stockholms Stadsteater (the Stockholm City Theatre). The plays of Unga Klara always deal with subjects of great concern to their young audience, for example mob behaviour, divorce and adult drunkenness. During the process when the play takes shape, the group usually collaborates with a single school-class, sometimes also with an author. The group consider their theatre work an ongoing form of research. They also take inspiration from public discussion of pedagogy and psychology. Books by Alice Miller, Bruno Bettelheim and Philippe Ariès have been of great importance to their plays.

Since the beginning of the 1980s Unga Klara has had a stage of its own in the City Cultural Centre in the heart of Stockholm. This stage is not an ordinary theatre with benches in a row. It is an empty room that can easily be transformed into almost any shape. It is rather small; the average audience seldom exceeds two hundred people.

The acting style of Unga Klara is brisk. The actors move quickly between expressions of different moods and avoid traditional ways of psychologizing. All the tools of theatre are used – props, lighting, costume. Grown-up actors usually perform in children's roles. The plays written by Unga Klara have become very popular all over Sweden. In particular the early ones – for example *Medea's Children* (1975) – were performed by many independent groups as well as regional theatres. The plays have also been translated and performed abroad.

THE GREAT DIRECTORS OF THE 1960s

Let us return to the beginning of the 1960s to trace developments over the last thirty years. At that time Swedish theatre life was still dominated by the big institutions in Gothenburg and Stockholm. Many of the directors who had exerted great influence on the theatre during the first half of the decade were still at work. Olof Molander, the famous Strindberg interpreter, worked in a realistic style and laid great stress on every detail. Strindberg's dramas were always located in Stockholm at the turn of the century, and the autobiographical view was stressed. The tone was always very solemn. In 1965 Molander ended his thirty-year Strindberg cycle with *To Damascus I-III* (all three parts in one) at Stockholm's City Theatre.

Alf Sjöberg, another of Dramaten's giants who had begun working right back in the 1930s, now stood at the height of his career. He went on producing vital theatre till 1980 when he was killed in an accident. For almost fifty years he remained avant-garde. His way of working was eclectic and most theatrical. His first vital impulses were derived from the Russian theatre of the 1920s, and his approach to theatre remained global. In the 1960s he introduced Brecht and the Absurdists to Dramaten. The first Brecht play produced was *Schweyk in the Second World War* (1964), followed by *Mother Courage*. Sjöberg also introduced Witold Gombrowicz to Sweden and produced *Princess Ivona* (1965) and *The Marriage* (1966).

The third influential director was Ingmar Bergman, who had been working in Malmö and Helsingborg in the south of Sweden during the 1950s. For the first time Bergman was working at Dramaten and for three years he was head of the theatre. This period (1963–6) became an extraordinarily vital one, as Bergman introduced many important changes. Wanting to make Dramaten the best theatre in the world, he collected the majority of Sweden's best actors; he also introduced a more democratic way of working and stressed the responsibility of the actor. A small council of five actors allowed the employees the opportunity to exert an influence upon repertoire politics and casting. Bergman laid great stress on playing to a young audience and introduced special performances to schoolchildren during the daytime. He also tried to reach an audience used to cinema, and on some occasions the same performance was shown twice a night. On those occasions the charge for tickets was very low, only 5 kronor (50 pence). During this period the rehearsals were sometimes open to the public.

Bergman was succeeded by Erland Josephson, an actor and dramatist who had worked with Ingmar Bergman for decades, especially in films. During the Josephson era the discussion about theatre democracy reached its high-point. The same was true for almost every theatre institution in Sweden. This was the age when the actor demanded more influence and the authorities of yesterday were despised.

Most of the Swedish dramatists who were performed during the 1960s were well established and had been performed earlier. Few of them were women. Lars Forssell, active already in the 1950s, became one of the most prolific dramatists of the 1960s. *Christina Alexandra* (1968) was staged at Stockholm's City Theatre, *Show* (The Goat, 1971) at Dramaten. The first play is about the Swedish queen, the other about the American satirist Lenny Bruce. Some new dramatists much appreciated during the 1960s were poets by origin: Werner Aspenström, Sandro Key-Åberg and Harry Martinson. In 1959 Martinson's space-opera *Aniara* had been performed at Operan; in 1964 his Chinese play *Tre knivar från Wei* (Three Knives from Wei) was staged at Dramaten.

Peter Weiss lived in Sweden but wrote in German. During the 1960s his plays were much produced, both abroad and in Sweden. *Marat/Sade* was directed by Frank Sundström at Dramaten in 1965. In the Auschwitz drama *The Investigation* German Nazis are put on trial. The play was produced by Dramaten in 1968 under the direction of Ingmar Bergman. Gunilla Palmstierna-Weiss constructed the scenery for most of Weiss's plays.

In Gothenburg a small group of actors in the City Theatre began working on their own. This group created a couple of revue-like plays about social conditions in Sweden. In the first one, *Flotten* (The Raft, 1967), neutral Sweden was portrayed as a raft driving through a choppy sea at five knots, trying to find out which way to go. In *Hemmet* (The Home, 1967) and *Sandlådan* (The Sandbox, 1968) the target was the Welfare State; is it really true that people are equals?

The revue form was much appreciated during this decade. Dramaten's *Oh What a Lovely Peace!* (1966), written by the well-known humorists Tage Danielsson and Hasse Alfredson, became a great success. This duo continued to produce together the same type of satiric, humorous and very warm revues for many years until the death of Danielsson. The authors not only wrote the texts; they also acted, directed and produced their revues.

Among foreign authors often staged during the 1960s may be

mentioned the French Absurdists, especially Beckett. *Waiting for Godot* was played at Dramaten, Genet's *The Balcony* at Uppsala-Gävle City Theatre under the direction of Frank Sundström. Many English dramatists were produced, for example Pinter and Jellicoe. Wesker's plays were very popular and the author visited Stockholm several times and directed a couple of plays himself. Other prominent guests visiting Sweden in the late 1960s were La Mama, Living Theater and Grotowski's Theatre Laboratory. These visits were to be of great importance for the development of the independent theatre movement in Sweden.

THE INDEPENDENT THEATRE GROUPS OF THE 1970s

During the 1970s discussion of theatre democracy became still more intense, especially within the institutions. Many heads and directors had their power put in question by actors demanding more influence. Theatre work sometimes almost came to a halt because of endless discussions about how to work. The strongest challenge to the institutional way of working came from the independent theatre groups which were growing in number and importance. The 1970s were to become the decade of the independent theatre groups.

Many of the first independent theatre groups started within institutions, however. The group already mentioned at Gothenburg's City Theatre belongs to this category. At the end of the 1960s another group was formed at Dramaten, the NJA-group. During the summer of 1969 they moved to the north of Sweden, to a steel factory in Luleå called NJA, owned by the state. Here they interviewed the steel-workers about their life. *Nils Johan Andersson and Others*, the NJA-play, was worked out as a revue and deals with the poor conditions of the workers in a Swedish iron factory. Later on the play was shown at Dramaten, but the group was not permitted to perform their play in Luleå during the miners' strike. The group wanted to go on working as a special unit within Dramaten, developing their working method. When this was not possible they left the theatre. First, they chose to work as a unit within Riksteatern under the name Proteatern. Later on, they left this organization and began working as an independent group under the name Fria Proteatern. This group remained together for twenty years until 1991.

Musikteatergruppen Oktober (The Music Theatre Group October), was founded in the early 1970s in Lund in the very south of Sweden.

Most of its members were students. They began by producing Brecht's *The Mother* and continued with a play they wrote themselves, *Sven Klang's Quintet* (1975). This play is about a dance-band in a small Swedish town back in the 1950s. Sven Klang, a 30-year-old car dealer, is the leader of the band; three members are teenagers but the fifth one, Lasse, is older and has a different background. He comes from Stockholm and – more important – to him music is much more essential than it is to the rest of the group. When the three teenagers are confronted with the anti-authoritarian Lasse, a conflict develops between them and Sven Klang. This play became a great success and was also filmed. A few years later, in 1978, October was invited to move to the town of Södertälje, south of Stockholm, and to work there for three years. During this period the town promised to fund one-half of the group's performances. The remainder of the actors' salaries had to come from touring.

In Södertälje October got the opportunity to work with the same public for a long time. Peculiar to this town is the fact that every third inhabitant is an immigrant and at least fifty nationalities are represented. This was one important prerequisite for the group when they started working, and during several of their productions they maintained close contact with these immigrants. In one production, *Södertäljebor* (Södertälje-Settlers), actors from three nationalities joined together and three different languages were used. When the play was performed the audience was selected very carefully so that all three nationalities were represented in the audience by about the same percentage.

October has now been resident in Södertälje for four periods of three years, and in the future the group will probably become transformed into a regional theatre. This is one of the rare occasions when an independent group has had the opportunity to work full-time in a certain area for a long period of time.

Byteatern (the Village Theatre), an independent group in the small town of Kalmar in the south-east of Sweden, began working in the 1960s and has recently been transformed into a regional theatre. They use a combination of puppets and actors. In 1990 their production of Ibsen's *Peer Gynt*, directed by Björn Samuelsson, attracted great attention: four actors played all the roles, along with about a hundred puppets. In winter Byteatern play in the harbour theatre; in summer they go on tour with the boat *M/s Helene* along the east coast.

Another independent group still in existence dating back to the 1960s is Nationalteatern (the National Theatre) in Gothenburg.

Their acting style was from the beginning rather provocative, like the group's name. Today the group is supported by the city and has a stage of its own. During the 1970s the group played in leisure centres, and some of their performances to adults took place in pubs. Many members of the group were musicians, and in the 1970s National-teatern was considered one of the best rock groups in Sweden. They were very popular among teenagers and they also produced interest-ing theatre for children. One double LP, *Cabbage Rolls and Bloomers* (1976), combined songs from four different plays into a fairy-tale much loved by young children. Today the group works in a more traditional way. In 1987 Nationalteatern performed a fairy-tale, *Peter Pan*, under the direction of Med Reventberg. After that the group also turned to opera.

In 1977 several of the best independent groups combined to carry out the 'Tent Project', a joint production of gigantic size, presenting one hundred years of Swedish history on stage. The play *Vi äro tusenden* (We Are Thousands) had many similarities with circus. Movement, lighting effects and acrobatics were used in a tent housing more than a thousand spectators. *We Are Thousands* was shown all over Sweden during the summer, and the performance went on for the whole day. In the interval the audience could be seen seated on the grass around the tent with their picnic hampers. A few well-known actors from the institutions participated in the production, and this was one important way in which the two theatre forms intermingled with each other. Some institutions used to the old way of producing theatre drew inspiration from The Tent Project, and in 1978 Dramaten carried out a project about atomic power, called *The Storm*.

Another strong movement that dates back to the 1970s is a new type of semi-documentary amateur theatre about the historical conditions of a certain landscape or town. *The Play about the Norberg Strike* was performed in 1977. In this play Arne Andersson, a trained director from Riksteatern, worked together with amateurs. The play was staged in the open during the summer and attracted many visitors to Norberg. The play was seen as a signal for something new; later on a lot of plays of the same kind were produced all over Sweden.

Many of the new dramatists who were introduced during this decade were in their thirties, a few of them were women. Some were members of the women's liberation movement. At Stockholm's City Theatre the plays of Margaretha Garpe and Suzanne Osten were staged. *Jösses flickor – befrielsen är nära* (Gee Girls – Liberation Is Near, 1974) was one of them. Both at Gothenburg's City Theatre and at Dramaten, Agneta Pleijel's *Kollontaj* was performed (1979). This play is about the Russian revolutionary Alexandra Kollontaj. At Dramaten the play was rewritten and directed by Alf Sjöberg as one of his last productions in 1979.

Many of the new plays took advantage of biographical material well known to the public. So did Per Olof Enquist in *Tribadernas natt* (The Night of the Tribades, 1975); this play dealt with sex roles and derived its special interest from portraying August Strindberg. In *Haren och vråken* (At The Hare and Hawk, 1978) Lars Forssell discusses the right of the Swedish people to act as a folk tribunal: the soldiers of Gustavus III are confronted with the people from Bellman's songs.

The foreign author most often performed was no doubt Dario Fo, who also visited Sweden on several occasions. Vaclav Havel and Edward Bond were new acquaintances. On television Ariane Mnouchkine was introduced to the general public with her film *Molière*.

Finally, the traditional solemn way of directing Strindberg slowly changed during this decade. Alf Sjöberg made his contribution with *Lord Bengt's Wife*. He retitled the play, stressed the main female role and called it *Margit*. At Gothenburg's City Theatre Lennart Hjulström directed the historical plays *Gustav Vasa* and *Gustav III* and laid stress on the revolutionary message of the plays.

THE 1980s

Regional Theatres

During the 1980s a new regional theatre began working in about a dozen counties. Some of the actors and directors were former members of independent theatre groups. This is another important way in which results from the independent theatre movement have merged with the tradition of the institutional theatre. On some rare occasions it has happened that an independent theatre group has been transformed into a regional theatre. In 1981 Skånska teatern, a group working in Landskrona in the south of Sweden, moved to the county of Gävleborg, 200 kilometres north of Stockholm. This experiment is of great interest from many different aspects and has turned out very fruitfully. The resulting Folkteatern i Gävleborg has become the most successful of all Swedish theatres during the 1980s.

Skånska teatern learned much from their work in Landskrona that proved useful on arrival in Gävleborg. They had been working in close contact with the same audience for several years and had also developed contacts with local authors who had not worked in theatre before, for example Mary Anderson, whose play, *Maria from Borstahusen*, had been performed in 1977. Most of the plays Skånska teatern had formerly produced were written by people outside the group, and unlike many other independent groups they laid great stress on the classics. Three plays by Rudolf Värnlund, a neglected Swedish dramatist from the 1930s, had been produced and performed in sequence on the same day. They had also played Shakespeare, Holberg and Forssell. Their translation of *A Midsummer Night's Dream* attracted considerable attention. When this play was staged the audience had to move between different performance areas – a factory, a circus tent, a citadel. Amateurs played an important part in the performance; they were used in the 'Pyramus and Thisbe' sequences.

With about 35 employees the new regional theatre – Folkteatern i Gävleborg – was rather large. Many actors came from Skånska teatern but some had worked in the institutions and knew their tradition. This difference in experience was expected to be fruitful; through this both categories could learn from each other. The reality did not turn out the way people had expected, however. It soon became evident that it was hard for these actors from different backgrounds to work together. The former members of Skånska teatern also had difficulties in adapting to the new hierarchical system. Peter Oskarson had accepted an appointment as head of the theatre, but was not very happy with his new role. For about five years the theatre did not function very well. In 1987 they found a solution. For the next three years the board of directors allowed the theatre workers to carry out an experiment, to function more like an independent group. The ensemble got permission to work without a head (this post was left vacant). Nor did they have to perform a specific number of performances and productions, decided beforehand. During the next three years Folkteatern was allowed to concentrate on a single project each year.

During the first year, 1987/8, Folkteatern decided to work with an old Swedish epic, *Den stora vreden* (The Great Wrath), myths and sagas dating back to the eighteenth century. The myths had been collected by the author Olof Högberg at the beginning of the century. The first necessity was to have his novel dramatized. After that every actor trained himself in story-telling. Alone, without the support of others, they arrived in a place where people had already gathered – a market for example – and tried to win an audience for their story. This was not always an easy task.

After that the actors went abroad to learn from other theatre traditions, from other ways of telling a story. A few actors stayed with pupils of the Peking Opera, studied and learned. Another group went to Kerala in India. When they returned home each group had learned something – they had witnessed another way of expressing oneself. Their knowledge was unknown to the rest of the ensemble and they could demonstrate what they had learned to each other. And, more importantly, they could observe their old way of working from a distance.

The Great Wrath was performed in an old steel factory in the village of Iggesund to an audience of about four hundred people. The performance went on from three in the afternoon till ten at night. The stories were unknown to most people, and so was the acting style. This powerful theatre was far removed from the psychological style of acting. Movement, dance and music predominated; dialogue became less important. And the bright colours of the costumes bore a slight resemblance to Asian dress. The music and dances stemmed from the north of Sweden, however. This folklore culture had to be learned from the beginning, just like Chinese acting. To most Swedes – including these actors – this old tradition was unknown and looked upon with disrespect. When the actors learned how to dance the polska, the halling and the schottisch they changed their attitude.

During the second year Folkteatern i Gävleborg chose to work with a story from the beginning of the nineteenth century about a religious sect having to emigrate to the United States because of their faith. In this production too they used local material. The play was written by the poet Margareta Ekarv and called *Drömmarnas barn* (Children of Dreams). In the third year *Hamlet* was staged in a similar manner to *The Great Wrath* with music and dance from the Swedish tradition. The play appeared in a new translation, and the main role was played by a pop star from Gästrikland. Peter Oskarson directed all three productions.

What has happened at Folkteatern i Gävleborg can be interpreted as the result of a major clash between many different theatre traditions. Or let us put it this way: when a group trained to work together under democratic forms and with great trust in each other suddenly has at its disposal the economic resources that the new cultural policy can furnish, the result may be hard to predict. And let us not forget the important role played by the board of directors. This board with its representatives from different political parties dared to give the theatre maximum freedom. And it all happened in a county – not in the national theatres in Stockholm.

Directors, dramatists and actors

At the beginning of the 1980s Ingmar Bergman returned to Dramaten after a period of directing at the Residenztheater in Munich. Now he produced two Shakespeare plays, one Ibsen play and several Strindberg plays. In *Miss Julie* Jean knows how to use the opportunity offered by Julie to obtain a better position in society; in *A Doll's House* Torvald is portrayed as young and rather naïve. Nora, on the other hand, is aware of her power from the beginning.

Many Bergman productions from the 1980s were set in one colour and extremely beautiful. This was true of the scarlet *King Lear* (1984) and the golden *Madame de Sade* (1989), written by the Japanese Yokyo Mishima. In many plays Bergman left one of the actors on stage all the time; in *Hamlet* Ophelia could be seen tumbling about during the whole performance. In *A Doll's House* Bergman left all the actors on stage; those who were not included in Ibsen's dialogue could be seen sitting on chairs in a sort of half-reality.

Unga Klara has always switched between children's theatre and plays for grown-ups and won a public for both. *Affären Danton* (The Danton Affair), a play which deals with the French revolution, was performed in 1986 for grown-ups. Suzanne Osten dramatized and produced a novel by an American writer, Joan Bowles. In *Lusthuset* (The Summer-House, 1988) the main female roles – the two mothers – were played by males. One year earlier Osten had staged a play by Eva Ström, *Paddakvariet* (The Toad Aquarium) where the children's roles were played by grey-haired middle-aged actors and the parents by actors of the proper age. This type of casting adds an extra dimension to the performance, a type of *Verfremdung*. *The Toad Aquarium* dealt with a theme often presented by Unga Klara, children's suffering when their parents get divorced. (A decade earlier Unga Klara had treated the same subject in *Medea's Children*, an extension of Euripides' play.)

Suzanne Osten has also established herself as a film director with four or five films. In the first, *Mamm* (Mother), she shows her own mother failing to get her film synopsis accepted. *Bröderna Mozart* (The Mozart Brothers) tells of the difficulties of having an opera staged in the theatre climate of the 1980s when a director is not considered an authority any longer. Osten uses the same actors from film to film, actors she works with on stage also.

Mixing professional actors and amateurs in certain productions has remained popular during recent years. Arne Andersson, the director of *The Play about the Norberg Strike* (1977), went on working with amateurs in Brecht's *St Joan of the Stockyards* (1984). This play was staged in a disused mine in Norberg.

The most interesting Swedish dramatist of the 1980s has been Lars Norén. His plays have been produced in all parts of Sweden and also performed abroad. Many prominent Norén productions have been produced by Göran Melander at Gothenburg's City Theatre. One of Norén's best plays, *Natten är dagens mor* (The Night Is Mother to the Day), was first produced in Malmö in 1982. Suzanne Osten directed one important Norén production, *Underjordens leende* (The Smile of the Lower Regions, 1982), and in Uppsala Christian Tomner did a remarkable production of the same play.

Many young actors, such as Staffan Göthe and Magnus Nilsson, trained in the informal way of working common among independent groups, have established themselves as authors during the last decade. Magnus Nilsson wrote *Guds djärvaste ängel* (God's Bravest Angel, 1986) for his group, October. This play is about the encounter of two famous modernist Finnish poets, Edit Södergran and Elmer Diktonius. Staffan Göthe began writing for children: his play *The Girl in the Aspen Tree* was written in the 1970s and has been produced in almost every part of Sweden. In 1986 a play for grown-ups, *La strada del amore* (The Road of Love), was produced in Gävle. His last trilogy, about the Cervieny family, is a modern version of Strindberg's *A Dream Play: En uppstoppad hund* (A Stuffed Dog) and *Den perfekta kyssen* (The Perfect Kiss) depict a generation that has lost much of its faith in a society of solidarity and equality.

Lars Norén is the dramatist most often produced today but Staffan Göthe, Magnus Nilsson and Bengt Ahlforss are among those who are always in the repertoire. The demand for Swedish drama is today amazingly high – perhaps higher than ever. This must be interpreted as one of the consequences of the new cultural policy: most theatres today prefer performing plays from their own region. Some regional theatres have declared that they intend to lay even more stress on new Swedish drama in the future. Authors unaccustomed to drama have found themselves invited by the theatre to write a play about a local personality or a historical event. Sometimes they have also been employed by the theatre for a couple of months. In many cases the regional theatres have served as drama schools for dramatists unaccustomed to the theatre medium. Several of the new Swedish dramatists have a thorough knowledge of theatre however. They are actors by origin and have often started writing in a situation when the theatre has been short of good scripts. Usually they have started writing for children and ended as dramatists for grown-ups. These authors/actors are privileged in many respects; they know their colleagues and can easily be produced. And they are well aware that words are only part of the language of the theatre.

The discussion about theatre democracy has been very intense for a long time now. Actors have gained more influence and the relationship between actor and director has changed. The director of today has little in common with those of the 1950s. Many of the well-known directors of that time used threat as their weapon. Such methods are not used any more; the director of today must be good at listening and be able to strengthen the personal skills of the actor. These faculties are usually possessed by women; therefore it is not surprising that many of the new directors are female. Suzanne Osten, Med Reventberg and Gunnel Lindblom all began working as actors and they know from experience the needs of the ensemble.

Allan Edwall is a good example of the actor good at everything. He is still working as an actor but has also written several plays, dramatized many novels and produced film scripts. He has worked as a film director as well as a theatre director and has started a theatre of his own. At Teatern vid Brunnsgatan in Stockholm he plays all the roles himself to an audience no larger than fifty people.

Today the head of the theatre has less influence than earlier; he has to share his power with the actors. Another important division of power is that between the artistic direction of the theatre and the theatre board. During the 1970s this question was much discussed, but today a working management has been agreed. The main tasks of the board of directors are to appoint the head of the theatre and to furnish the theatre with money. The board also decides the number of productions the theatre has to put on each year. The board is not allowed to decide the repertoire, however. This is always the privilege of the artistic direction of the theatre.

CONCLUSIONS

During the last ten years many regional theatres have started working all over Sweden but the total size of the audience has not been influenced by this. Fewer productions are given today than earlier. This can be explained partly by the growing costs of producing theatre, partly by the difficulty of gathering a big audience in small villages. The average size of an audience in the region is only about a hundred people.

Children's theatre has been more successful in finding its way to the public. 'Theatre in schools is the only functioning community-theatre in our country, in the sense that all schoolchildren, regardless of social or cultural background, can encounter theatre as art,' says the journalist Margareta Sörensen. We know that some of the schoolchildren will never go to the theatre as adults. This is one of the reasons why it is so important that the theatre encounter should be impressive and marvellous – unlike everything else the child has seen before.

Children's theatre in Sweden has managed to develop a new repertoire in close contact with its audience. This is true also of some of the regional theatres. Folkteatern i Gävleborg is one example. The co-operation between the board of the theatre and the artistic direction already mentioned gives one example of what may happen when the theatre's need for time is taken in account. The balance between the board's wish to furnish the region with as much theatre as possible and the theatre's wish to develop their skills is a delicate one. Freedom of experimentation is a necessity to keep theatre vital. And one of the goals of the new cultural policy should be to make possible a continuous renewal of the art. If such a freedom can be guaranteed and if the subsidies remain at the same level as today, nobody can predict what will happen to Swedish theatre tomorrow.

BIBLIOGRAPHY

The Council of Europe has recently published two reports on Swedish cultural policy: *Swedish State Cultural Policy. Objectives, Measures and Results*, Stockholm 1990, and *National Cultural Policy in Sweden*, Stockholm, 1990. Both books are in the National Cultural Review's programme of the Council of Europe's Council of Cultural Co-operation.

The Swedish Institute in Stockholm currently publishes reports on Swedish theatre. See, for example, Henrik Sjögren, *Stage and Society in Sweden. Aspects of Swedish Theatre since 1945*, Stockholm, 1979, and Kent Hägglund, *Theatre for Children. A Contemporary View*, Stockholm, 1989.

The series *Nordic Theatre Studies. Yearbook of Theatre Research in Scandinavia* is published by Munksgaard International Publishers of Copenhagen and has appeared in various volumes: 1, *Women in Scandinavian Theatre*, 1988; 2/3, *Theatre Studies in Scandinavia. Traditions and Developments*, 1989; and 4, *Theatre Policy*, 1991.

10

POLAND

(*Dead Souls Under Western Eyes*)

George Hyde

To describe post-war Poland as a totalitarian state would not be far from the truth; yet this oppressed nation has produced art, theatre, literature, music and film equal to any in Europe. The contradictions of Polish history,[1] culminating in the post-war period of Communist rule, have stimulated creative work and produced a responsive critical milieu of great sophistication. In the post-war period, despite the strings that were attached, which were in any case not always very effective, the arts throve on huge subsidies. If I devote most of my attention in this chapter to what may be called 'alternative' theatre (the term is even less precise in the Polish context than it is in the British) this is not meant as a criticism or disparagement of the other, more 'institutional' kind, which was often highly innovative; and there is, for instance, the distinctively Polish phenomenon of Józef Szajna's Studio Theatre in the Palace of Culture, where a radical avant-garde vision became part of a thriving 'official' institution. It is also no part of my intention to denigrate the work of the many highly original playwrights whose output either does not belong to the avant-garde, or, like that of Tadeusz Różewicz, for example, or Slawomir Mrożek, works on the interface of 'legitimate' and 'alternative' styles. But in Poland, as elsewhere, there have been some notably radical ways of constructing aesthetic (especially theatrical) spaces, and of deconstructing or subverting 'the tradition', that co-existed very uneasily with institutional culture, especially where the 'culinary'[2] art of theatre was concerned. It is these 'alternative' groups, or some of them, that are the subject of this chapter, which for reasons of space has had to restrict its coverage very severely.

THE 'CONDITION OF POLAND' QUESTION

If Polish theatre flourished in the way it did between 1960 and 1980, it was partly because of its rich and very distinctive indigenous traditions. Czesław Miłosz evokes these in his reminiscences of Polish Lithuania:

> Poland, as I look at it in retrospect, had better organised theatres than many 'Western' countries . . . the principle of repertory theatre was universally recognised, and the work of director and actor was regarded as a kind of service to society. Hence Wilno's large theatre . . . co-operated closely with the schools and the university. The avant-garde quality of its stage direction and set design, its use of anti-naturalistic devices, introduced us early to the concept of magic as the essence of the stage. Classical dramas were performed . . . as well as Polish Romantic dramas (which can be ranked with some of the most bizarre works of theatrical literature). . . .[3]

The points that Miłosz makes here can be made again, more or less unchanged, in connection with contemporary Polish theatre. The two principal avant-garde post-war Polish theatres, Grotowski's[4] and Kantor's,[5] for example, different as they are in other ways, are unimaginable without a troupe of actors and actresses dedicated to realizing the imaginative vision of the dramaturge (or director), in both cases anti-naturalist, 'magical' and dealing very freely with Classical and Romantic traditions. More common in European theatre than in British, this kind of shared vision and activity has made it possible to address the problems of a fragmented and morally bankrupt society, caught in a vice between consumerism and the 'Dead Souls' of Soviet Marxism, with a peculiar intensity. A distorting mirror is held up to a distorted reality in the hope that, if only for a moment, something true might get said. It is the urgency of this appeal, in the absence of a free press and media, that constitutes the power of the Polish theatre of the 1960s and 1970s. It is also what still speaks so powerfully to us, caught in the aftermath of European socialism, and watching authoritarian policies impoverish education and the arts in the name of market values.

WHICH PEOPLE'S THEATRE?

Latent in Miłosz's phrase 'service to society' it is not hard to make out the perennial vexed Polish question of 'the folk'. The Romantic plays which Miłosz invokes here, and which constitute a powerful, eccentric kind of 'great tradition' of Polish theatre, agonized over the apparently insoluble problem of the identity and deliverance of the Polish nation, in the context of over a hundred years of partition and foreign rule (not to mention internal strife); and one of the sources of that 'anti-naturalism' of which Miłosz speaks is certainly the fact that Romantic closet drama[6] from Mickiewicz to Wyspiański, haunted by ghostly presences and obscure cthonic powers, continued to embody the consciousness of 'the race' (a nation with no nation-state) long after the end of the Romantic period as such. This is by no means just a literary matter: Poland perhaps has more dead than most nations, and they will not rest. They participate in the work of Grupa Działania and Gardzienice, two companies whose 'happenings' I shall discuss later in the context of the 'return to the people'; and death is the recurrent theme of the two major 'dramaturges' of the period, Jerzy Grotowski and Tadeusz Kantor, especially the latter, who has a positively Baroque theory of the relationship between art and death.[7] Polish theatre, in other words, was 'a people's theatre' long before the Communists hijacked the phrase, and the avant-garde in the post-war years keeps reminding us of the gulf between their popular affiliations and current, Marxist ideas of an art which belongs to the people.[8]

Clearly, 'the people' will form an important ideological focus in a state ostensibly devoted to nurturing and furthering the interests of workers and peasants; indeed, a major part of the energy of post-war Polish theatre was generated by rival bids for authority in this domain. Witold Filler puts the 'official' view amiably enough:

> From her very inception People's Poland considered the theatre one of the most important means in the process of building a socialist culture. Barely a week after the proclamation of the July Manifesto (22nd July 1944) the first performance was held in liberated Lublin: the frontline theatre of the First Polish Army staged Stanislaw Wyspiański's *The Wedding* [*Wesele*]. The decree of the Polish Committee of National Liberation on 15th Sept. 1944 mentions 'the State's patronage of the writers and performers in the field of the theatre'.[9]

Filler thus makes 'People's Poland' (a convenient political fiction) the agent of national renewal – a tautological proposition in which the question of the Party's right to the term 'People's' is deliberately disregarded. The major play to which he refers (by Wyspiański, in theatre the Polish Yeats) is a Symbolist piece which explores the great void at the heart of late nineteenth-century Polish society – the 'bourgeois' idea of nationhood which the peculiar class structure, as well as Poland's history of political oppression, did not allow to develop, or which was overlaid by massively overdetermined national symbols (in this respect Poland resembles Ireland, another nation with a great theatrical tradition). At the centre of Wyspiański's play is the marriage, based on autobiography, of an intellectual to a peasant girl, and the key events of the action take place during a kind of dionysiac wedding feast which is haunted by the ghostly presence of the *chochoł*, the 'straw man' (actually an unusually large straw mulch used in Poland to protect young trees and bushes against severe frost, and often seen dramatically silhouetted against a winter sky, as in Wyspiański's famous painting). This Expressionist *chochoł* became synonymous with the undisclosed reality of the Polish nation, biding its time, suppressed during the nineteenth-century insurrections but still undefeated; and inevitably it also acquired some of the knowingly ironic, even masochistic, resonances characteristic of the latter-day Polish 'Romantic revival'.[10]

GROTOWSKI AND THE LESSONS OF POVERTY

There are good reasons, then, why Filler should call Polish theatre a 'theatre living the life of the people', even if Poles have learned to distrust phrases of this kind. But it would also be true to say that the significance of the word 'the people' in the Polish imagination and tradition has little to do with the idea of a 'People's Theatre' as used by (for example) Bradby and McCormick.[11] In the earliest period of his theatrical work, Jerzy Grotowski was already striving to give some content to the notion of 'the life of the people' on the basis of a Marxist reading of history, but his ideas, subject to the most heterogeneous influences, soon evolved into something very different from the bland official optimism of my quotation from Filler. Grotowski's 'poor theatre' is polemical, of course; born of Poland's historical traumas, it invokes Poland's real poverty in order to challenge 'culinary' modes; it also steers a kind of 'impoverished', quasi-monastic, self-denying course between Soviet Marxism's 'Dead Souls' and artistic formalism. Superimposing its own disciplines, as much religious as theatrical, upon the Romantic stereotypes of the plays with which (as often as not) it works, it returns to the irreducible human realities of the body and the spirit, and the complex relations between them, locating here the only 'mythic' reality which it can draw upon, but confronting this dramatic 'raw material' rather than absorbing it or sheltering behind it. This deconstructed theatre is a quasi-religious *via negativa*[12] designed to empty out the surfeited self produced by modern 'kleptomania',[13] and to challenge the spurious realism that exhausts itself in objects. The stage is the empty space in which communion is generated, spilling over into the audience, whose privileged distance is transgressed or engulfed or shown up for the fragile line of defence that it is.[14] There is little room in these early manifestos for detailed theories of the function of theatre in society, but a critique of culture is nevertheless implicit, and sometimes explicit, in Grotowski's minimalism. In the early 1960s, influenced by psychodrama and by Eastern religions, he begins to speak quasi-mystically (though never losing touch with theatrical realities) of the body's centres of energies, and of role and text as 'scalpels' and 'trampolines' to help the actor strip away, stretch and expose the body, the self, and his or her experience as nakedly as possible. At times, we hear echoes of the familiar Brechtian polemic with the impostures of bourgeois theatre (a polemic which is also based on an effect of 'estrangement', though Grotowski's version is not overtly politicized);[15] but there is also a (subterranean) challenge to the totalitarian thrust of Soviet Marxism, which had little time for the individual, and none at all for ideas of holiness beyond its own iconography. Grotowski's ideas sometimes remind one of Gandhi, perhaps because, like Gandhi, he has absorbed the ideas of Tolstoy, among others. Poverty is offered as a powerful challenge to mechanical reproduction in the 'consumerist' form of television and other media. Grotowski does not need to say, as Polish students said in 1968 and again in the 1980s, that 'television lies': instead he chooses to emphasize, as no 'Western' director (probably) could afford to, that theatre can exist on its own terms, regardless of its public 'image', because it has a sacred task quite different from any objectives the media might set themselves.[16]

The inherent didacticism of this, typical of much of the work of alternative Polish theatre, puzzles Western audiences. It can be accounted for partly as a riposte to the moral bankruptcy of the Polish United Workers' Party from at least the mid-1960s onwards and partly as an echo of the nineteenth-century 'Polish complex' stated in classic form by Wyspiański's *The Wedding* and in modern guise in Tadeusz Konwicki's powerful novel.[17] 'Art belongs to the people', said Lenin; but theatre, according to Grotowski, exists to restore to us a full sense of being human, freed from Party slogans about perfectibility and a better tomorrow. (Like many Polish artists, Grotowski began life with a more positive attitude towards Marxism, out of which his ideas may be said to have evolved.) We discover our 'humanity' painfully, through encounters – with texts, with others, and with ourselves. Without such meetings, socialism is meaningless; with them, it may turn out to be needless. In his hostility to the *dirigisme* of Polish political and social life, and the consequences of this in the way that Polish society has fragmented and turned in upon itself, Grotowski increasingly drew upon eclectic models of encounter, both spiritual and physical, in which myth acts through the present, and is embodied in historical and textual processes. The denial of basic human truths and rights by Marxism's relentless scientific materialism produced, in Poland, a kind of backlash, sometimes quite atavistic.

AUSCHWITZ: TERMINAL THEATRE

The Second World War, for example, was endlessly invoked by the Party throughout its period of rule as a backdrop to its monopoly of power, and in order to generate and reinforce anxiety. When Grotowski takes on the concentration camp theme, as he does in *Akropolis*,[18] he deconstructs the official rhetoric of 'martyrology' (an odd but ubiquitous 'official' Polish coinage) and sets bodies wantonly on the rack, in rags, in heaps, strained and anguished: 'The inmates belong in a nightmare and seem to move in on the sleeping spectators from all sides.'[19] The 'texts' on which the theatrical performance is based are the fantasies and dreams (mainly scriptural) of the 'dead' inmates. In Grotowski's theatre, literary texts have no privileged life of their own. Like Kantor in this if in nothing else, he sees the text (Wyspiański's *Akropolis* or another) as intrinsically 'dead' structures of fixed (authoritarian) relations which the performance interrogates. Props share in the general 'poverty' by doubling up roles and being pressed into service to signify a number of large concepts (in much the same way, Kantor creates 'bio-objects', inert things which bear the imprint of human contact, need, endeavour). It would be simplistic to interpret this as an image of Polish conditions; yet a desperate sort of improvisation was necessary for survival in a country where one had to use influence to obtain even a pot of paint or a bag of nails, and these trivia of a 'degraded' reality have also left their imprint on social relations and on art. When language merges into noise and/or silence in Grotowski's scenarios, and characters are depersonalized in order to demolish the remnants of a constricting rhetoric, we are witnessing an extreme image of Polish reality, which the director has interpreted in terms of Artaud's savage geometry of death.

The Laboratory Theatre had to move forward by subverting even itself. In the course of the 1970s, Grotowski, who was now describing *Towards a Poor Theatre* (1978) as 'only a travel diary', experimented briefly, as a logical development of his methods, with direct audience participation, and rejected it in favour of a different and more radical model of shared work based more on psychotherapy than on theatre. The end of art was still moral, but drama was no longer something to live up to, but something to live through (cf. Pasternak's indictment of Soviet socialism: 'Man was born to live, not to prepare for life'). Grotowski's work took on the utopian form of a kind of 'Paradise Now', though in practice it lacked the untidy and equivocal Romanticism of the Living Theatre.[20] In 1973, at the group's new headquarters at Brzezinka, in the countryside 40 kilometres from Wrocław, there was the first 'meeting' or 'special project', after three years' preparation, which including building and digging. The Polish title given to the event, *Święto* communicates the idea of sanctity, lost now in the English equivalent, *Holiday*. Selected followers of the Laboratory Theatre were invited to participate. Leszek Kolankiewicz, cited by Jennifer Kumiega, describes the special project thus:

> For the first few days we do household work. We do not talk about what is to happen here. Habits brought from the city slowly die out: the defensive attitude (necessary there), the dullness of the senses, and indifference. . . . Gradually we become sensitive to one another, we feel our constant, tangible, warm presence. We grow into one, moving, many-peopled body. The work here is hard: we dig a deep pit, grub up stumps of trees, chop wood, carry coal and stones. . . .
>
> Our collective body touches the ground more strongly, as it were, and – because it is collective – nestles in it more closely. We learn to inhabit. We build a large shed which will be our Home. We bring from the woods, and take from the river, trunks of trees and bring armfuls of branches. The work goes on all day and long into the night. . . . On another day we disperse in the forest.[21]

The extreme overcrowding, stress and pollution of Polish city life, as well as the utter darkness and remoteness of the Polish countryside, have generated this monastic (Christian or Buddhist) variant of the spirit of secrecy, the spirit of the *chochoł* symptomatic of withdrawal, waiting, concealment and resistance, but encountering these with new and creative forms of communal life. Kumiega goes on:

> Inside, the activities were naturally of a more confined, intense nature, often involving improvised music, drumming and dancing. There were occasionally a variety of properties, brought in from outside – straw, sand, earth, water in barrels. . . . The only occasion on which words were employed by the organizers apart from practical usage, was infrequently in the form of brief, poetic and metaphoric injunctions, used as a spur to action.[22]

As the project took shape, 'therapy' sessions developed, as well as meditations, 'game' events and group activities of various sorts, where the 'actors' shared their skills, refined over many years, with their 'guests'. Grotowski made a virtue of the inaccessibility of these events to the public at large for, in the Polish context, at least at the time of which I speak, no great virtue attached to accessibility and availability, since what was accessible and available was bound, almost by definition, to be second-rate.

INTO PARATHEATRE

In 1975, under the auspices of the Theatre of Nations Festival, Grotowski presented a 'University of Research' in Wrocław, at which there were visiting companies, films and workshops, with the paratheatrical activities of the Laboratory Theatre extending into night-time sessions entitled *The Beehive* (*Ul*).[23] Already Grotowski was beginning to move still further away from theatre as such, or towards a synthesis of theatre and psychodrama, symbolized by his sacred mountain with its flame burning eternally upon it, symbolic of the creative process. Those who worked with him at this time confirmed the power of his faith in his vision, and in 1976 the Party paper *Trybuna Ludu* (The People's Tribune) published an interview in which Grotowski outlined his ambitious three-part project: *Night Vigil, The Way* and *Mountain of Flame*. The first of these events, as described by Kolankiewicz, was characterized by group activities involving chanting and choreographed rhythmic movements.[24] *The Way* developed the idea of the pilgrimage, in this case a planned trek through the forest towards a remote objective. A hill outside Wrocław was the *Mountain of Flame* with a castle where the group was mustered and organized into a variety of exercises based on the simple principle that had come to underlie all Grotowski's activities: 'You, others, and some kind of space' (Burzyński).[25] Grotowski saw all this as a kind of return to origins, a necessary 'openness' about relationships, impossible in Polish life, and an exercise in 'disarmament', an issue linking East and West and one which relates the private space – since we are 'armed', even against ourselves – to the public. In this extraordinarily stripped-down form Grotowski's work continues to engage with Poland's precarious geographical and political situation, and with the need, which had grown no less urgent, to find a mirror for a society with no viable image of itself beyond official optimism.

The workshops continued, leading up to a new project in 1979, *Tree of People* (*Drzewo Ludzi*). Located in the Laboratory building in Wrocław, it retained the concentration and perhaps some of the exclusiveness, of the Laboratory, but its 'work-flow' (Cynkutis's word) incorporated 400 people[26] in a series of 'experiences' of living, working together and 'encountering', which were guided only to a very small extent. The year 1980 saw the preparation of a piece originally entitled *A la Dostoevsky* (the Russian writer, banned under Stalin, had for a long time been the doyen of subversives in Poland and elsewhere in Eastern Europe). This project saw the light of day as *Thanatos Polski* in 1981. Like *Apocalypsis cum Figuris*, it was a montage of texts, arguably influenced by the work of groups like the Poznań-based Theatre of the Eighth Day, using materials (among other things) by Miłosz and Mickiewicz which had an overt 'condition of Poland' theme. The new openness which could assimilate the work of the most important 'student' theatre of the 1970s was made possible by the political events of 1980–1, which suddenly, and largely unexpectedly, imposed an obligation to speak sincerely upon this secretive and anguished society. Theatrical 'action' could be seen to be reinforcing Solidarity-inspired strikes and demonstrations in the name of presenting, at long last, a truthful contemporary statement about the condition of the nation (we are talking about a country with no institutionalized political opposition). The religious or sacrilegious elements in the performance (Protestant cultures do not appreciate the creative potential of blasphemy) were not new to Grotowski's productions, or those of other Polish directors, but they were clearly reinforced by the fact of the leading role of the Catholic Solidarity in the early days of the movement to overthrow Communism. The Laboratory Theatre did not survive long beyond the imposition of martial law: in 1984 it was formally disbanded, not as a consequence of political reprisals, but because its work was done.

TADEUSZ KANTOR: DEATH AND THE DADA

This account of Grotowski cannot begin to engage with the worldwide influence of his workshop methods, which may have sought inspiration both in the East and in the West, but gave back much more than they had taken. The utter seriousness with which he confronted the theatrical space, which he boldly conceptualized as a kind of existential space at the heart of contemporary experience, and the major contribution he made to the perennial Polish debate about the artist's responsibility to the people, are beyond dispute. Like other such 'encounters', Grotowski's leave behind an aura rather than a body of texts, but his work has been continued by those who have learned from it. The same cannot be said of Tadeusz Kantor, another dramaturge with a devoted company of talented actors and actresses wholly engrossed in realizing his vision, who died in 1990 and left, as far as one can tell, no heir, unless it is Krzysztof Miklaszewski, who has recorded much of his work very expertly on film. In some respects, there is an overlap between his work and Grotowski's, since they are both working with the intricate and eccentric traditions of post-Romantic Polish literature, and specifically the legacy of closet drama.[27] The crucial difference between them, in a word, would be Kantor's word *zagęszczenie*, or density. If Grotowski's theatre is 'poor', Kantor's is 'wrecked',[28] littered with dense layers of symbols, associations, resonances from literary and artistic works belonging (mostly) to the modernist canon. A sculptor and painter by training, strongly influenced by Dada and Surrealism and by the Art Informel (Tachisme) of Matthieu and others, Kantor began his theatrical career with a war-time underground production of Wyspiański's *The Return of Odysseus*,[29] an event which contains the seeds of his fascination with all the components of the theatrical space, and to which he constantly returned in his thought towards the end of his life. The 'random' stage (which he conceives of differently from Grotowski, but no less radically), the 'malleable' auditorium (again there is a superficial resemblance to Grotowski), the set of complex relationships between the text, the actors and the audience, props (the 'bio-object') and the metaphysic which holds them all together, combine with a blend of overt showmanship and subtle transformations of Edward Gordon Craig's aesthetic of the *'Über-Marionette'*.[30]

His experimental theatre, called *Cricot-2*, in honour of a pre-war avant-garde theatre, was founded in Kraków in 1955, and in the early days his work was inextricably linked with the texts of the Polish avant-gardist Witkacy, which he 'minced' (his own word) for his theatre.

Most of Kantor's innovations are contributions to his theory of what he calls 'real' space. His production of Witkacy's *The Little Manor House* was set in a real laundry, *The Water Hen* was staged in an old poorhouse, *Lovelies and Dowdies* (partly) in the cloakroom of the theatre instead of the theatre itself: and in a key essay appended to *Wielopole/Wielopole* he lists some of the 'real places' that have lodged in his memory and imagination, including the railway station (where he waited for Odysseus in *The Return of Odysseus*) and a Post Office (where, in his own words, 'A thousand units of information are caught in a state of weightlessness between sender and addressee': a reference to a happening involving a giant letter and a group of 'postmen'). These places/spaces are linked by what he calls 'a sort of elemental ordinariness ... a familiarity ... a forlornness ... nostalgia, melancholy, sadness ... transitoriness ... poetry/A rooted sorrow, "poverty" ', and they constitute a 'lower order reality'. Reality is defined by Kantor as 'the medium through which fiction finds utterance'.[31] Unlike Grotowski, Kantor believes that fictions, much as we hate them, are all we have, and for Kantor Grotowski's use of space is the nadir of naturalism (or illusionism) and contradicts the basic principle of theatre, which is that the audience belongs to the world of the living, the text to the world of the dead, where the actors are trapped (though not without a struggle). Theatre trespasses, for a licensed period, upon the private space of the spectator, but in doing so it outrages decency and good sense. Thus the audience passing through the cloakroom of the theatre (where, in *Lovelies and Dowdies*, it was waylaid) finds, in Kantor's words,

Something terrifying about it.
If we give rein to our fancy
we might even say
that for the duration of the performance
we are 'in part' left hanging
rubbing shoulders, higgledy-piggledy, with persons unknown,
identified only by numbers
deprived of our liberty
our individuality

humiliated
treated with contempt . . .[32]

This is very far removed from Grotowski's celebration of the kinds of 'encounter' of body and spirit, actor and audience, made possible by the theatrical space. Transgression, yes; but Kantor insists that the audience are, after all, free to leave the world of the dead, bearing the stigma of their experience. The designated space of the stage, therefore, is always with us, however mobile it may be in practice. It is what guarantees the possibility of entering the illusion of 'the real', since it 'frames' the world of dream and recollection (and nightmare and anxiety) that is crucial to his theatre (he would say, to all theatre, since his is only an extreme case of a universal condition).

Poland is itself, by virtue of a series of grotesque historical 'accidents', both a real and a virtual, 'constructed', space. The 'density' of Kantor's theatrical space reminds us of Poland's traumas by reminding us of our own, in a series of obsessive parallelisms and reduplications of the real and represented worlds, littered with objects caught, as Kantor says, 'between the scrap heap and infinity', many of which refer directly to Polish historical events. These are as ambivalent as the marionettes which have always played a major part in his productions, confronting us with the inauthenticity of our own gestures towards 'identity'. Derived in part from Craig, and owing a lot to Bruno Schulz, they have developed some very specific contemporary forms:

> The mannequin in my production of The Water Hen (1976) and the mannequins in The Shoemakers (1970) had a very specific role: they were like a non-material extension, a kind of ADDITIONAL ORGAN for the actor, who was their 'master'. The mannequins already used in my production of Słowacki's Balladyna were DOUBLES of live characters, somehow endowed with higher CONSCIOUSNESS attained 'after the completion of their lives'. These mannequins were already stamped with the sign of DEATH.[33]

KANTOR'S THEATRE OF DEATH

The preoccupation of Polish art with death is striking. It is tempting to explain it, or perhaps explain it away, by reference to the Holocaust; but significantly Kantor (who has his roots in the rich Jewish-Christian traditions of eastern Poland, and was lucky to survive the war) could never have done what Grotowski did, and stage a play in a death camp. This would have been, for him, gross literalism. The inescapable fact of mass extermination is turned, in Kantor's world, into a huge metaphor, invoking the age-old interaction of the living and the dead, a rich source of images in both Catholic and Jewish culture. Passed through the fine sieve of modernism, what this means is really what Proust and Kafka both told us, and what Freud spelt out 'scientifically': that we keep telling ourselves stories to make sense of our knowledge of our own death, which throws an ever-lengthening shadow between us and what we were or wanted to be. The death camp is imprinted upon the modern world and its immortality games. The 'density' of *Dead Class* (1975) codes the layered ephemerality of the self, which goes on repeating itself in forlorn images of memory and desire even while it hears the doors slamming shut behind its back. Poland, of course, has an institutionalized version of this: what we call Hallowe'en is, for that culture, the potent *zaduszki*, All Souls, when the dead walk. *Zaduszki* forms, moreover, the centrepiece of Mickiewicz's masterpiece *Dziady*, wherein art and society join hands in a ritual *kaddish*. Kantor's *Dead Class* works with this rite *à rebours*; the wax effigies represent the 'dead' (anterior, transgressed) selves of the live actors, or the characters they impersonate (since they are all, as in *Wielopole/Wielopole*, hired hacks, whores, and con-men) and the living and the dead vie with each other for possession of a common space in the represented world (the Old People in *Dead Class* 'carry dummies seemingly growing out of their bodies, effigies of themselves, pupils in black school uniform, uniforms with the faces of children'). The alternation of the living Beadle with a dummy 'reinforces the impression that the black schoolroom is but an imitation, the external shell of something whose real existence is long a thing of the past'.[34] The dummy self also tells us about a lost authenticity of being, standing for the vestigial, traumatized childhood self, victim of the adult's regime of *upupenie*.[35] Thus the doubling of actor and dummy compromises both, as they sit side by side on the school benches; it goes without saying that although there are specific Polish sources for this motif, its application is universal. Similarly, the Priest in *Wielopole/Wielopole* has a waxwork double not only to embody his 'dead' self, but also to foreground the duplicity of representation (actor and dummy are alternately cranked into view on a bed machine by the treacherous family). Dummies figure extensively in the episode of the Platoon not only because a soldier is an automaton but because it is the soldier, fallen in battle after battle in Polish history, who best represents the world of the dead. Kantor's father died in the First World War.

The set of *Dead Class* (which Kantor describes as *wrak*, 'the wreck' or 'wreckage') is a schoolroom in which endless drills and repetitions inculcate a kind of 'knowledge' (biblical, historical, philological and so on) without rhyme or reason – a nightmarish running-on-the-spot related to Poland's anguished perception of roles and systems being imposed on her by others. Text and props are both symptomatic of 'the wreck', or 'junk', and, in Kantor's own words,

> Junk is what's left after a violent act of destruction. Evidently it has nothing in common with imitation or repetition, there is nothing arty about it. Junk is the thing it was, but stripped altogether of its everyday functionality and usefulness. Nothing could be more useless. Which is why it is so peculiarly in touch with its past. A tragic past. Its function is only recoverable in recollection. In *Dead Class* the school benches are junk of this sort. But it is not their appearance that makes them junk. They become junk by virtue of the actors playing the old men (and women) who make futile efforts to return, at the close of their lives, to the schoolroom. As things in themselves they are dumb and dead, capable of initiating nothing, even infinitesimally, illusorily, that might slake their insatiable thirst to recover lost time.[36]

The scene of the 'catechism' of rote learning echoes Witkacy and the grotesque 'violation through the ears' sequence of Gombrowicz's *Ferdydurke*.[37] These futile learning-processes combine and contrast with the anxious search for an identity which inspired this compulsive repetition of their childhood humiliation in the first place (cf. Schulz's story *The Old Age Pensioner* from the collection *The Sanatorium Under the Sign of the Hourglass* (1937), which served Kantor as rich source material). Kantor's Dada machines, which he calls 'bio-objects' by virtue of the fact that they rattle about in the gaps left by the departure of truly human activity, express the chillingly contracted and foreshortened life processes of his absurd vision. The Family Machine enacts – grotesquely accelerated – the cycle of life and death, while the Mechanical Cradle, resembling a child's coffin, clatters obscenely in time to the rhythms of the Family Machine. This mechanical superimposition of past, present and future mocks the fetishized family pieties of Polish (and *a fortiori* Polish-Jewish) society; but it is also a comment on the immortality games we all play. The lavatory is the place (we are told) where our characters enjoyed their 'first taste of freedom'; but if there is no freedom within the represented space there is no certainty of any outside of it (as evidenced, for example, by the Woman Behind the Window, who becomes violent and abusive because she is excluded from the scene she observes). 'Escaping' into the so-called 'simultaneous orgy' the characters fall into a re-run of Witkacy's *Tumour Brainard*, re-enacting Tumour's meeting with the Malays: these 'primitive' people are incapable of freeing themselves through transgression, a Malinowskian point which is reiterated in the *Colonial Expedition* sequence (again from Witkacy).[38]

In Kantor's dense wasteland of cultural fragments (where the old dramaturge himself took on the role of a daemonic Tiresias) movement and gesture are absurd, incongruous, out of phase. Word and image fail to coincide; language is maimed and deformed, 'reified', just as the fragments of texts are. Incantation, Dada noise, improvised shouts and grunts are interspersed with literary texts, and with German or Yiddish, so that the human voice, too, becomes an object or an obscure instrument. Towards the end of Part Three of *Dead Class*, for example, there is a chilling moment when the function of the Mechanical Cradle is unexpectedly interrupted and changed (I quote from Jan Klassowicz's scene-by-scene transcript):

The old man's 'dummy' dialogue (Kantor's word, to underline its meaninglessness) ends with a violent quarrel . . . 'I filed for divorce today . . . get out of my sight, you goddam bitch. I am lord of the world!' The Old Woman: 'So that's how it is? So, all I've done for you is nothing, is it? And am I to be kicked around as a reward for my humiliation. And you dare insult what is most sacred in me? There, you double clown!' She takes out and mercilessly shows around what was in the cradle – it looks like testicles, but in fact it is dried-up, dead wood – two wooden balls. All action stops dead for a moment as everybody looks spellbound at this still-life image, the brazen mockery of death. The Old Woman hands the balls to the Old Man who draws back and takes them automatically, and then, frightened, puts them in his pocket. The cradle rumbles on but its sound is different now, hollow. The Stranger, who has been eavesdropping all the time, cries out: But Mrs. Brainard, you mustn't do things like that. It's barbaric.[39]

The problem is resolved by the Old Man With A Bike taking the balls; he 'looks at them tenderly' and says

'Wouldn't even spare a child, the sons of bitches.' He walks stiffly to the cradle and delicately puts the balls in. The cradle keeps rumbling.[40]

This absurd exchange reminds us of a fact that Kantor underlines in more than one context, namely that his theatre is always, from one angle, the 'big top', a circus or vaudeville where farce and knockabout take on metaphysical resonances. As in the circus, we enjoy not only the spectacle and the illusion but also the pleasurable sense of contrivance and device, the machinery that keeps the whole thing running. Backstage, or far up in the tent's great dome, there is something elemental,

subjugated, apparently, by the gilt-and-velvet splendour that shuts it in, the splendour of balconies, caryatids, boxes and stalls. Beyond the idyllic blue sky towers an impenetrable wall. Beyond the sunlit greenery of trees and the marble palaces, great latticeworks of rope, massive winches, poles, breathtaking ladders suspended over dark precipices, iron causeways, batteries of spotlights, cables, ropes, and lines. This is where the action is, in this inferno. This machinery, kept going by the dirty hands of the 'workers', is what sustains the splendid trumpery, the glory, the swagger, the braggadocio, the imposture and the affectation, the fine tissue of deceit displayed on one side only, aimed at the public.[41]

Kantor's Baudelairean flair for allegorizing the everyday world is nowhere more apparent than in *Wielopole/Wielopole*, where he is at his most autobiographical. Poking away at the façades of things, burrowing (like a child) in the holes and corners of family life, where everything is 'estranged', represented as alien, reaching into the cobwebby recesses of memory for the brilliant, distorted images it surprisingly yields up, Kantor constructs (or deconstructs) a life story which is also a set of variations on some of the obsessive patterns of Polish history, and reworks, in bizarre forms, many of the cherished symbols of his culture. It is no more a direct satire on Polish reality than *Dead Class*, yet, like *Dead Class*, it is unimaginable except as a distorting mirror held up to the distorted reality of the country Sylvia Plath described as 'scraped flat by the rollers of wars, wars, wars'.[42] A backless wardrobe, the site of childhood fears, and the place (perhaps) where a Jew survived the war, lets a Platoon pass to share the domestic space of the family. Memory is the photographer/machine-gunner, who freezes each traumatized shot as she records it, tantalizing us by asserting the reality of what Baudelaire called the 'anterior world', a world which we can never repossess. All private and personal spaces have been transgressed by the Platoon, a bizarre *corps-de-ballet* which takes Marian Kantor (the Father) off to the war (specifically the First World War, but in principle all wars) before the marriage ceremony has been completed, turning Helena (the Mother) almost instantly into a victim of the hostilities, leaving her to the not-so-tender mercies of the Family. Nothing escapes Kantor's absurdist vision of the psychopathology of family life, with its mad aunties and its washed-up Uncle Staś, who has come back from Siberia to be greeted with contempt.

MEASURING UP TO THE POWER GAME

There is a macabre appropriateness, therefore, in the fact that Kantor's 1978 production, *Où sont les neiges d'antan?*, should be so strangely prophetic of the *stan wojenny*, or martial law period (the Polish phrase actually means 'state of war', and Poles spoke bitterly of General Jaruzelski's 'war' against the Polish people). This production, revived subsequent to martial law, was Kantor's most esoteric to date, and might well have taken for its epigraph not Villon, but Rimbaud's 'J'ai seul la clé de cette parade sauvage'.[45] Like all his productions, it is 'free from conventionality and from good sense', but unlike the others it has very little in the way of a script to hang its action on: just the murky 'texts' of some of Kantor's own obsessions and the traumas they feed off – and the perennial subtext of Polish history. The acting space is unusually long and thin, giving the impression of a parade ground, and there is a reviewing stand (the Polish word *trybuna* is a very resonant one). There are three black screens: two like conventional wings, the other a sort of backdrop. The auditorium passes around the ends of the 'stage'. Against the backdrop there is a chair with a skeleton dressed in Jewish clothes; at one end of the space is a device known as 'the trumpets of Jericho' which heralds the climax of the play, at the other a heap of earth and a shovel.[44]

The action is an angry and enigmatic series of variations on this space and these 'objects'. It is initiated by a figure in white who pulls on a rope and is joined by eight men, also in white, who become identified with the Russian Volga boatmen (the serfs, in other words, of the song). This is the first of many (sardonic) images of collective work. The rope soon imposes its own dynamic, and we see a tug-of-war, stretching it out as far as the skeleton. It now divides the acting space, carrying all sorts of resonances, but serving above all as an image of forces that cancel one another out, uncertain allegiances, random groupings. It also corresponds to Kantor's all-important boundary of the living and the dead, which theatre knowingly transgresses. 'Leaders' come and go: a fat man, for example, who leads the passive mob in white up and down, a manoeuvre followed by frantic, uncoordinated movements, and flight from the group. It is like a mad parody of social and political processes, but no madder, perhaps, than martial law itself and the panic it produced as it deliberately set out to turn the Polish nation against itself. One of the eight finds a tailor's ruler, and 'threatens' the group with being measured. He laughs as the group melts away to avoid this humiliation. The former leader of the group becomes a rival 'measurer', the true 'Geometer', measuring the rope, cursing the audience and (ritually) appropriating the skeleton's cloak.

Like the Dumb Show in *Hamlet*, Kantor's melodramatic, manic commentary on the usurpation of power and the travesty of rationality that is supposed to justify or rectify it leaves little unsaid. State socialism was much more than just another form of government. It drew heavily upon the iconography both of this world and of the next to justify its mysterious ways. It generated its own Aesopic language, which dealt in indirections and allusions rather than calling a spade a spade.[45] Making any sense of its collapse into absolutism, or of its disintegration and dissolution, is a thankless task; but Kantor seems to enjoy his joke at the expense of the allegorists and interpreters. The jovial man out walking at the beginning of Part Two carries the debris of shattered ideologies stuffed into a bag on his back (recalling Edgar in Kantor's production of *The Water Hen*).[46] Like the characters in *Dead Class*, he seems belatedly to have realized that he is now stuck for ever with his 'dummy' self. The Twins (an inimitable component of Kantor's group) try to help him shove things into the bag. A *miłośnik prasy* (this means something like 'compulsive newspaper reader') appears: as he reads, he throws away his papers, which the Twins pick up. After the Reader comes a Digger, who grabs the shovel and shovels some earth. The Rimbaudesque *parade sauvage* is Kantor's and no one else's, and we will not find an easy key to it by reading off these images against contemporary Polish history; and yet it all looks remarkably like a skeletal prefiguration of the psychotic reality of Polish life during martial law, when the idols of the tribe were dusted off yet again. As in Shakespeare's *Hamlet*, something profoundly disturbing is going on at the interface between the personal and the political worlds, though it is hard to say exactly what it is.

In the final stages, a girl in a bridal veil, anticipating the wrecked Helena of *Wielopole/Wielopole* (a displaced image of the mother-as-child), engages in a series of farcical mistaken identity games with the Twins. People with buckets, passing them down a human chain, and a Rabbi, recalling the burning of the Warsaw Ghetto, make way for the 'unnameable' strutting figure (Himmler) who also enters the action of *Wielopole/Wielopole*. The brutal irrationality of martial law has sparked off traumatic drama – images of 'authority' from the time of the Nazi occupation – as it did in actual fact for many Poles; and it does not surprise us that the bride being dressed for her wedding is actually dead. The Jericho Trumpet, operated by two Jews, sounds, as the Groom pulls up the Bride on a mattress; its first notes make themselves heard through the opening bars of a tango, and two Cardinals enter, dressed in red, dancing to the exotic music. Kantor appears, also moving jerkily to the rhythm of the tango. He, too, tries to bring a kind of order to the proceedings, when suddenly it all vanishes. The dead bride remains, and the men in white enter and try to turn their smocks inside out to make a shroud for her; but the clothing all unravels to the rhythm of the tango, which grows noisier and noisier and then gives way to the deafening sound of marching. The shroud falls on the girl and they all kneel. The 'unnameable' appears again (cf. *Wielopole/Wielopole*). The rope pulls Kantor back to behind the screens, and as he disappears, the marching ceases.

ANOTHER SAVAGE PARADE

Kantor was criticized for not denouncing martial law, but his political response is in his texts, in the nightmares he sent to trouble the sleep of the People's Republic. Shortly before he died, he bitterly condemned the entire period of the rule of the United Workers' Party,[47] but paradoxically, like every satirist, he found his richest material in political folly and irresponsibility, and it would have been artistically inappropriate for him to speak out. As the years passed, and he became ever more conscious of time running out both for him and for Poland, the knowledge reinforced the metaphysical bent of his work. *Let the Artists Die Like Dogs* (1985) harps on death with an ill-mannered obsessiveness. In an interview given to Michał Kobialka he makes this movingly personal statement:

> Someone, who is another I, is walking up to me. In a moment we will pass each other or bump into each other. I am thinking about this moment with growing uneasiness. However, it does not escape my perception that I am not walking forward but in the direction of the depth where I started a moment ago. I am walking forward back.[48]

Approaching the looking-glass land of death, he sees advancing upon him the 'I' he has become, with an endless depth stretching out behind him. This is his new insight: only in death do we meet ourselves as we truly are – which is why his theatrical pimps and whores, and the artists whose company they keep, hold the keys to the kingdom. The artist holds on only with the utmost difficulty to what is his. This is why state patronage was even more cynical than the withdrawal of state patronage: it is a more effective way of silencing the artists (Kantor tells us that Dante's 'Abandon hope', addressed – of course! – to artists, was printed on the front pages of newspapers in 1948). The Hungarians cancelled an exhibition and performance of Kantor's work. Why? Silence: one doesn't ask, or one didn't. It is this silence that surrounds *Let the Artists Die Like Dogs*: the silence of the cemetery, the prison, and the text. His play undertakes a journey, not into the past, like *Wielopole/Wielopole*, but forward/back beyond the frontiers of death: a journey continued in *I'll Come Again No More* and *Today is my Birthday*.[49]

The *terminus ad quem* for *Let the Artists Die Like Dogs*, the culminating ensemble piece towards which Kantor's action is moving, is a grotesque deconstruction of the sixteenth-century *Weit Stoss* (*Wit Stwosz*) altarpiece in Kraków, with its central image of the Assumption of the Blessed Virgin. As usual, Kantor's interpretation of his images is highly personal: not least the ghastly horseman, Pilsudski on his legendary white charger, the strong leader Poles were praying for as the Soviet Empire began to disintegrate. Kantor's vision of the Inferno in Part One (a vision of eternity) is not distinct from the small childhood room of *Wielopole/Wielopole*, since, as Dante points out, the damned are condemned to relive for ever those experiences which damned them, and this is what Hell is. There is some comfort in the (Proustian) domestic scale of the drama of damnation and redemption, however, and in its absurdity. The company's extraordinary pair of identical twins, near the beginning of the piece, lose each other and go in search of each other, and in this (farcical) way dramatize Kantor's own quest for himself. 'Real I' sits on the stage, while 'I dying' is in bed so that (as Kantor tells us) he can confront the future 'me dying'. He is also there as a 6-year-old, playing soldiers. The child soldier is followed by 'the unnameable', the carnivalesque Pilsudski, and ranks of lead soldiers. Asclepius appears, only to be mocked by the Twins; then a group of Players, led by the Jailor, wearing a three-cornered hat inscribed 'Let the Artists Die Like Dogs'. In Act Two the room is invaded by spectres from History and from Death, followed by the ubiquitous Players: the room has become a kind of night shelter, and the 'real' play can begin: a scene of torment, the Hanged Man with his scaffold, the Trickster/Pimp, the Man Washing his Dirty Feet (complete with Basin), the Blatant Tart from the Cabaret, etc., the Sister, the Mother, and the Identical Twins, the little Boy and (of course) his Hero on Horseback: this is the Inferno (or the Carnival) of Everyday Life. The Dying Man describes his agony, interrupted by the parade of heroes from the child's fantasies (the Troupe of the Theatre of Death), followed again by the Players. The Author prepares the way for a second Circus of Agony. Kantor describes these latter sequences as a 'Vicious Circle', a typically Polish theme. The Author is left with the gallows, and exits saying 'And thus I spent my sixty-four years'. The Hanged Man sings a defiant song and exits too.[50]

Act Three begins with the Players and the inhabitants of the room intoning a rustic hymn. As in a dream, the room's only door begins to move closer to us. Weit Stoss enters: come back from the Dead, dressed in bohemian style, but with a Cross under his arm, he dances with the Cabaret Tart, and starts making his Altarpiece, which changes into a Prison Cell, then a Torture Chamber. The Apostles are played by the local inhabitants, and the Sister becomes the Virgin. The Jailor has changed into a Hotel Page (carrying Stoss's bags) and then into a Concentration Camp Executioner. The Tart becomes the Angel of Death, and the other Players are similarly transformed. In Act Four the Vagabond-Players make their last bid for survival: the fates of the Whores and Pimps accompany the death of 'Him to whom the Overture said goodbye', the 'unique one'. The Night Shelter becomes a Prison. The Angel of Death tempts the Prisoners. Weit Stoss gives his (travesty) message to the world: the last work of the Master of Kraków is The Barricade, with all that implies. As with all Kantor's work, it is the images (terrifying skeletal horses, split Cricot packing cases forming a barricade, and dozens of others) and the way they are processed that compose the real 'text'.[51]

YOUNGER AVANT-GARDE GROUPS

Kantor was one of the major artists of his generation, but it would be wrong to suggest that the Polish avant-garde stage was simply the preserve of Kantor and Grotowski alone. The rivalry between them was of course so extreme that it would be hard to find evidence of any mutual influence; but it is always hard, where Polish directors are concerned, to identify cross-currents, or to form an overview of developments, for several reasons. One is the deliberate built-in ephemerality about much of their work which had something to do with censorship, and something to do with an avant-garde version of authenticity (and keeping one step ahead of the censorship). Another is the polemical thrust which made every group the mouthpiece of an instant philosophy of theatre, in the modernist manner, critical of the ruling ideology, provisional, and generally obscure. Nevertheless, the most interesting alternative groups in Poland of the 1960s, 1970s and 1980s owe something to Grotowski, or Kantor, or to both, and may in turn have exerted some small influence on these two. Although I have drawn a sharp contrast between Kantor and Grotowski, it should be said that 'poverty' complements 'density' in the complex allegories of Polish theatre (and Polish life). In fact, they form the twin poles of the two contrasted groups which end my study, Gardzienice and the Theatre of the Eighth Day. The former clearly gravitates towards Grotowski, forming part of the 'return of the people', associated with Grotowski's later work, which I defined mainly in terms of a fascination with folk rituals as the basis of new 'encounters'; while the latter, with its rich, surreal, biting satire, symbolic density and literariness, is rather more akin to Kantor (though I am not aware of an explicit debt). Both these theatres are 'alternative' in a rather different way from either Kantor or Grotowski, and many of their similarities to one or the other of these directors spring from their use of the rich fund of symbols and images generated from the Polish heritage and Polish realities. Always in conflict with 'the system', they are, like Kantor and Grotowski, unimaginable outside of the context of a country where the arts had a strong following, were well supported financially, and constituted both a safety-valve and an opposition. Both had from the outset student affiliations, and wore a kind of student 'camouflage' when it suited them.

The Gardzienice group was founded in 1978, and when it is not on one of its very successful tours it operates in and around the village of Gardzienice, near Lublin, in eastern Poland, a rather desolate agricultural area where there were once many Jewish settlements. Grupa Działania, in some ways similar, flourished in the late 1970s on a 'utopian' programme of paratheatrical events in part drawn from the material circumstances of life in Lucim, the village near Torun where they settled, and in part from a participational aesthetics familiar in modern theatre, breaking down the boundaries between actor and spectator in a, by Polish standards, relatively relaxed and open manner, reminiscent of street theatre and some kinds of touring theatre in this country. They went further, however, than most of their Western equivalents: artists working with the group actually changed the environment, altering the visual aspect of the villages themselves with paintings and sculptures. Gardzienice revived and reinforced the traditional, not-long-dead ceremonies of the village, and devised new ones in keeping with a community's 'roots', so that Poland's backwardness, which Communism (against its own declared intentions) reinforced, served as a dramatic resource. The aim was to build an alternative to 'mass' culture. In contradistinction to the educational projects with theatre in Britain which in other ways it resembles, the Polish group struck that Polish vein which one might rightly call atavistic, and even in some sense nationalistic, if these words did not have such negative connotations for us. Although neither of these groups has a formal religious affiliation, where Gardzienice is concerned one has to reckon with the persistence of Catholicism (to say nothing of the still strangely ceremonious, even ritualistic ways of the Poles), in order to grasp how such a reaction against the official Dom Kultury (House of Culture), implanted by the Party for largely propagandist reasons in every rural area, might have been possible.[52]

GARDZIENICE: THE POETICS OF THE MUDDY FIELD

From its beginnings in 1976, Gardzienice has pursued an independent course, with a well-defined programme. Its founder, Włodzimierz Staniewski, formerly a member of the Kraków STU and a collaborator with Grotowski, had a vision from the outset of how his work might contribute to the revival, and survival, of an authentic national culture, in the face of the onslaught from the media and from the dubious institutional 'folk' culture encouraged by the Party. Staniewski's faith in his vision has been borne out by the work of the group and its accompanying statements and manifestos, as well as by the sympathetic 'anthropological' contributions of its academic followers. He left Grotowski after five years, in 1979, because, in his own words, he found himself in a 'dangerous and threatening situation': a pregnant phrase, which may refer to nothing more than a need to free oneself from the influence of a charismatic figure, but probably also registers a dissatisfaction with Grotowski's elitism. In Gardzienice's neo-realism, theatre confronts Poland's rural poverty as if it were a resource, in practical and provocative ways. There is little time for self-communing, though the Grotowskian revaluation of the idea of the 'holy day' (*Święto*) has left a strong imprint on their work. For Gardzienice, work in the community means precisely that.

Zbigniew Osiński,[53] the foremost Polish authority on Grotowski, defines Gardzienice's principal endeavour as the effort to unearth authentic folk culture in those rare places where it still survives, especially in the minds and hearts of older people in the countryside, and to use it to create an environment in which the group can develop its own theatrical ideas in relation to the life of the community (pragmatically as well as artistically). For all its optimism, it is a movement born of desperation, and responds to the tragic fact that the spirit of the community has been killed off both by ideology (persistent attempts, strongly resisted, to Sovietize the peasants) and consumerism, two powerful forces for control. Gardzienice offers an image of the flowers that might grow on the grave of these contradictions. The Russian cultural historian Mikhail Bakhtin,[54] a Christian whose 'coded' writings defied Stalinism, provides whatever additional theory is needed. This is (*mutatis mutandis*) that theory of carnival which has recently become fashionable among Western scholars who for different reasons are denied the riches of a religious culture and its potential for significant acts of transgression. The earliest work of the group (whose actual 'repertoire' has deliberately been kept small, to allow for the continuous process of osmosis that shapes their interaction with a range of different environments) was based on Rabelais' *Gargantua and Pantagruel*, a production inspired by Bakhtin's imaginative study of Rabelais in relation to the ecclesiastical culture of the Middle Ages.

Osiński speaks of this, quite rightly, in terms of 'grasping the entity of human life (joy and suffering, coarseness and lyricism, the fear of death)', but he also stresses, with good reason, its 'opposition to the official/formal and hierarchic kind of relationship between men'. Bakhtin, the successor to the Russian Formalists, builds his theories (especially the influential concept of the 'dialogic principle') on an aesthetic derived from Shklovsky's emphasis on art's capacity to 'make strange' and thereby to repossess forms of discourse (and thus experience) that have become automated and empty.[55] Another major influence identified by Osiński is that of Evgeni Vakhtangov, the Russian actor, director, and educationalist. Gardzienice took as their credo a quotation from Vakhtangov:

> The country-folk experience the surrounding reality, let it pass through the prism of their soul and reveal it truly experienced in folk art by means of images kept in memory. . . . Art ought to meet the country-folk soul. When it meets the soul of an artist who understands the words of the folk-soul it ought to result in a thoroughly folk product.[56]

Osiński compares this with Gardzienice's

> An artist ought to make an attempt at profound understanding of country folk and not at teaching it. He ought to rise to those people realizing their level and not in a conceited manner trying to raise them to himself.[57]

The third influence is the eminent pre-war director Juliusz Osterwa and the 'Reduta' group. As Osterwa said:

> An idea. It is only worth mentioning if it realises itself in the shape of pottery, not only aesthetic but also practical.[58]

Less exclusive than Grotowski, more far-reaching than Osterwa's theories, Gardzienice extends the workshop principle into the community, making the culmination of any series of performances a fully communal activity, drawing upon the skills, crafts and trades of the village, as well as their folklore, songs and symbols. The theatrical space is carved out of the shared space of the village and its fields by means of a series of planned rhythmic interventions which run through the whole, catching up all the threads of its pseudo-narrative in a hyperbolic, associative, and accumulative series of overlapping scenes. But equally, in a quotation from Bakhtin, Staniewski speaks in more hysterical terms of the way that

> All objects are drawn by the motion of life which makes them the living participants of events. The objects take part in the

story, they are not contrasted with action as its passive background.[59]

Osiński notes that there is, inevitably, a degree of ambivalence about the (very powerful) intervention of this 'intellectual', symbolic, and quasi-religious activity into the rural community. Staniewski acknowledges the dangers; he speaks of what he is doing as potentially an 'aggressive move against strangers', and he realizes great care must be exercised to avoid preaching or bullying. Sometimes there is some resistance: some performances have met with indifference, some with hostility; but most, he tells us, have involved the community in significantly creative ways. There is also some danger of sanctimoniousness: but here again, when Włodzimierz Pawluczuk compares the Gardzienice 'expedition as a way of being' to the biblical Abraham's 'expedition' to the promised land,[60] a Polish reader is less likely to blench than an English one is. Gardzienice may appear didactic, but the Rabelais production, and the more recent *Avvakum*, foreground not the didacticism but the transgressiveness of the whole operation in ways that are thoroughly congenial and comprehensible to the Polish mind, urban or rural. Pawluczuk quotes Bruno Schulz, an 'intellectual' writer with a deep awareness of the roots of story-telling and the permanent validity of myths and symbols:

> Did the reader ever hear anything about parallel time strands in double-stream time? Yes, there exist such side branches of time, a little illegal and problematic, to be sure, but when one carries such contraband as we do, such overtime events, not to be classified – one really must not be too fastidious.[61]

Under the duress of the expedition and of working together, a rhythm is established, actions become meaningful for their own sake, ritualized, and the artist's rather intellectual 'contraband' acquires a 'density' of meaning comparable to that of which Kantor speaks. Sheds and barns, lit by candlelight and torchlight, become mystical sites lost in the (very dark and pretty trackless) Polish countryside. In this way, Gardzienice, like other contemporary Polish companies, and despite a marked pragmatic bent which is not altogether typical of Polish artists, still wears the mantle of Mickiewicz's Messianic Romanticism. Pawluczuk's description of the Ostrów Północny expedition of 1979 stresses the difficulty and danger of the journey, which becomes a kind of Pilgrim's Progress across what sounds like a half-savage country. Inevitably, there is also an encounter with and a journey through language, since (as Pawluczuk demonstrates through examples) Gardzienice is forced to create a new rhetoric simply in order to destroy the old rhetoric; a process which is, of course, endless. The arrival at Sanniki, and the place itself (with its pathos and nakedness), is part of what Holy Theatre is about:

> The performance took place in the middle of the village, in the scenery of old farm buildings. The background was an old, dilapidated shed, not used for many years. Earlier, such sheds were haunted, now the shed itself haunts. It is a symbol of decay and death looming like fate over the neighbourhood. In and around Sanniki there are many such sheds totally abandoned, ruined and rotting, as if exerting their last effort to keep on the surface of existence.
>
> And this ruined shed, one of the many sheds – symbols always and inseparably evoking sadness and melancholy – that evening this shed came alive, arose from the dead, became bright with many lights, gained a specific lustre. Here the Sanniki dwellers assembled. In front of the shed many fires were aflame. . . . The door opened abruptly and a fiery cart, covered with hundreds of candles, came out. This in itself was enough for a burst of great joy, I might say – enthusiasm among the gathered people. But then a sad, melancholy tune about unhappy love flew out.
>
> The sadness lasted briefly. The drums were touched, there was a rustle and thunder and the performance was transformed into a dynamic eruption of flames, movement, physical agility, rhythms and words, crude, I'd even say obscene, but in such harmony with the whole, that all obscenity evaporated like water from a cake leaving a strong crispness. Old women shake their sides with laughter. Men joke, roughly but quite decently.[62]

AVAKKUM OUT OF DOSTOEVSKY: A RUSSIAN SOURCE

The Gardzienice project, initially hedged around with all the secrecy characteristic of People's Poland, has now acquired a public face and an international audience. Its 'folk' rituals (or 'Native Culture', as Staniewski calls it) have inevitably encountered the realities of mechanical reproduction, despite all its efforts to avoid this, and the grainy, atmospheric photographs in *The Gardzienice Project '89*[63] cannot help making the poverty of the village and its ramshackle buildings look spuriously 'collectable' (though many villagers can doubtless remember a time when you could still buy wood, bricks, paint etc. over the counter, and when people took pride in looking after their houses). Moreover, Gardzienice now tours as well. The current major performance of the company is *Avvakum*, combined at Cardiff and elsewhere with *Gathering* (their basic induction to principles and methods). It comes as no surprise to find that the text is religious, but it is perhaps somewhat more surprising to find that it is Russian, until one remembers that Poland's 'Western' eyes still habitually look East for spiritual inspiration. *Avvakum* is a Russian wasteland of Dead Souls, and in addition to its other functions it says on behalf of the Russians that which they are still in no position to say on their own account. Halina Filipowicz's paraphrase brings out the contemporaneity of this play about the seventeenth-century leader of the Old Believers:

> The Old Believers, radical optimists convinced that the Russian people are capable of purifying their spiritual life, believed in the inevitable victory of the ancient traditions of the Russian Church despite Nikon's barbarically enforced innovations . . . the pessimists abandoned all hope for a spiritual renewal and preached mass suicide . . . thousands of men, women, and children drowned themselves or fled to the woods where they cast themselves into the flames in a deranged rite of purification through water or fire. These orgies of death were often accompanied by nightmarish bacchanals . . . Avvakum was declared a heretic and thrice deported with his wife and children to Siberia, where he spent twenty-five years.[64]

There is no mistaking the specifically Polish reference of this contemporary mystery play, however, Avvakum the prophet and saint is the artist/visionary who, throughout Polish history, has kept the sacred flame burning, and has been rewarded with death or exile and vilification. The 'modernizers', prophets of the socialist utopia, are recognizably Dostoevsky's 'devils' (or those possessed by devils) careering to their destruction in a frenzy of lies and excess. Staniewski follows Christian eschatology in his insistence on the need to die into life, and for him the place of exile is the place of prophecy. From the obscurantism, violence and degradation of Russian history, as much as from its profound spirituality, the Western mind can learn more about itself and about the snares and pitfalls of its own rationality than it will ever discover from sources closer to home. Over the religious lamentations, prayers and hymns hangs the Dostoevskian spectre of human futility, as well as the spectre of Communism, which, as those two sad gentlemen, Messrs Marx and Engels, truly said, haunts Europe, not in the way they thought, nor even in the shape of Heine's 'dark hero', but in the familiar guise of the ghost of an alcoholic down-and-out groping his way to the nearest vodka store.[65]

This image, supplied to me by the poet and literary theorist Tadeusz Slawek, might have been lifted from a production by my last group, the Theatre of the Eighth Day. Their intriguing name is an act of homage to the important Polish prose writer Marek Hłasko, whose novella *The Eighth Day of the Week*[66] is a classic of the neo-realism of the 1950s and 1960s which is currently undergoing a revaluation. The 'eighth day' is the one we spend the other seven looking forward to (or in some cases back to), the one that never was and never will be, but which all puerile utopias, Eastern Marxist and Western consumerist, capitalize upon. If we label Gardzienice alternative theatre, Eighth Day belongs in some sense to the amazingly vigorous, innovative and widespread student theatre movement that flourished in the 1960s and 1970s and far exceeded the brief suggested by its title. To do it justice, one would have to examine the work of a dozen companies, including Pstrąg, Provisorium, Academia Ruchu, Teatr 77, and the very different Scena Plastyczna of Leszek Mądzik, as well as the Lublin Konfrontacje, a very lively Festival of Student Theatre. The ZSMP, or Socialist Union of Students, was (despite many disputes) very well funded throughout the period of Communist rule; and although, as Aldona Jawłowska shows in her excellent study,[67] there had always been a complicated relationship between the Party organization and cultural bodies in the universities, there is no doubt that Party funds were available, often in a lavish scale, for student theatre. It is doubtful whether this kind of theatre will survive the demise of the United Workers' Party, which is a nice paradox (but one which can be met with all too frequently in Polish cultural life today). It should also be borne in mind that Eighth Day, like some other 'student' groups, used this designation as a convenient device, students being granted a certain licence, and also being in receipt of generous funding. Its composition was never exclusively student.

Eighth Day was founded in Poznań in 1977, and made its first big impact with a show (the right word, I think) called *Prezecena dla Wszystkich* (Bargains for All). Eighth Day is remarkably free of programmes, metaphysics, totalizing visions, holiness or holism; yet of course it *is* 'more than theatre', in Jawłowska's beguiling phrase, and it takes a no less catastrophist view of the state of Poland (and the world) than any of the other directors whose work I have described. Jawłowska describes their first production as an attempt to 'show the rules of the game as they apply to Polish society in the seventies', and they are pretty savage rules for all but a small mafia. The production reflected a feeling that the Party had succeeded in its principal objective of 'dividing and ruling' by fostering in society a subtle evil of compromise, dishonesty and resignation.[68] The play, like their other productions, was a huge collage, like some sort of giant cabaret, with neither protagonist nor plot, but illustrating through hyperbole, irony and the grotesque, and with a surreal flow of images, the distortions that had poisoned social and personal life as a consequence of the hollow rhetoric of authoritarian 'optimism'. The title was unambiguous: 'bargains for all' evoked the shabbiness of Polish life, attributable to the Party's neglect of human needs in favour of spending on (largely superfluous) heavy industry. The universal corruption that followed meant (among other things) that the dollar became all-powerful. People solved most problems by opening a bottle, and alcoholism features in a vivid sequence which dramatizes the double-think of an ideology which uses drink as a necessary safety valve, instrument of control, and source of revenue, while hypocritically condemning drunkenness and treating alcoholics as common criminals. Equally, 'the crowd' or 'the mob' act and speak with the irrationality of any oppressed group defending its own interests and anathematizing every kind of departure from the (unbearably narrow) social norms. The rhetoric of 'building a new tomorrow' is mocked in configurations of actors representing workers and peasants going through the motions of building the Grand Hotel, one of them becoming more and more desperate, to the accompaniment of the kind of official 'work song' composed in the 1950s (the period in which Wajda's devastating *Człowiek z Marmuru* (Man of Marble) is set).[69]

The sequence of lurid, strident images continues, growing more and more surreal, with a grotesque Priest elevating the Host, which is a gold coin; it is followed by pious platitudes about family life, and a parodic babble of advertising jargon of the bland 'informational' sort used in the socialist countries to persuade people to accept what was available and not ask for anything different. Bogus folklore (as propagated by dance groups, etc.) also comes in for satire, while cabaret-style dancing girls display slogans like 'Freedom', 'Fair Play', 'Fraternity', and 'Socialism', and sing hit songs. A possible echo of Kantor enters with the doubling of actors with dolls in the final procession. Eighth Day, in programme notes accompanying the performance, protests that it does not wish to impose any views on the audience, and simply wants to make us laugh and cry at the follies of contemporary society, thereby arousing in spectators a heightened moral awareness. But the blandness of this statement must be understood in the context of the group's devastating 'comic strip' imagery of the breakdown of dialogue in society, and thus linked to the 'state of arrest' which generated it.[70] The theatre's primary targets might be defined as the abuse of language and the values (or lack of them) of the new executive class. It is not directly aimed at the Party – this would have been impossible in the late 1970s, in any case – but Party functionaries are nevertheless pilloried in the guise of the philistines who have settled for a quiet life and are playing the system and making the right noises when called upon to do so, and encouraging the great majority of the population to follow their lead. It may be another irony that a semi-underground theatre in a People's Republic should speak to a large (and ecstatic) audience in the language of humanism, but we need to keep reminding ourselves that no formal political opposition to Marxism was possible at the time, and theatre took on this role.

Ach, jakże godnie żyliśmy (1979) (Ah, How Splendid Life Was Then), as Aldona Jawłowska rightly remarks, asks the same question about the validity of 'paradise on earth' that the earlier production asked (as did many student companies throughout the 1970s), but more bitterly and in even more lurid images.[71] The questions may be more agonized, but they are just as unanswerable, communicating a Dostoevskian hunger for belief, the terror of ultimate things, and a sense that social institutions are caricatures of themselves, and scarcely need to be travestied in performance. What in this 'puerile utopia' (and the production combines an adolescent rawness with its sophisticated satire) can reconcile us to our own death? or, still worse, to the knowledge of the futility of our sacrifices, whether to 'the cause' or to our own nearest and dearest? Humanity wants 'paradise now'; its dreams are unrealizable, but this refusal of the consolations of historical inevitability is a desperate refusal that constitutes a value in itself. The production takes a perverse delight in the lies and hypocrisy of a society riddled with contradictions undreamed of by Marx or Engels. This play is even more of a collage than the other, and contains everything from a kind of 'degraded' social realism to borrowings from Romanticism and passionate ironic tirades.

The play opens with a 'naturalistic' scene in a railway waiting-room, with the passengers engaging in a very 'unnatural' debate about the existence of God. A drunken girl obsessively re-runs the murder of two local men. A traveller enters, half-opening his case from time to time, in which there is a picture of an idyllic scene, house, garden and all (Eighth Day makes impressive use of images 'quoted' within the represented world). Men rebel to no end, deserting God's prison (the existential condition) in order to rush into the prison of History, trying to build a world out of hatred. Mozart's Requiem blasts out, underlining, with consciously blatant irony, the symbolism of the desperate search for God. A great inflated belly of Nemesis descends from the clouds, spewing pink piggy-banks, and a string of shining toy lorries comes out of the shadows, cruising along one after the other, until they reach a point where the road is broken and they fall into the void. The action shifts to a lower part of the stage, and to a workers' council, drinking and singing its own praises in Russian. The 'people', they say, are bored, they need a few martyrs and holy men. After discussing how to stir things up, they shift to problems of production: how can we encourage the consumption of more potatoes? These Swiftian caricatures of the 'folk' and the 'production line' are bitter comic-strip responses to the flattening and squeezing of reality by the 'organs' (of Party power) and the media – the raw material of People's Poland in terminal disarray. Eighth Day's Manichaean running on the spot passes rapidly over images of revolution, liberation, fantasy and reverie, death and isolation, to come to rest, chillingly, on the figure of the *Übermensch*, dreaming (yet again) of transcending and transforming this broken world. The concluding scene takes place in darkness, with one of the actors speaking as a 'disinherited son', claiming nothing but the right to speak, offering the audience only the right to listen, but not insisting on their agreement. A Genet-like debt to cabaret is apparent in the take-it-or-leave-it off-handedness with which the production throws big issues about, capturing like nothing else the mood of the end of the Gierek era. It is full of the bitter conviction that politicians only take power in order to abuse it, and of the black, self-destructive Romanticism of the national self-images being recycled in the period. Eighth Day may have helped to make Solidarity possible; but it also prefigures martial law, and from our present vantage point has the air of a Last Judgement.

CONCLUSIONS

It is difficult to predict the future of Polish theatre. The political situation in the country is odder than ever, but the oddity is no longer so rich in dramatic potential, and the days of lavish funding for the arts are over. Mazowiecki's short-lived new deal has given way to Wałęsa's uneasy and rather autocratic democracy, which lacks the charisma of Gierek's doomed era, but is still bankrupt, and has found little alternative to repeating the United Workers' Party's exhortations to consume less and work harder. Now that the Party itself can no longer be blamed for the dreariness and hardship of life, it is more difficult for satire to find its targets, and the silent majority doubtless feels (as to some extent it always did) that it can do no good to rock the boat. Poland's theatrical traditions will persist, of course, but the moment of which I have spoken has gone for ever. Freedom of speech is a wonderful thing, but history has never shown any evidence of a necessary relationship between it and creativity. Meanwhile, the economy has taken a nose-dive unparalleled since the war. A new 'realism' is in the air; and the issues are no longer so directly political, or expressed so symbolically, or so embedded in the national culture and the mythographic past of Romanticism. The new tone may have been set by the superb *Decalogue* series of films by Krzysztof Kieślowski: sharply focused, harsh and aimed directly and practically at the different kind of moral void threatening the emergent Polish society of the 1990s. The era of the Party is already beginning to look – for those who did not suffer too much – like an intelligible, and even collectable, human aberration. As Tadeusz Slawek put it not long ago, in lurid imagery redolent of Eighth Day,

> This monster has been with us, its claws are still there, its fangs flash in the dark (a bit more blunt these days), its cloak is a little bit tattered, and on the whole the vampire looks a bit like Bela Lugosi, dangerous but pathetic, treacherous although predictable. It still sucks blood all right, but now we have a supply of wooden sticks, and garlic has also produced good crops this year. . . . What is threatening is *people*. . . . We have been turned into a pale shadow of men: human relationships have been severed since everybody is a competitor in a sugar/gas/

butter/cheese line; the dominating model of life is that of cheap, vile, and brutal cunning . . . social life has lost all the charm of human tenderness even when measured only with a yardstick of conventional good manners.[72]

If my account of the work of selected Polish theatre groups in the post-war period is partial and inconclusive, this is for reasons of space, and because the time for a complete evaluation of the extraordinary achievements of this embattled national culture has not yet arrived. Anyone who experienced the excitement of those 'alternative' productions in the claustrophobic context of the ailing Marxist state cannot help being apprehensive about the long-term effects on Polish culture of standing in line; but the queue this time is the one outside the Common Market headquarters, and the price of entry may turn out to be higher than any the Communists could have devised. Bereft of their subsidies, even the more 'institutional' theatres are having to reassess their production policies, while journals and publishing houses turn abroad in their search for subsidies, advertising copy and investment. Worse: the once highly valued and avidly collected classics of 'forbidden' writing moulder in bookshops the way the works of Marx and Engels used to. This is the price of freedom anywhere in the world, but the Communist aftermath has left a hunger for the forbidden fruit of Western 'decadence' that will not be easily satisfied, and writers and artists, long treated with special wariness and respect, have been thrown into the market at the deep end.

NOTES

1 See Norman Davies's extraordinarily illuminating two-volume study of Polish history, *God's Playground*, Oxford, Clarendon Press, 1981. Davies sees with unusual clarity how closely Polish literature and Polish history are connected.
2 Bertolt Brecht used this term to describe the kind of commercial theatre that 'dishes up' a spectacle, by contrast with his Epic Theatre, which deconstructs it.
3 Czesław Miłosz, *Native Realm*, Harmondsworth, Penguin Books, 1988, from the chapter entitled 'City of my youth'. Miłosz's account of the wilder shores of the Polish imagination, *The Land of Ulro*, Manchester, Carcanet Press, 1985, is equally indispensable.
4 Jerzy Grotowski, *Towards a Poor Theatre*, ed. Eugenio Barba, London, Eyre Methuen, 1969.
5 Tadeusz Kantor, *Wielopole/Wielopole*, trans. and ed. G. M. Hyde and Mariusz Tchorek, London, Marion Boyers, 1990. This is the most

accessible volume in English, and contains numerous theoretical pieces.

6 'Closet drama' is a generally accepted term (see Alex Preminger, *Princeton Encyclopedia of Poetry and Poetics*, London, Macmillan, 1975, p. 142) for a kind of drama 'designed for reading in the study (closet) or to small groups rather than for performance on the public stage'. The Romantic period was particularly rich in closet drama, and Shelley's *The Cenci* (1819) is an instance of an 'unstageable' play that later staged. In the Polish context, closet drama flourished as a direct consequence of political oppression.

7 G. M. Hyde, 'A New Lease of Death', intro. to Tadeusz Kantor, *Wielopole/Wielopole*.

8 The key texts are Adam Mickiewicz's *Dziady* (1832) and Stanisław Wyspiański's *Wesele* (1901); but cf. also Stanisław Ignacy Witkiewicz (Witkacy), *The Shoemakers*, in *The Madman and the Nun and Other Plays*, trans. and ed. D. G. Gerould and C. S. Durer, Seattle, Washington University Press, 1968.

9 Witold Filler, *Contemporary Polish Theatre*, Warsaw, Interpress Publishers, 1977, ch. 2, p. 17.

10 A prime instance of this recycling in contemporary Polish literature is Tadeusz Konwicki's, *The Polish Complex*, Harmondsworth, Penguin Books, 1983.

11 David Bradby and John McCormick, *People's Theatre*, London, Croom Helm, 1978.

12 Grotowski's use of this term from St John of the Cross is heterodox, since he incorporates in it states of trance and ecstasy which St John specifically excludes from the 'negative way' that leads to the knowledge of God.

13 Grotowski's use of this term relates it not only to consumerism, but to the habit of recycling in post-modern culture.

14 See Peter Brook, *The Empty Space*, Harmondsworth, Penguin Books, 1972.

15 A theatrical paradigm appears at the heart of Russian Formalism (see my forthcoming book, *Formalism*, Routledge).

16 See Christopher Innes, *Holy Theatre*, Cambridge, Cambridge University Press, 1981.

17 Konwicki, *The Polish Complex*.

18 Jerzy Grotowski, op. cit., on Wyspiański's play *Akropolis* (1904), contribution by Ludwik Flaszen, pp. 61–71.

19 ibid., p. 63.

20 See Innes, *Holy Theatre*.

21 Leszek Kolankiewicz, cited in Jennifer Kumiega, *The Theatre of Grotowski*, London, Eyre Methuen, 1987, p. 172.

22 Kumiega, *The Theatre of Grotowski*.

23 ibid.

24 Kolankiewicz, cited by Kumiega, op. cit., p. 188.

25 In an article in *Odra* (Nov. 1984) entitled 'Grotowskiego Teatr po Drodzie', Tadeusz Burzynski defines Grotowski's essential (unanswered) question as 'Jak być, aby naprawde być?' ('How to be, so as really to be?').

26 Kumiega, op. cit., p. 204.

27 See Kantor, *Wielopole/Wielopole*. The best study of the development of

Kantor's art is still Wieslaw Borowski, *Kantor*, Warsaw, 1982 (in Polish).

28 The Polish word 'wrak' has the sense of 'debris' and 'wreckage'.

29 Stanisław Wyspiański, *Powrót Odysa*, 1907 (in English as *The Return of Odysseus*, trans. Howard Clarke, Indiana, Indiana University Publications, 1966).

30 Edward Gordon Craig, *The Actor and the Über-Marionette* (1907), in E. G. Craig, *On the Art of the Theatre*, London, Heinemann, 1911. Craig's theories and theatre designs were much more influential in Poland and Russia than in England.

31 Kantor, *Wielopole/Wielopole*, pp. 150–1.

32 ibid., p. 152.

33 Tadeusz Kantor, *The Theatre of Death: A Manifesto*, in Catherine Itzen and Bohdan Drozdowski, eds, *Gambit 33-34: Special Double Polish Theatre Issue*, London, John Calder, 1979, p. 101.

34 Tadeusz Kantor, *Dead Class*, in Itzen and Drozdowski, *Gambit 33-34*, pp. 111ff.

35 A coinage used by Gombrowicz in *Ferdydurke*, 1935, formed from the Polish word 'pupa' (a variant of 'dupa', 'arse'). The word means, more or less, 'to sit people on their arses and preach all kinds of nonsense at them'. Adam Czerniawski and I have been debating the best English translation for this: he favours 'bottomize' (i.e. 'lobotomize') while I prefer 'bummify' (i.e. 'mummify'). Or the two words might be combined in one, 'bottify' (by analogy with 'mortify').

36 Kantor, *Dead Class*, in Itzen and Drozdowski, op. cit.

37 Gombrowicz's importance cannot be overstated: this major avant-garde writer defines better than anyone the Polish avant-garde's anarchic spirit of contradiction.

38 Bronisław Malinowski, the eminent Polish anthropologist, was a close friend of Witkacy, who accompanied him on one of his Far Eastern expeditions. There is good reason to believe that Witkacy's 'anthropological' fascination with the compulsive mechanisms of social (and sexual) ritual springs from Malinowski's work.

39 Kantor, *Dead Class*, transcribed by Jan Klassowicz, in Itzen and Drozdowski, op. cit., p. 134.

40 ibid.

41 Kantor, *Wielopole/Wielopole*, (material excluded from English edition).

42 Sylvia Plath, 'Daddy', in *Ariel*, London, Faber, 1965.

43 Arthur Rimbaud, 'Parade', in *Les Illuminations*, Paris, 1886.

44 Tadeusz Kantor, programme notes to *Où sont les neiges d'antan?* Cf. Krzysztof Miklaszewski, 'Cricotage z Villonem w Herbie', in *Rozmowy i spotkania z Tadeuszem Kantorem*, Kraków, KAW, 1984.

45 The term 'Aesopic language' was applied by Russian literary and social critics of the last century to the self-imposed indirections employed by writers in response to Tsarist censorship. It persisted, for obvious reasons, after the revolution, and during the Communist period spread throughout Central Europe (reinforcing a native strain).

46 Kantor's production of Witkacy's *The Water Hen* (1967), which is probably his masterpiece, gave Edgar two suitcases full of his psychological 'baggage'.

47 See Georges Banu, ed., *Kantor: l'artiste à la fin du XXe siècle*, Paris, Actes Sud, 1990. Cf. G. M. Hyde, 'Tadeusz Kantor', in *Plays and Players*, April 1991.

48 Tadeusz Kantor, interview with Michał Kobialka, 'Let the Artists Die?', *TDR* 30: 3, Fall 1986.

49 See the interview with Barbara Sawa in *Polityka* 39, Nov. 1988.

50 Tadeusz Kantor, *Let the Artists Die Like Dogs*. The 'unnameable' here is equated by Kantor with Pilsudski, in *Wielopole* with Himmler.

51 ibid.

52 Milan Kundera lampoons Stalinist folklore in his novel *The Joke* (1967); English version, London, Faber, 1982, while at the same time expressing his sense of how complex a part of the Czech inheritance folk music is.

53 Zbigniew Osiński, in *Radar* 12, 1979, reprinted in the documents accompanying *Theatre and Folk Traditions*, Lublin, 17–19 May, 1980.

54 Mikhail Bakhtin is known for the 'dialogic principle', a phrase widely misunderstood and misapplied in the Anglo-Saxon world. Deriving from the work of the Russian Formalists, it formed the basis of his study of medieval culture, *Rabelais and his World* (1940), Cambridge, Mass., MIT Press, 1968, which makes extensive play with the concept of 'carnivalization', the suspension and subversion of cultural codes.

55 Viktor Shklovsky, 'Art as Technique', in L. T. Lemon and M. J. Reis, trans. and eds, *Russian Formalist Criticism: Four Essays*, Lincoln, University of Nebraska Press, 1965.

56 Zbigniew Osiński, op. cit.

57 ibid.

58 ibid.

59 Włodzimierz Staniewski, Lublin documents (cf. n.53).

60 Włodzimierz Pawluczuk, *The Expedition*.

61 ibid.

62 ibid.

63 Gardzienice Theatre Association, *The Gardzienice Project '89*, Cardiff, Centre for Performance Research, 1989.

64 Halina Filipowicz, 'Avakkum in context', ibid.

65 See also n.72 (a personal letter from Tadeusz Slawek).

66 Marek Hłasko, *Osmy dzień tygodnia*, Warsaw, PIW, 1957 (tr. Norbert Guterman, *The Eighth Day of the Week*, Heinemann, 1957).

67 Aldona Jawłowska, *Wiecej niz teatr*, Warsaw, PIW, 1988, Section Two.

68 This 'Orwellian' dimension to life in Gierek's Poland was matched by the black but creative irony of the people, toned down after Solidarity and subsequent developments.

69 Wajda's work in the theatre deserves a special study of its own. His *Man of Marble* was the biggest cinematic event of the Gierek years.

70 See Miłosz, *Native Realm* passim.

71 Like other Polish theatre, Eighth Day makes creative use of the highly original work of Polish graphic artists.

72 Tadeusz Sławek, poet and theorist, in an unpublished letter.

BIBLIOGRAPHY

Banu, Georges, ed., *Kantor: l'artiste à la fin du XXe siècle*, Paris, Actes Sud, 1990.

Bradby, D. and McCormick, J., *People's Theatre*, London, Croom Helm, 1978.

Brook, P., *The Empty Space*, Harmondsworth, Penguin Books, 1972.

Craig, E. G., *On the Art of the Theatre*, London, Heinemann, 1911.

Davies, N., *God's Playground*, 2 vols, Oxford, Clarendon Press, 1981.

Filler, W., *Contemporary Polish Theatre*, Warsaw, Interpress Publishers, 1977.

Gombrowicz, W., *Ferdydurke*, trans. Eric Mosbacher, Harmondsworth, Penguin Books, 1990.

Grotowski, J., *Towards a Poor Theatre*, ed. Eugenio Barba, London, Eyre Methuen, 1969.

Innes, C., *Holy Theatre*, Cambridge, Cambridge University Press, 1981.

Itzen, C. and Drozdowski, B., eds, *Gambit 33-34: Special Double Polish Theatre Issue*, London, John Calder, 1979.

Jawłowska, A. *Wiecej niż teatr*, Warsaw, PIW, 1988.

Kantor, T., *Wielopole/Wielopole*, trans. and ed. G. M. Hyde and M. Tchorek, London, Marion Boyars, 1990.

Konwicki, T., *The Polish Complex*, Harmondsworth, Penguin Books, 1983.

Kumiega, J., *The Theatre of Grotowski*, London, Eyre Methuen, 1987.

Miłosz, C., *Native Realm*, Harmondsworth, Penguin Books, 1988.

—— *The Land of Ulro*, Manchester, Carcanet Press, 1985.

Shklovsky, Viktor, 'Art as Technique' in L. T. Lemon and M. J. Reis, trans. and eds, *Russian Formalist Criticism: Four Essays*, Lincoln, University of Nebraska Press, 1965.

Witkiewicz, S. I. (Witkacy), *The Madman and the Nun and Other Plays*, trans. and ed. D. C. Gerould and C. S. Durer, Seattle, Washington University Press, 1968.

Wyspiański, S., trans. Howard Clarke, *The Return of Odysseus*, Indiana, Indiana University Publications, 1966.

11

GREAT BRITAIN*

Ralph Yarrow and Anthony Frost

INTRODUCTION: THEATRE, SOCIETY, EXPERIENCE

The issues most prominent in developments in theatre in Britain in the period 1960–90 are in part specific to the British cultural scene, in its historical and political contexts (the end of censorship in 1968, governmental attitudes to the arts in the 1980s), and in part related to trends in Europe as a whole and to changing critical and practical understandings of theatre (performance theory, focus on theatrical semiosis, the increasing prominence of 'physical theatre').

These issues can be approached under several headings, which inevitably interrelate and recontextualize each other: the interfaces of theatre and society, politics and performance, aesthetics and economics, are complex and open up issues about the kinds of significance ascribed to the arts, and the extent to which we value the culture of the physical and sensitive capacities – which, as Don Cupitt has pointed out, has not received great prominence in the West overall and has certainly been accorded a quirky status in Britain.

'Theatre' comes from a root meaning 'to view'; it offers new and multiple perspectives. The etymology of 'drama' concerns action. If theatre and drama change and renew themselves, it is because they are about change and renewal, about the activation of different perspectives and understandings and about their infiltration into the assumptions a society encodes in its forms of language and behaviour. The major changes in the period 1960–90 lead in the same direction. The freeing of possibilities for actors, the rethinking of the nature of performance, the search for new and formally appropriate models,

* Based in part on a discussion among members of the University of East Anglia Drama Sector recorded in the Audio Visual Centre in August 1989 (participants: Franc Chamberlain, Anthony Frost, Prof. Julian Hilton, Jon Hyde; Chair: Dr Ralph Yarrow).

the insertion into new contexts of communication and learning, mean that theatre in this period is particularly concerned to develop ways of expressing the option available to human beings to make sense of their lives in and through the physical process of living and acting in the world.

As an analogical language, theatre is perhaps the most complete; it reproduces and reflects the ways we behave individually and together through all the channels of perception and expression open to us through intellect and senses. Its enactment is social, in that it is a publicization of private realities, an exercise in communication, a communal event; its organization is social in that it is conceived and performed by individuals who have to negotiate and work together to produce an experienceable result. Theatre *is* society; not surprisingly too, its managerial and organizational structures have been debated and reviewed by those who make them up. The implications of such changes are psychological, in that they relate to how we feel, understand ourselves and behave; political, in that they compose a model of social organization and decision-making; and aesthetic, in that they make up a shape or structure that expresses the perception of whatever 'realities' the work and the working methods encompass.

Theatre is a live event: not so much in the sense that it imitates or mimes a reality everyone can agree on; but more directly and radically in the sense that it is *present*. We as audience share the time and space, and thus the emotional and problematic experience, of the performers as themselves and/or as characters. We are present at a reality that is not in any meaningful sense 'fictional' (though it may be thought of as 'virtual'): it involves, challenges, amuses or horrifies us, it engages our being more profoundly than many of our other everyday actions, and it has probably more significant effects on our assessment of ourselves and the world we live in, and consequently on the way we make choices and act.

Now live events are by their nature unpredictable and disturbing. That is a major part of the justification for theatre; it is also a major reason why it has been regarded with suspicion by most established authorities. So it is appropriate to indicate that the first cluster of concerns may be grouped around the consequences of the removal of theatrical censorship in Britain in 1968; not simply the fact that it was henceforth possible to get 'dirty' plays performed, but more importantly the removal of ideological and physical taboos which affected both content and performance style.

ACTORS, ACTOR-TRAINING, ACTING STYLES

Before 1968 it was in effect impossible to improvise on the British stage, because improvisation could not be submitted to the censor; thus work that relied on spontaneous invention by performers, or more particularly participatory interchange between performers and spectators, and in addition work that relied mainly on physical articulation (the use of mime, physical *gestus*, movement, dance, rhythm, sound and so on) could not legally be presented, though it was often tolerated. Hence one of the most significant post-1968 developments in Britain is the increasing public presence of such work.

The ramifications of this extend into many spheres; on the one hand, the need for appropriate actor-training leads, as in for instance France, Holland and Switzerland, to a growth of companies formed by performers trained in the methods of (e.g.) Jacques Lecoq or Jerzy Grotowski; on the other hand, there is a growth in importance of small-scale touring theatre and a concomitant explosion of the Edinburgh fringe (and other forms of 'fringe'). There is also a parallel with the growth of international theatre festivals, workshops and so on, from Avignon to Glasgow. Other important dimensions are represented in Britain by the establishment of venues devoted primarily to avant-garde production, like the Traverse in Edinburgh, and by performance research as represented by the Centre for Performance Research (CPR) in Cardiff. Both have offered British performers and audiences the chance to participate in the making of new forms, ranging from the disturbingly gothic neo-Romanticism of Kantor to the 'barter' model of Eugene Barba's Odin Teatret (a mutual exchange of styles or modes of performance, like that practised by Peter Brook during his *Conference of the Birds* project in Africa, when his actors presented a performance in exchange, for example, a tribal dance or ritual).

By extension, such ways of working have connections with more specifically 'political' developments in the organization of theatre, for example changes in management structures in theatre companies (collective enterprises, sometimes working with writers as in the case of Joint Stock and Caryl Churchill, or Mike Leigh and his actors). Such cases are by no means restricted to back-street theatre, as the names already cited indicate; other relevant examples would include the operational style of Peter Brook (exported, it is true, to Paris as perhaps a more congenial scene) and the formation of companies such as the British Actors Theatre Company and Not the National Theatre, whose personnel have more than passing acquaintance with the major 'established' British companies.

We need to say a bit more about the kinds of development for performers and performance (and consequently for performance theory) that have grown out of the increasing importance of improvisatory methods.[1] British actors and directors in the last thirty years have been principally affected by three approaches: that of Jacques Copeau, which, as adapted by Michel Saint-Denis, formed an integral part of the training provided by many Drama Schools; that of Keith Johnstone (*Impro*) who was closely associated with the Royal Court Theatre, an important centre of new writing and new performance;[2] and that of Jerzy Grotowski (*Towards a Poor Theatre*), which, although perhaps respected more as a somewhat extreme model for artistic devotion than as a practical guide for many, nevertheless profoundly influenced styles of work and concepts of the actor/audience relationship in the case, for instance, of Peter Brook.[3]

To these we should add, particularly in the last decade, the increasing recognition of the importance of the approach of Jacques Lecoq, responsible at his Paris school for training many of the most inventive companies and performers of recent years. Although there are direct lines back to Copeau from Lecoq, his work emphasizes more an intense physical readiness and is more consciously 'post-modern' in the sense that he understands the development of a plurality of resources to be the chief structural aim of actor-training; his goal is a performer/performance of maximum flexibility. It may indeed be said that the basic aim of all improvisation is the freeing of the actor's resources, both physical and intellectual, from the temptation to fall back on habit and towards an ability to be totally present – *disponible* in Gide's sense of open, available, charged-up but not as yet active.[4]

The increasing use of training methods based around such approaches has produced a shift in performance style away from the declamatory, the star system, or the Great British Accent, and towards a multi-disciplinary mode. Mime, dance and other skills of a more physical kind are seen as equally important performance options, though improvisation certainly need not devalue attention to text; it is, as in the case for instance of Copeau and Grotowski – as indeed of Stanisłavsky before them – used precisely in order to make the approach to the text more multi-layered, more resourceful.

Physical and improvisatory theatre is closer to the carnivalesque, in Bakhtin's sense of inversion of the norm with revolutionary implications.[5] Perhaps hard times, up to a point, are precisely the oppositional incentive that stimulates the growth of such a theatre. Certainly Lecoq would see it this way, and Dario Fo and Franca Rame also come to mind. Their influence has been important. It also helps to emphasize another aspect of 'alternative' – an inadequate and inaccurate term – theatre; its multi-cultural catchment. Just as innovative writers and directors like Brecht, Artaud and Grotowski have discovered alternative performance models in Eastern theatre, so too performance theory has drawn – especially in the case of Schechner – on anthropology and cross-cultural awareness; and in recent years organizations like the Pan Project (director, John Martin) and the CPR (director, Richard Gough) have been created specifically to foster connections across ethnic and generic boundaries. Such an opening to different contexts, different conceptions of theatre, different physical audiences, may be one of the most important aspects of the process of adaptation that has been occurring. We will consider below whether perhaps a new 'textual' model may be appropriate rather than the relatively static structure embedded in the 'well-made play'. If it is so, the development of companies and venues that can take up the challenge is a vital part of the process.

DIRECTORS

Alongside this development, sometimes coinciding with it, sometimes tangential, run the swings between 'actors' and 'directors' theatre which occur during the period. Directors do sometimes learn from, and with (or sometimes as), actors. Even those who come from the old stable of the star-performer system, or take over venues that have operated it, change their ways. Olivier was flexible as a performer and inventive as a director; Peter Brook may at the start of his career look like the model of the superior intellectual directorial figure, but his style shifts considerably towards ensemble-participation – particularly in his international work, but also in celebrated collaborations with the RSC or the National Theatre; Peter Hall's appointment at the National suggested a willingness to move away, even if gradually, from the models of fixed repertoire and top-down management usual in the post-war period. Joan Littlewood (Theatre Workshop, E15) marks one end of a scale in many respects, but much changes in the relationship between actors and directors in virtually all forms of theatre – fixed, touring and so on – in the period. Directors themselves are more frequently found operating in teams or tandems, either with co-directors or with designers, lighting designers, *dramaturges* and/or writers, and so on (Hall/Pinter, Dexter/Wesker, Nunn/Hands, Hall/Barton, and so on). The old hegemony of the actor-manager or impresario gives way to an increasing variety of modes of operation which operates both in 'established' and in more mobile situations. These are reflected in performance style, as for example in key productions like Brook's with the RSC (*Marat/Sade* in 1964, *US* in 1966, *The Dream* – as it came to be known – in 1970) or Littlewood's *Oh What a Lovely War!* (1963). From the 1970s many companies developed physical performance styles based on mask, mime and techniques involving audience contact, conscious theatricality and other markers of a tradition deriving in part from popular and carnivalesque forms: examples include Trestle (mask), Moving Picture Mime Show, Mediaeval Players, Theatre Machine and Declan Donnellan's Cheek by Jowl.

FINANCING AND HOUSING THE ARTS

Another set of issues is linked by economics. Although money is not the necessary condition for the production of theatre – or any form of art – its presence or absence is a major constitutive factor in determining the sort of theatre that can be produced. It can be argued that the unequal distribution of resources to theatre in Britain (that is, the vast majority to 'national' companies performing in fixed locations, mainly in London and large conurbations, and offering a repertoire of relatively traditional plays in not-too-disturbing enactments) has been a major factor in the growth of an 'alternative' theatre scene. The very factor that support has in the main gone to the development and maintenance of 'plant' (fixed spaces described as theatres) – even though design for such spaces has increasingly favoured flexibility and even though administrators might reasonably point out that grants have become less and less adequate – has tended to underwrite the traditional idea of the well-made play performed to well-dressed and well-behaved audiences. (Even new writers who have succeeded have often been those who follow this model to some extent – we could instance here the early work of David Hare.)

The question of financial provision needs a closer look, however. It is true that from the late 1950s until the early 1970s there was a spate of theatre building and renovation. Some of this was supported by national funding via the Arts Council, but most came from local authorities. During this period theatres like the Victoria, Stoke-on-Trent (1962),

(1962), the Nottingham Playhouse (1963), the Birmingham Rep and the Crucible, Sheffield (1971), the Sherman, Cardiff, and the Leicester Haymarket (1973) were all built. Arts Council funding for theatre was running at over £17 million. By 1990 it was £31 million; to maintain level funding at the 1974 level, over £76 million would be necessary. (One quick side-glance; this total amount of subsidy is about the same as the figure received by *one venue* in Switzerland, though admittedly that is the Zurich Opera House . . .) None of this £31 million was available for maintenance, and many of Britain's permanent theatre spaces, from small Arts Centres through to the 'new' National Theatre, are in desperate need of repair. The National, less than 20 years after construction, needs to spend £20 million on repairs and to use £3 million of each year's income for maintenance; the Royal Court is appealing for £800,000 and the Young Vic for £350,000. Any chance of saving the excavated remains of the Rose or of building replicas of other Shakespearean theatres at Southwark has to rely on national and international fund-raising appeals and agitation. Celebrated battles between directors and management during the period have focused as often as not on financial issues rather than artistic or organizational questions; John Neville (Nottingham) and Peter Cheeseman (Stoke) both clashed with the managers in 1967 in this way. All such financial problems nevertheless relate closely to issues of programming and aesthetics; compromises often have to be made. Life in the 1980s and early 1990s was and is difficult for theatre structures; it has only become marginally easier for performers during the period. In 1974 it was still the case that at any one time 75 per cent of actors were out of work. Getting an Equity union card still requires extreme ingenuity, to say the least; and though there are more venues and more types of work available (particularly 'fillers' like advertising and voice-overs), apprenticeship as a performer is frequently as long, exhausting and hazardous as being a junior doctor, and very much less adequately rewarded.

Regional Arts Councils with limited funds have been vital in supporting and encouraging smaller-scale and innovative theatre in Arts Centres and similar venues up and down the country, but here too inequalities inevitably occur. However, at least the system has staggered on and new work has been performed, in spite of the gradual collapse of the policy optimistically set out in the 1980s' document for the Arts entitled *The Glory of the Garden*.[6] Other areas covered in this book (West Germany and Poland, for example) have an even less distinguished record in this respect. Established theatres have in general also had a hard time getting bums on seats, West End tat notwithstanding. In addition to plant-related problems, crisis has hit many of the established 'rep' venues: Nottingham, Leicester, Bristol and Sheffield, amongst others, were in grave financial difficulties in 1990. There is also a related problem in the traditional insularity and anti-intellectualism of public taste in Britain. (Not that there might not be comparable problems in other locations; the preference for insularity and excessive intellectualism in Paris, perhaps . . . but specific nationally supported initiatives like the Théâtre Nationale Populaire have to some extent been set up in order to address these problems in France.)

VOICES, WRITING, TEXTS

Some further problems were highlighted at a conference of directors and writers in 1989. According to David Edgar, creative energy is mainly to be found in touring theatre, TIE (theatre in education), performance art and multi-cultural ensemble work. Michel Vinaver claimed that there was, as in France, too much 'directors' theatre' still; the conference was presented with statistics which showed that less new writing was performed than in the 1970s (down from 12 to 7 per cent); instead, there were many more adaptations – like Lloyd Webber's version of Eliot's cat-poems and Hugo's *Les Misérables* (20 as opposed to 5 per cent); and, not surprisingly, more musicals (11.5 as against 6 per cent). Theatre in London has become increasingly dominated, especially in financial terms, by Lloyd Webber musicals. And *The Mousetrap* approaches 40. In 1989 more than half the shows in British established theatres were pantomimes.

Perhaps the fundamental question is whether what Peter Brook calls 'dead theatre' has gained ground at the expense of other categories, or whether the undoubted plurality ('post-modern' might be a rather too daring term for Britain) of offerings, styles and performance venues is evidence enough of vitality. The *Revels History of Drama in English* (1978) concludes that 'the English stage has had a great and unexpected revival since 1956'.[7] It may still be the case that there are lots of little revolutions going on in theatre in Britain (perhaps adequate even in 1989 in a country that has not witnessed a full-scale political performance of that kind quite so recently as most others in Europe?); it may also be the case that, as Adorno pointed out and as Benjamin and Keats, amongst others, perceived in Shakespeare, the most influential revolutionary statements are implicit rather than explicit. In that context revolution of *form* rather than of message is the more radical course, precisely because the form of the play directly affects the physiological, psychological and affective response of the audience. This necessarily links with a consideration of new writing.

It may be helpful first to indicate some of the landmarks. Osborne's *Look Back in Anger* marks perhaps the beginning of one form of innovation in 1956, though it should be remembered that Beckett's first plays were written just before this. However, in one sense the story of British theatre since that time has been the problem first of accommodating to naturalism (roughly 70 years after most people in Europe had got over it) and then finding something to replace it. The 1960s is largely a period of trying on for size issues of social relevance that Ibsen and Hauptmann had explored in the 1870s and 1880s (in the case of the latter particularly, asking the same questions about the appropriate form of drama in which to ask them, involving issues of – for instance – dialect, documentary detail and psychological modelling); they had been taken up in a slightly different sense in the 1920s and after by Brecht, Piscator and others (political relevance, role of audience, use of alternative performance-spaces in factories, halls and so on). In this light the extraordinary insularity of British culture is particularly evident.

Now indubitably the early work of Osborne, Wesker and so on was useful in enabling British theatre to catch up and to face up to issues of, for instance, political importance, which it had skilfully managed to avoid (or been 'persuaded' to avoid) until then (with occasional exceptions, as in some of Shaw). Arden, for instance, was able to draw on some aspects of Brechtian technique and couple them with a powerful sense of indigenous language and incident in *Serjeant Musgrave's Dance* (1959). This then left the writers of the 1960s and after in a position to begin to come to terms with other kinds of development which had also occurred in European theatre.

It is debatable to what extent that challenge has been met, although there is in the later work of Osborne, in Pinter, Arden, Bond, Brenton, Hare, Edgar and others an awareness of, for instance, epic and Absurd theatre and skilful use of many techniques for shocking, involving and challenging audiences. Some of the major landmarks were plays like Pinter's *The Birthday Party* in 1958; Bond's *Saved* and Orton's *Loot* (1965); Bond's *Lear* (1970). They seem to have taken on board modernist theatre's concern with questioning received modes of social and cultural behaviour and discourse, its challenge to the 'prison house

of language' (Jameson)[8] which tends to prescribe and limit experience and understanding, and to dislocate conventional securities like
D. H. Lawrence's 'old stable ego of personality'.

In spite of all this, it is not clear that any radically different
structures of performance have emerged in scripted theatre of this
kind. Perhaps that is because we have a need to believe in the sorts of
things the 'well-made play' confirms about our view of ourselves and
our world; this aesthetic necessity speaks of a felt need for coherent
plot or consistent personae – which could be interpreted either as a
mark of the genuine validity of these models and their consistency
with the experienced world, or on the other hand as evidence of a
powerful desire or nostalgia for their veracity, for confirmation of the
status of purposeful and teleological action and progress, both in
terms of individual psychology and social and historical process, into
which we have been accultured during the previous centuries. It may
be that we go on wanting to believe in these 'overarching narratives'
(Lyotard), and we therefore require our cultural experience to
replicate them.

To undo that kind of deeply felt psychological and cultural
conservatism is a long job. That may, to do them credit, be why the
work of the writers mentioned in the previous few paragraphs has not
resulted in a complete paradigm-shift of attitudes to performance, but
has nevertheless succeeded in instituting significant shifts in the ways
plays are received by audiences, and to a lesser extent in the ways in
which they are physicalized by actors. (This has occurred in spite of
the fact that new writing often received only short runs at established
theatres, with the notable exception of the attitude pioneered by
George Devine at the Royal Court, which has continued to support
new writing and young writers.) It may nevertheless be the case, as
Artaud claimed, that theatre is the most effective (or at least the most
public and communal) means of instigating actual physical change by
working through the sensibility and the physiology, as well as being
able to present a (Brechtian) challenge to the intellect to analyse
underlying social patterns and undertake consequent existential
choices. In this way the writers mentioned are, each in their own way,
contributing towards the development of a theatre that engages the
whole person (of both performer and spectator) – a development that
practitioners linked to physical theatre pursue more overtly. If there
is a consistency amongst the different strands of new British theatre,
perhaps it is in this activation of the complex of activities which may
be called 'involvement' in the act of theatre.

That, in a sense, is only another of the periodical restatements of the collision of private experience and public reality offered by all theatre. Certainly the writers mentioned above – to whom should most importantly be added the increasingly powerful presence of women writers like Caryl Churchill, Sarah Daniels and Pam Gems – represent a consistent attempt to formulate theatrically effective approaches to the shifting perceptions and attitudes to individual and social life in Britain; they work by analogy and by documentary detail, through satire and aesthetic distance, shock and sympathy; their style could be described as realistic, Absurd, Brechtian, feminist, Marxist, improvisatory, and so on. Theatre has always been eclectic, because one of its chief weapons is the presentation of multiple roles and perspectives, the physicalization of a dialectic of positions and interpretations; the British theatre of the 1960s and after is no exception.

Whose are the most important theatre voices of this extended thirty-year period? It is far easier to point to playwrights from the earlier half than from the latter. And this is not merely due to a loss of critical distance: something has happened. Voices have been stilled. Most of the main playwrights have gone silent in the last decade, their work becoming introspective, their attention turning towards other media. In the latter half of the period the locus of creative energy is collective not individual, directorial more than authorial, physical rather than textual.

The watershed of Osborne's otherwise indifferent *Look Back in Anger* in 1956 marked a major return to the *drama* – to self-expression through the written play – which lasted perhaps for twenty years. Within two years Osborne himself had characterized his piece as 'a rather formal, old-fashioned play'. The earliest audiences, too, seemed to share this opinion. Then extracts were shown on *Monitor*, the BBC arts programme. The 'Jimmy Porter' or 'Angry Young Man' craze began. The energy of Jimmy's invective, the mere sound of his voice rather than what it was (or was not) saying, prompted many young writers to turn to the stage rather than to the novel, or to poetry as their primary medium.

Partly this reflects a shift in energy within the arts, and an eventual counter-shift is a natural dialectical expectation. The growing accessibility of video during the 1980s has shifted the focus away from both the stage and the large screen. But anger, or at least opposition to restriction and prejudice, cannot be kept out for long. Improvisation mocks the censor; the imperative need to find a voice mounts another challenge. The dominant voices of the late 1970s and 1980s make use of anger, not just to sound off about imagined stuffiness or exorcise the guilt of inverted snobbery like Jimmy Porter, but to question codes and modes, however apparently liberal. Sarah Daniels's *Byrthrite* (1986) cuts up Caryl Churchill's 'feminist success' *Vinegar Tom* to propose a more radical attack. Similarly, John McGrath jettisons the Brechtian dialectic of Arden's *Serjeant Musgrave's Dance* by exposing his audience to the raw violence of Ulster's bloody legacy in his *Serjeant Musgrave Dances on* (1974). Steven Berkoff (e.g. *East* in 1975, *Greek* in 1979, *Decadence* in 1981, *West* in 1983) juxtaposes the voices of high and low culture (Shakespeare and the East End) to reflect both the traps of peer-group inarticulacy and the possibilities of springing open such linguistic traps (John Godber has done something similar). Here too a highly physical and aggressive performance style reinstates theatre as the kind of confrontation that the small screen can only – perhaps dangerously – render less problematic.

The latter half of the period has seen the emergence of new, previously unheard voices, sometimes in the form of new writing, often through ensemble play creation; gay voices in Gay Sweatshop; women's in Joint Stock and Monstrous Regiment; Afro-Caribbean and Asian in Temba and Tara Arts. But are these new voices readily heard? Where do new plays and playwrights go? Upstairs? (To a Sunday Night without decor, or to the smaller Theatre Upstairs – frequently inactive – at the Royal Court, rather than the risky main house.) Round the back? (To the inexpensive, less prestigious studio, or to the tricked-out rehearsal room, or physically separate shed where failure might not embarrass the main company – though success can always be transferred in.) Down the pub? (To student theatre, or lunch-time theatre or theatre in public houses.) On the Road? (Out in search of any venue that can be persuaded to have you: universities, colleges, Arts Centres.) Play-writing does not pay well in Britain. The income of a playwright – except for that of a very select few – will need to be eked out by other kinds of work. Commitment to theatre writing remains largely ideological rather than financial.

Less gloomily, however, theatre has also always demonstrated the recently fashionable notion of 'intertextuality' in practice. The performed text is always an embedding of one text, code or semiotic system in many others; the written is surrounded or opened out by its intersection with the visual, the gestural and so on. All such 'texts' continually redefine and work off each other in performance.

Similarly, contemporary work in theatre incorporates, perhaps even more clearly than in other genres, conventions from previous modes: the 'Shakespearean' is itself an accretion of historical styles, not a single constant; 'quoting' is not limited, as in fiction or music, to a single mode; a contemporary work might present a 'Revenge' motif on a 'medieval' stage using a 'Craig' design and featuring an actor with a 'Chaplinesque' walk. . . . The plurality of style and mode evident in British theatre in the 1980s and 1990s was and is an indication of this; whilst traditional critics might lament the absence of a single discernibly characteristic form, the plurality may itself be evidence of an experimentation that is not simply born of desperation, but is an appropriate way of encountering the range of available modes and of working with them to provide responses. The shapes that emerge may be fluid, they may suggest energies in motion rather than fixed contours; but such configurations may be relevant to a view of both existential and physical reality as the play of form (*pace*, for instance, humanistic psychology and quantum physics). Julian Hilton has suggested, both in the discussion on which this chapter is based, and in his *Performance*,[9] that the new form of drama may be non-linear, dislocative. What we have been considering so far seems to support this. The notion of 'text' as something relatively fixed is in the process of giving way to the foregrounding of 'play' (to which Shakespeare was no stranger). Not that linear and rational activity is thereby superseded; rather, it is incorporated into a pluralistic functioning of mind and body that exemplifies a more 'holistic' sense of human reality and draws consciously and purposefully upon the fact that we think, perceive, feel and act in highly complex interactive ways, for which the multi-dimensional model of theatre is able to offer a convincing and useful parallel. The interweaving of signs by which communication in drama occurs, activates an equally complex, and ideally equally conscious, reaction in the spectator: we come consciously alive in the process to more of our latent, and in so-called 'normal' activity under-used, range of sense-making.

Life there certainly is, both in the 'established' and in newer writers; and the story of the 1970s and 1980s in particular has also been the story of the reaffirmation of the communality of the activity called 'theatre'. The period has been notable for the directions taken by, for instance, the relationships between directors and actors, the nature and method of operation of theatre companies (including the growth of collectives – Monstrous Regiment, Joint Stock, Gay Sweatshop – and touring as opposed to civic theatre), the development of new venues, the pluralization of performance styles and the role of drama in education.

EDUCATION

Education is a useful point from which to continue, since it also opens out the usually overlooked area of amateur theatre. There may or may not be a direct link between interest in taking part in drama and various uses of it in education; as TIE, as a contribution to interactive teaching techniques (whose implications extend far beyond primary education, for instance), or as evidenced in the growing numbers of candidates for drama and theatre studies at GCSE and A level, and the demand for places at colleges, universities and drama schools. At least two issues are relevant here; first, the educational realization that the participatory and performative mode is a highly efficient channel of teaching and learning; and second, the more basic but equally important recognition that it is fun, and that it leads to positive social and psychological benefit. Thus the increase in demand occurs in spite of government marginalization in funding and recognition of the arts. Similarly, in spite of apparently adverse conditions (universal television ownership, apparent decline in community-based activities, financial problems for the British Theatre Association and so on) the number and quality of amateur productions in Britain is at least holding its own. Schools and colleges produce much excellent and often imaginative work; there are well established and thoroughly competent amateur companies performing regularly in many towns and cities; and many other enthusiastic groups from Young Farmers to the Women's Institute continue to put on plays and organize competitions. Many local and regional authorities have undertaken initiatives to promote theatre and related arts for young people, with generally good responses; new theatre companies continue to come (and go) as evidence of a widespread desire to be involved. This, from the vantage-point of the early 1990s, suggests that the shifts and developments taking place in theatre during the previous three decades have contributed to a continuing and perhaps extended interest in drama as a way of discovering and expressing personal and communal significance.

BRITAIN IN EUROPE?

Just because Britain is an island, does it have to be insular? Europe-anism has traditionally been viewed with xenophobic suspicion by the

British theatre no less than by the British political establishment (often reflected in the popular press). The indications are, however, increasingly positive. At the time of writing, a Spanish theatre company is performing a German playwright's redaction of *Hamlet* in London. Is the apparently increasing internationalism of British theatre simply a marginal activity – the trailing hem of the Fringe? What are the other signs?

First, foreign exotica have always been exciting to theatrical *cognoscenti*, but ever since the demise of Peter Daubeny's World Theatre Seasons we have been looking for a successful way to import the best of world drama on a regular basis. Thelma Holt of the National Theatre and Lucy Neal and Rose de Wend Fenton of LIFT (London International Festival of Theatre) have strongly promoted internationalism for a number of years.[10] Foreign companies have long been welcome at Edinburgh's Festivals, both mainstream and Fringe. LIFT is doing its best; but it is London-based, and many productions are classic texts (chosen because they are sure-fire hits?).

Second, there are foreign directors – Yuri Lyubimov at Leicester, Robert Lepage at Glasgow, Rita Russek at Chichester – but no Giorgio Strehler, no Roberto Ciulli, no Otomar Krejča – to name but three. English actors need to be exposed to their methods; their current rejection of the director's status needs to be confronted with the best that Europe can offer. Productions, translators, collaborators could provide access to and audiences for these European co-workers. Importing their productions (at Festivals like LIFT or Edinburgh), or inviting them to come and work could capitalize on the freedom of movement across national boundaries implicit in the single market after 1992.

Third, there are foreign plays in translation: these are increasing, but mostly at the margins – all the professional productions of Franz Xavier Kroetz to date have been at the Bush or the Traverse. Botho Strauss has had one West End run (with Glenda Jackson) in 1983. Fo's plays have suffered in translation, and his reputation has been altered by that translation. Roger Planchon's *Blues, Whites and Reds* was offered at Birmingham Rep in the early 1970s – what since? Perhaps one solution is to attack the problem on a textual level. We need more, better, faster translations of contemporary European drama.

The difficulty here is compounded by the failure to provide showcases for the best work of British directors and companies, let alone European ones. In Germany, each spring, there is a *Theatertreffen* in Berlin. This is a non-competitive celebration of German-language theatre from the two former halves of Germany, Austria and Switzerland. Plays are selected on merit, usually on grounds of critical acclaim, and companies are invited to participate. Plays that have gone out of the repertory are restaged if necessary. Great regional prestige attaches to an invitation. In a divided, federal, regional system the plays of Dresden are presented side by side with those of Zurich or Wuppertal. Audiences gain from a short season of the very best, most challenging, most controversial plays.

Similarly, Mülheim annually plays host to the competitive Stücke festival of new German drama (with a DM20,000 prize for the best play, in 1990 won by Georg Tabori's *Weisman und Rottgesicht*), and Roberto Ciulli's Theater an der Ruhr (which is based at Mülheim) has created an accompanying *Theaterlandschaft* ('theatre landscape') which has brought Yugoslavian, Polish and Turkish theatre into the heart of industrial Germany. Ciulli believes that 'theatre which does not travel is limited in the artistic, cultural and political sense. . . . So he travels with his company and brings other companies to Mülheim.'[11] Ciulli is in the vanguard in the emergence of a truly European, cross-cultural theatre.

Britain lacks the freedom, the facilities and the will to create such a 'theatre landscape'. Not that we do not tour (The National Theatre under Peter Hall could play the *Oresteia* at Epidauros, for example). But where do we celebrate the best of our new dramatic writing in this manner? Where do we send the best of our regional theatre so that it can be widely seen? Where do we invite foreign theatre artists to work with us?

There are encouraging signs and portents. Covent Garden has just become (in September 1990) the venue for a new international theatre festival. Performances concentrated this year on local street theatre, but an associated event (the International Playreading Series), held in the adjacent Theatre Museum, presented staged readings of plays by foreign authors unknown in Britain – with the long-term aim of mounting a production of the best play at the next festival in 1992. The sponsors of the project were the International Theatre Institute, the BBC and the Directors' Guild.

More up-to-date information – primarily of a visual kind – of the best in contemporary European theatre would be beneficial; as occurred, for example, with the visits of Brecht's Berliner Ensemble in 1956 and Grotowski's Teatr Laboratorium (Laboratory Theatre) in 1968. Nothing has a more profound effect on the directorial imagination than images from another director's work. And the boldness of the European theatrical imagination (at its best in the work of a Ciulli, say, or a Stein) can liberate creativity in British theatre too. The pan-European quarterly publication *Euromaske*, edited in Yugoslavia (at present in English language only) by Dušan Jovanović and Dragan Klaič claims its purpose 'is not academic but pragmatic and professional'. The aim is to supplement specialist journals and 'to cover, analyse and evaluate all important developments in the performing arts in Europe from an international, trans-cultural and post-ideological standpoint'.[12]

Fourth in the list of signs of internationalism would be 'foreign' working practices – a long (properly paid) rehearsal period, cast research and lectures, a dramaturge working on the text, the set in the rehearsal room from day one. Some of these have been offered (e.g. to Lyubimov) by Peter Lichtenfels at the Leicester Haymarket. Without the provision of what are seen in much of Europe as basic facilities, the best of European theatre practitioners will have little interest in crossing the Channel. Time is of the essence here. In a three-week rehearsal period there is little or no time to reflect upon the ideas and themes of the play, or to experiment with variant approaches, or acquire new performance skills. There is no time to read, discuss or do real research.

The problem may in large measure be perceptual. The pages of *Plays and Players* record a large number of foreign (mainly European) plays beings offered. Yet one hardly perceives them. The focus is on the capital, or on the large, prestigious festivals. Perhaps we need a process of increasing decentralization. A fully decentralized National Theatre (on the Swedish model) is unlikely in Britain. The weight of history is against it. It took two hundred years and more to get the edifice on the South Bank into place, and we are not suggesting its removal. But we are arguing for an increased dispersal of resources to the regions (under the revised Regional Arts Associations) and an increased sense of responsibility to the regions from the centre. The Royal National Theatre on tour. The Royal Shakespeare Company on tour. And not only with the English Classics, but with modern European theatre too. Theatre needs the vision and the backing to contribute to an awareness of that part of our culture that Britain shares with Europe, as well as developing its own hallmark.

NOTES

Information has been drawn from articles in *Plays and Players*, *Time Out* and the *Observer*, and from Peter Roberts, *Theatre in Britain*, rev. edn, London, Pitman, 1975.

1 A. Frost and R. Yarrow, *Improvisation in Drama*, London, Macmillan, 1990.
2 Keith Johnstone, *Impro*, London, Methuen, 1981.
3 Jerzy Grotowski, *Towards a Poor Theatre*, Copenhagen, Odin Teatret, 1968, trans. various, London, Methuen, 1969.
4 André Gide, *Les Faux Monnayeurs*, Paris, Gallimard, 1925: see esp. pp. 25, 59.
5 Mikhail Bakhtin, *Rabelairs and His World*, trans. Hélène Iswolsky, Cambridge, Mass., Massachusetts Institute of Technology, 1968.
6 London, Arts Council Publications, 1982.
7 *Revels History of Drama in English*, ed. T. W. Craik, vol. VII, *1880 to the Present Day*, London, Methuen, 1978: 264.
8 Fredric Jameson, *The Prison House of Language*, Princeton, Princeton University Press, 1972.
9 J. Hilton, *Performance*, London, Macmillan, 1987: 153.
10 *Plays and Players*, Sept. 1987.
11 Ognenka Miličevic, 'The career of a conscious outsider', *Euromaske* 1, 1990: 56.
12 *Euromaske*, 1, 1990: 3.

BIBLIOGRAPHY

Frost, Anthony and Yarrow, Ralph, *Improvisation in Drama*, London, Macmillan, 1990.
Hilton, Julian, *Performance*, London, Macmillan, 1987.
Roberts, Peter, *Theatre in Britain*, London, rev. edn, London, Pitman, 1975.
Roose-Evans, James, *Experimental Theatre: From Stanislavsky to Today*, New York, Avon Books, 1970.
Journals: The *New Theatre Quarterly* (edited by Simon Trussler and Clive Barker) specializes in mainly twentieth-century theatre scholarship. *Plays and Players* (monthly, edited by Vera Lustig) specializes in journalistic articles on contemporary drama and on performance reviews. *Euromaske* (quarterly), published in Yugoslavia, in English, has articles on contemporary European theatre and drama by journalists and scholars from several countries.

INDEX